PRAISE FOR *AN OBAMA'S JOURNEY*

"With gut-wrenching honesty, Mark Obama Ndesandjo exorcises demons from his past while delicately balancing diverse cultures that straddle three continents. His candor covers failures, successes, racism, a scandal or two, musical joys, charitable pleasures, and amazement at watching from a distance as his rival sibling performed political miracles."
—JOHN CAIRNS, AUTHOR OF *ALL ABOARD! PLANET EXPAT*

"An Obama's Journey is a touching story of one man's transnational search for identity, cultural understanding, and forgiveness. It's a riveting, stunningly honest read that transcends being the biography of the president's half brother; from his early years in Kenya to his coming of age in the United States and final passage to China, Mark Obama has a remarkable tale to tell in his own right."
—JENNI MARSH, *SOUTH CHINA MORNING POST*

"Like any great autobiography, this book is about more than a person. It is about humanity and relationships and holds lessons for all to learn. I enjoyed reading the full and nuanced description of Africa's beauty and savagery and about its curiously admirable indifference. Mark captures the heady days before the tech bubble in America and lands in China just in time to witness the vibrant new life the Chinese are creating for themselves. The musical evocations and explanations that begin each chapter are unusual in an autobiography, perhaps even unique, and set the mood and themes well for that chapter, as well as introduce more texture to the book that helps round out the story. The few, but well-spaced, scenes where he meets Barack crackle with electricity. Their evolving friendship is fascinating to watch. Masterly writing, with poignant anecdotes and insightful, quotable thoughts."
—FRITZ GALT, AUTHOR OF *CHINA GATE*

"Mark Obama's story inspires as it reveals how he has managed to use his tumultuous childhood experiences to uplift and guide orphans to overcome their own childhood obstacles. He is a survivor of the sometimes unbearable, unhappy, and uncontrollable circumstances that are thrown at us at an early age. Like a true survivor, he uses his talents of writing and music to influence those around him into shaping a more positive future for themselves and the world around them."
—SARA ATZMON, HOLOCAUST SURVIVOR AND ARTIST

An Obama's Journey

My Odyssey of Self-Discovery across Three Cultures

Mark Obama Ndesandjo

LYONS PRESS

Guilford, Connecticut

Helena, Montana

An imprint of Rowman & Littlefield

Lyons Press is an imprint of Rowman & Littlefield

Distributed by NATIONAL BOOK NETWORK

Copyright © 2014 by Mark Obama Ndesandjo

All photos courtesy of the author unless otherwise noted.

British Library Cataloguing-in-Publication Information available

Library of Congress Cataloging-in-Publication Data is available on file.

ISBN 978-1-4930-0751-6 (hardcover)

∞™ The paper used in this publication meets the minimum requirements of American National Standard for Information Sciences—Permanence of Paper for Printed Library Materials, ANSI/NISO Z39.48-1992.

*For the unnamed boy with the spade-like hands and
in memory of David Opiyo*

Contents

CONTENTS

INTRODUCTION

THIS BOOK IS NOT ABOUT HOW TO ACHIEVE A FORTUNE OR ANY OTHER measure of worldly success, so if you're looking for fresh insights into making millions, you will likely be disappointed. It is not just about brothers and fathers, sisters and mothers. Nor is it about revenge and hate. It is primarily about a search for meaning, a memoir of family connections, self-discovery, and ultimate redemption.

The characters and events portrayed and the names used herein are based on my personal recollection. Clearly my recollection is not perfect, and, if in error, I beg the reader's indulgence.

One of my brothers called me the "crazy one"; my sister-in-law Michelle Obama referred to me as the "wayward one." At first I was a little miffed by these descriptions. After some thought, I realized that, despite an element of exaggeration, there was some truth in them. I wrote this book in an attempt to make sense of the zigzagging trail of my life to date, to understand myself better but also to record my quest to make a difference in this world. As Gandhi once said: "The best way to find yourself is to lose yourself in the service of others."

I was born in Kenya, lost myself in America, and found myself again in China. The once-tangled skeins of my life do not, with the benefit of hindsight, seem as tortuous as they once did. I see more clearly now where my path began, although I do not yet know where it will end. This book is dedicated to those who are lost and need some fresh insight into their wanderings in their eternal quest for identity. I hope that young people in particular will be able to learn from my mistakes and hopefully avoid some of the pitfalls that lie ahead of them on their particular paths through life. Perhaps some of them may even be inspired enough to seek to be of service to others.

—Mark Obama Ndesandjo
Shenzhen, China, 2014

Note: I refer to my brother, Barack Hussein Obama II, as Barack Jr. in the book, as I remember some family members did, to help distinguish his name from our father's.

Our lives improve only when we take chances—and the first and most difficult risk we can take is to be honest with ourselves.

—WALTER ANDERSON

Oh, you're the wayward one.

—MICHELLE OBAMA

PRELUDE

Winter in Beijing, 2009

SOMETIMES, IN THE DARKNESS OF MEMORY, OR AT TIME'S AMORPHOUS boundaries, the faces of kin merge with my own. It is easy to become confused, figuring out where one ends and the other begins.

My mother and I both have big noses. My brother, President Barack Obama, has big ears. My father had large hands. My family tends toward these eye-catching extremities, just short of being ugly but large enough to be noticed.

My wife and I had just arrived at the St. Regis Beijing when Barack arrived to greet us. We had passed through security and were standing in a small reception room somewhere on an upper floor. It was decorated with pink paisley wallpaper and faux-antique French furniture upholstered in green and scarlet. Above a white marble fireplace hung a modernistic acrylic painting like an out-of-focus photograph. Plush sofas and hard-backed chairs were arranged randomly, giving it a hybrid office/living-room feel. The ambiguous nature of this closely protected meeting place was enhanced by the dim lighting from the table lamps and consulate staff passing in and out inconspicuously like mute specters.

Hearing a sound behind me, I turned to see someone standing in the doorway, cast into shadow by the bright light from the corridor outside. I recognized the outline of those big, mouse-like ears that always seem to stick out. He stepped into the light, and I saw his calm, serious face. The lines on it seemed to have deepened since the last time we had met, during his inauguration week. Even though he is only an inch or two taller, he nevertheless managed to tower over me, just as he had in 1988 when we met for the first time. I felt suddenly overwhelmed to see my brother Barack Obama, president of the United States.

He had made me a promise during his inauguration week: "I will meet you and your wife in China."

Until I met Barack in Beijing, I had never viewed him as the president. Instead, I just saw him as my brother—a little taller and older than me, true, but still just a brother. When he walked through the door and saw me, he instinctively held out his hand. Feeling momentarily insulted, I hugged him instead. Soundlessly, he hugged me back. I detected a faint smell of cigarette smoke and knew that, in spite of his and Michelle's best efforts, today he had been playing truant. At the moment we embraced, he could have asked for anything and I would gladly have given it to him. This, finally, was the moment of closeness we should have shared decades ago. There had been something cold and accusatory about our encounter in the summer of 1988 in Kenya, characterized by his lawyerly reasoning and almost anthropological inquiry into our common history—and our father, Barack Obama Sr.

"What *I'm* wondering is what's going on in Barack's mind right now," a friend had commented to me after I had published my novel, *Nairobi to Shenzhen*.

I had already alienated my sister, Auma, who was furious I had publicly spoken of our dysfunctional father, whom she had idolized for so long. Upon meeting Barack Jr., she had likely told him little of the domestic violence within our family.

At best, I thought, Barack would ignore the ruckus. At worst he would give me the cold shoulder.

What indeed was my brother thinking?

"How are you doing, Mark?" he said. I examined his face more closely. His skin had a yellowish, leathery tinge, as though the fire within had burnt out. His eyes looked somewhat weary but also resigned, like one who sees burdens for what they are—ineluctable, requiring his constant vigilance and duty, always there.

"Great threads, man," I said, not knowing how else to reply. He wore a beautiful silver-shaded navy-blue suit with crisp tailoring. I was seeing everything about him with acute clarity: every stitch visible, every crease thrown into relief. There was a bald strip on the left side of his head where he had been accidentally nicked by an electric trimmer. He wore a flag lapel pin neatly aligned with the knot in his brilliant blue-and-white-speckled tie.

The words rang again in my mind: *I will meet you and your wife in China, just not in Shenzhen. They won't let me have dinner with you.*

My brother had kept his promise.

But his mind was elsewhere, or perhaps it was too fully engaged in the moment, like the man who has consumed a cup of tea greedily, then drunk another and another, the pleasure diminishing further with each fresh cup. I was perhaps his hundredth cup of tea, after a year packed with more than he had ever expected to drink.

During our meeting Barack smiled just twice.

The first time was when he saw a picture of my mother. For the recent publication of my novel, I'd produced dummy copies of the book, which featured its jacket but had blank pages within.

"Let's get some photos of your family and paste them inside for Barack," my wife had suggested before we flew to Beijing.

I loved the idea. Eagerly, we selected photos of my father; my late brother, David; my mother; and myself—ones Barack had probably never seen before—and pasted them in. Beside each one, I wrote in longhand a short paragraph of explanation and reflection.

"How is your mother?" he asked.

"She's fine."

"Please send her my regards."

It was a slight smile, just the barest upturn of the lips and an almost imperceptible fluttering of the eyelashes, as if he felt too abashed to say anything more. This is Barack's real smile, the reflection of his personality when it is free from theatrics and politicking, arising from his own some-what stern and somber character. Our respective mothers and grand-mothers were powerful and unforgettable influences over both our lives, that smile said.

The second time he smiled was when we came to a picture of our father sitting at a desk studying.

In this photo, taken during his student days at the University of Hawaii, Barack Obama Sr. looks serious and fully absorbed in his work. A faint curve of pigment, perhaps an old flame's lipstick, is faintly impressed on the top part of it. This photo showed the side of my father that I had grown to admire late in life. In it I saw all the industry and focus on his studies that had pulled him ahead of so many.

My brother looked at this photo and smiled again—but only half a smile this time, tinged with implicit refusal to engage with me further on this subject. I had forgotten that in private, away from the public oratory, my brother could be a black Heathcliff, his presence a mono-syllabic and sullen wind that roared across the moor, cold and isolate. He didn't say anything, but I knew at that moment he could not forgive me.

At one of our previous meetings, in Austin during the campaign, I had given him a carefully chosen piece of Chinese calligraphy:

天涯咫尺
So close yet so far
So far, yet so near

My brother was so close to me in this Beijing room, and yet still so far away. I had hoped we would talk of Obama Sr., perhaps reach an understanding of how two sons of the same father could have followed such widely divergent paths.

Yet could I honestly have expected that some old photographs, or even the novel I had written, would get my brother to open up to me for the first time? How could the beliefs he had clung to for decades, the entrenched admiration of an adult for his father, be in any way altered by the views of a brother he barely knew?

How naive I had been.

It was a good question my friend had asked. But in the end there was no answer to it.

Whatever Barack thought of my novel and what it said, he would never tell me. Or at least not of his own volition. I was not courageous enough to press him for his opinion, for I was close enough to see what he thought—and at that moment my brother scared me. With the change that had overtaken his life, he was like a huge steel ball that could roll free and crush anything or anyone that stood in his path.

Sometimes by chance,
A look or a glance,
*May one's fortune advance**

That moment of withholding told me so much about his reluctance to *like* me, let alone love me as his brother.

Years earlier, when I was writing a particularly difficult passage about our father, I had burst into tears. My wife stared in astonishment at the sight of a grown man overcome with emotion.

"My family will hate me for this book, baby," I explained.

She hugged me and assured me they would not, while no doubt sensing I was right.

Later that day in Beijing, my brother replied to an interviewer's question about our meeting: "I don't know him very well. I met him for the first time *only two years ago.*"

Hearing myself referred to in the third person like that felt surreal. Maybe I should have made allowances for the bluntness of the interviewer's question, but the pain in my heart disregarded any such logic or excuse. After all, I had met him a number of times before.

He had become not my brother, but the president of the United States. This was the politicking Barack, in the media spotlight where politicians perform every day. Perhaps I'd thought there might be something about our family tie that would override the carefully bland, ready response, but the dismissive words were spoken.

For me the rest of our meeting went by in something of a daze. Before I knew it, he was off to see the president of China, and my wife and I were flying back to Shenzhen.

---

* *The Story of the Red Stone, or The Dream of the Red Chamber, Vol. 1: The Golden Days* by Cao Xueqin (Trans. David Hawkes, Penguin, 1974)

Later, after I had returned home and had time to think things over, I wrote Barack a letter.

Dear Brother,

It was great meeting you in Beijing! I hope you find some time to read this, for I know of the great challenges that daily demand your time . . .

Many years ago, you tried to start a discussion with me about life in general, and our father in particular. At that time I closed myself to you. Over a year ago our sister Auma told me, "There is a time for everything." I have been thinking about these two things a lot recently: our broken conversation and how "untimely" things sometimes are. Your election was untimely for me, but it started me thinking about what we had talked about long ago. I started to think of my home in Alego, a home which you briefly knew, but which I was immersed in for years. You were seeking our father's ghost. I was running away from it. I had tried very hard to forget my past, but failed miserably. By failing to understand myself I made terrible mistakes . . .

For a long time I could not accept our name. It was part of such sad memories. You changed that. You made me very proud and inspired me to go back . . .

Barack, I want to reconnect with all our family and you are a lynchpin. Without your support I can do it but it will be hard . . .

I wanted to say so much to you, Barack, but our time was so limited. I truly hope we can continue what we started long ago as I try to reconnect with my history and my memories . . .

Love,
Mark Okoth

He did not reply. I have never asked him if he read the letter. Nevertheless, despite the bittersweet atmosphere of our meeting, I still treasure the memory of that hug from my brother, that first smile, the feeling of being among family, warm and protected from the bitter Beijing winter.

But for both of us the beginning lay in Africa, where our differences, and our two remarkable journeys, first took shape.

Meeting Barack in Beijing. It was during this 2009 meeting that I first realized how much my writing about our family's domestic abuse had alienated him. Later, in response to an interviewer's question, he said he had met me for the first time only two years before. I never found out why he said this, even though we met for the first time in 1988.

CHAPTER ONE

Kenya: Where It All Began

MUSICAL EVOCATION

The Rite of Spring: Igor Stravinsky

There is an amazing section in this orchestral work by Russian composer Igor Stravinsky where the weirdly evocative opening melody is suddenly interrupted by unison strings in a violent, very loud, primordial rhythm. It commands the listener's attention while introducing a savage dance element that marks a maiden's sacrifice. It is said that during the 1913 Paris premiere, one man was so moved by the work he stood and instinctively started beating a tattoo on the bald head of the person sitting in front of him. To me Kenya is like this music: all about contrasting melodies of a rough and ready, unforgiving and often harsh nature, difficult to articulate in words, but full of a seductive beauty that dances in rhythm with the earth itself.

AFRICA IS A PLACE OF SUBLIME CONTRASTS AND SAVAGE INDIFFERENCE. To view for the first time a lion hunting and killing, muscles rippling in the sun, to see it pick up the body of an onyx with just its teeth—and all beneath the great blue bowl of a sky that seems to stretch to infinity— is a humbling experience. How do I convey what it means to grow up amid such beauty and such harshness? I can share only vignettes and memories that pass in and out of my consciousness, like sunlight through a diamond's facets. The years, days, and hours shift and blur like a mirage hovering over a burning-hot road.

Born in 1965, I lived in Kenya until I was eighteen. The scene of potent events that marked me for life also furnished me with the bricks from which I later built my spiritual house. Growing up there was both wonderful and terrible. Because I came from a mixed-race family, Africans denied me their brotherhood. To my face, children my own age called me epithets I hated, *half-caste, chotara*, and *white* among them. At one point I had grown to believe *half-caste* was a term of the purest abuse, rather like *son-of-a-bitch* or *asshole* multiplied one thousand times. Some people used it with the casual familiarity with which one might say *rose* or *chair*, but their insensitivity had the same effect on me as a white supremacist's invective.

"You're a half-caste, aren't you?" a man would casually ask me.

"Leave that *chotara* alone. I don't like him," my schoolmates would often say.

I was a white negro or a black *mzungu* (Caucasian in Swahili). I was black to all whites, yet white to all blacks—with no middle ground. Unable to bond with my black brothers, I quickly adopted the culture of my white mother and her more polite Caucasian brethren. Although there was a point beyond which most would not let me befriend them, others allowed me to make rudimentary social advances. For a long time that was enough. Once stroked lightly, I put the pedal to the metal and zoomed ahead—alone and self-reliant.

My fellow Africans can discriminate among themselves in a way as harsh as anything found in the United States. Outside of their immediate clans or tribes, they can flaunt power just as arrogantly and unfeelingly as their former British masters, but indiscriminately and with less self-discipline. This management of power between the more than forty ethnic groups of Kenya is a bastardized inheritance from former colonial masters, who, for more than seven decades, manipulated already nascent tribalism and nepotism—the twin sicknesses of the continent. The bureaucrats are the worst. Their power is wielded against whites as well as blacks.

———

Up until the new terminal opened in 2013, Kenya's Jomo Kenyatta International Airport remained much the same as it had been since 1958. Entering it, you were struck by an uncompromising display of sharp edges and harsh outlines, with advertisements for Coca-Cola and mobile phone companies covering the walls like an afterthought. Neon lights shined down harshly on travelers as they deplaned.

I remember the first few times I returned to Kenya in the late 1980s. I was in university in the United States then and would return occasionally to visit my family. Once off the plane, all travelers had to line up with their passports before three officials seated on a five-foot-high pedestal. The representatives of immigration control rarely looked at the people passing before them. When they did it was only briefly, like a spark of cold light, and with great solemnity.

"Passport."

I would place my American passport in front of the bent head. "Here you are . . ."

A long pause. Then: "Hmmm . . ."

I would be asked something brusquely. Sometimes I would ask them to repeat the question. Only then would they look at me. Sometimes their faces were oddly youthful; more often wisps of white hair were visible among the black. Often there was a palpable air of boredom. *Haki ya mungu* [Swear to God], *what the hell am I doing in this place?* they might have been asking themselves.

Yet always there was their delight in exercising power.

In the moment when our eyes locked, I felt naked and hated myself for my own weakness. A long minute would pass by in silence. I could hear the high-pitched screech of the neon strips blazing overhead.

"Hmmm . . . what is this?" the official would ask.

A cold sweat would start on my forehead. I would feel like an Arab traveling El Al. Yet this vigilance had little to do with security. There was no shared warmth, no connecting, with these people. They held all the power and they loved the feeling. They might even deny me entry. Then I thought of my mother. *She will get me through if there is trouble.* I could almost smell the fear of others in line behind me, or imagine their thoughts.

We will be sent back!
They will dump me in a jail with the smelly natives!

"Hmmm, what is this?" the official would ask me again.

"Uhhh . . . what? Ex-Excuse me?"

Ignoring me, he would show my passport to a colleague. Silence would fall. The people in line behind me would grow increasingly alarmed. The two immigration officials would confer solemnly together for a minute or two in Kikuyu or Luo while beads of sweat continued to roll down my brow. Finally, the bureaucrat would hand back my passport gingerly, as if it were infected. I would grasp it with relief.

"You can go." With a bored, demeaning gesture, he would wave me on.

Sometimes, after passing through these checkpoints, I would be furious. I was born here. Why put me through this every time? Am I really so different? But, as usual, I would just smile and say, "Thank you."

There were stories of people delayed for hours at the airport for no reason other than an official's capricious dislike of them.

Passport control became faster over the years, but there were always these subtle slights, the sense that, no matter what I did, Kenya was reluctant to welcome me back home. It was like being on an obstacle course where my family happened to live in the center. Over the years, I would navigate it with increasing skill, yet there were always unexpected bumps and rough moments.

My sense of angst would persist up to the baggage terminal. There I would grab my bags and stagger toward a customs agent. Most of the time I would pass through customs in less than a minute. Other times the questions would begin all over again.

I returned to Kenya in 2006 accompanied by my wife. This time the place seemed much friendlier.

"*Jambo*," I said impulsively in Swahili at the immigration desk. "I think you are from here." The visa officer smiled at me and quickly let us through. A short while later, a stocky lady at the baggage check waved me and my wife through with barely a glance. All I did was smile and say, "*Jambo, mama, Habari gani?*" [Hello, mother, how are you today?]

Perhaps it had always been this way and it was I who had changed. For one thing, I was speaking Swahili.

A Bantu language with Arabic, Persian, and other Middle Eastern and South Asian loan words, Swahili is the lingua franca of Kenya, and of many countries in sub-Saharan Africa. At an early age, I'd decided not to learn it. This was partly out of laziness, choosing to get by solely on English, and partly because I was arrogant enough then to consider it unimportant. And because the few friends I had were white, Indian, or spoke English, I had little incentive to change my ideas. It was sometimes hard being African, and the rewards for doing so—for me at least—seemed uncertain.

⌒⌒

Other than a few big cities such as Nairobi and Mombasa, much of Kenya is arable land or desert, with thousands of small towns and villages scattered across it. In many sleepy little towns, the influences of Western culture are plain to see. Posters on kiosk walls glorify the macho American movie heroes of *Rambo* and *Die Hard*, and the latest pirated movies blare from small rooms whose doorways are covered with a strip of black cloth. In the remotest areas, inhabitants may spend their Sunday evenings en masse before open-air cinema screens set up in the village square or else at the local cinema house. At dusk the streets seem to dance with scraps of paper and refuse blown hither and thither. Time after time a stranger to town will come across a stray dog meandering in and out of the darkness. As if drawn together by their mutual solitude, the two feel bound, almost tethered, to each other, before lurching back onto their separate courses.

What is this pervading African indifference I write of? It is a mannerism and a mood, a tone and perhaps even a virtue. It is found equally in the savannah, the twisted pathways and alleys of Nairobi's concrete jungle, and throughout Kenya's scattered country towns. On a visit to the north many years ago during my twenties, I took long walks alongside Lake Turkana at dusk, when the sun looked down tenderly upon the cooling blackened earth. The hills sloped away above the placid water, their sharp, jagged outlines seemingly at one with the immense scarlet-and-mauve rents in the pink sky. Against such a backdrop human beings seem irrelevant, motes against the timeless scene.

In that long-ago foray to Lake Turkana, I encountered El Molo tribesmen, survivors from the distant past. They lived in a few small communities of thirty to forty people, their total population numbered in the hundreds only. Their wooden houses looked skimpy but were strong enough for a place where nature demands resilience. Yet they were a vanishing people. The onset of Western culture and the tribesmen's exposure to diseases to which they had no immunity had seen to that. The children were beautiful, with polished brown skin and eyes that glinted with a sad, sweet merriment. Brightly colored beads dangled over their faces and across their chests. The people we met averted their eyes, shy before us. We, on the contrary, ought to have been shy, for we were the interlopers. We were the gangly, hairy strangers dressed in rude khaki and carrying clunky, noisy cameras.

While walking back to the boat one day, I heard a strange sound. Through the rattan wall of a small hut, I saw the outline of an old man, mumbling audibly to himself.

"He talks to himself every day," someone explained. "No one understands what he is saying. Maybe he is a little crazy."

"There is no one else left from his tribe. They all died long ago. He is the last one. The villagers look after him now."

This village had taken him in and sustained him with its charity. Day after day, as the people around him slept, he would mutter, throwing out his words into the indifferent night. He could have been sharing great thoughts and ideas, stories of ancient warriors or doomed lovers, the epic tales of his vanished race.

I realize now how fortunate I am to have what he lacked: the ability to express myself through music and writing. Without these abilities I would be like him, possessing a view of the world that is unique simply because no one else understands or cares to understand it. Fate had been savage to this man with so much to tell about his life and the extinct people who had left him behind, forever unheard.

Such is the indifference of the land where I was born.

Returning to the capital from my safari to the Turkana Basin, I remember the air turning cool and dry as we climbed higher, and in places it was increasingly polluted by clouds of exhaust fumes. The fields became green and the roads firm and smooth. The people changed too. Lean and wiry Turkana in tribal garments were replaced by short, plump Kikuyu in Western clothes, managing shops selling grocery items and liquor.

Merchants displaying Chinese-made television sets in their shops and providing travelers with tea would line the road, doing their bit to survive. Vendors selling woolen caps and rugs displayed their goods to tourists right off of the highland roads. As we approached, their wares would look like soft, pure white clouds in the grass. Bounced around on our hard seats on the Nissan safari truck, we wanted to stop and lie back on the soft wool and dream forever. But the wind bit into us with a ferocity that braced us and made us feel glad to be alive, and we kept moving.

The only constant was the Rift Valley, whose great and magnificent chasm carved from the earth stretched far into the distance and merged with the luminescent horizon. The Rift is the longest and deepest valley in the world, stretching from northern Syria all the way south to Mozambique. Those who marvel at the immensity of the Grand Canyon will be thunderstruck by the Rift Valley.

A visitor to Kenya is always struck by the beauty of its trees. Even dead trees have a unique beauty here. Their shriveled branches curve grotesquely upward, as if praying silently in the vast cathedral of the African sky. On the savannah there are the sausage trees (*Kigelia africana*) with their brewable fruits, whose thick fingerlike branches reach for the sky and whose latex sap supplies poison for the Maasai's arrows. There is the omnipresent acacia, whose broad branches extend like umbrellas to shade animals from the heat, and the *Diospyros crassiflora* that the tribes use as a purgative and for making furniture. Above all, I remember the trees of my home in the residential area of Westlands. As the wind from the Karura Forest rushed through them, I would hear a low tinkling sound, like thousands of little silver bells, and then, with a stronger gust of wind, a great sigh or exhalation.

Occasionally, when I was in my teens, friends and I would visit the great rich highlands of the Ngong Hills just a few hours' drive from the capital. Once prized by British farmers for their agricultural promise and declared off-limits to Africans, they are now farmed by rich and poor alike and produce much of the country's prized exports, including the Arabica coffee sold by Starbucks. We would rest here under a lone tree overlooking the lush valleys. At those times we would be quiet, thinking about the future of this beautiful land as the cool wind rushed over us. This is an environment you could never find in the United States or China. In place of their eternal noise and the constant hustle to chase after success, here all was peace, freedom, and stillness.

Growing up, I recall Kenya as a quiet, even sleepy, land. In spite of a rickety infrastructure perpetually on the point of collapse, its people continued their deliberate, traditional ways. At our home, my parents would entertain friends who, in spite of seeming impressed by my moderate successes in America and China, would be mostly indifferent to the hurly-burly of the West. Our Kenyan friends would speak straightforwardly, hold their hands to their sides without any displays of jittery or nervous energy, and calmly listen to each idea and opinion.

"America is so different," a Kenyan visitor to the United States might marvel. "In Kenya, when we have time we visit friends, have long lunches, just relax. Here everyone works so hard!"

This apparent meekness cloaked not only a relaxed optimism but also a tough, almost lupine intelligence that occasionally, though rarely, would show itself in the swift lash of sarcasm.

During my childhood and youth, the days jogged by at a steady pace. Sometimes I would go nearly mad at the measured tempo of life in Nairobi and would wait impatiently for something else to happen, even if I didn't know what. At other moments, I would look at the bird-of-paradise flowers in the garden, poised on their stems as if for flight, and imagine that their bright yellow and orange banners were wings that could carry me far, far away. And yet the time passed, like a discreet angel bearing secret gifts, inevitable, inexorable, and, for those with a sense of unfulfilled destiny like myself, always with that same maddening African indifference.

Many were seduced by my homeland (for Kenya—just like America and China—*is* my home) and came there in pursuit of a dream. Sometimes, as in the case of my mother, they eventually found it. Most were disappointed as life there turned out to be much harder than they'd expected.

Nairobi, its capital, was a city built on dreams. Sometime around 1900 the railroad from the coast reached it. Founded just a year earlier as a supply depot, Nairobi started to thrive as the mercantile center of the British colony of Kenya, known until 1920 as the East Africa Protectorate. The city's name derives from the Maasai *Ewaso Nyirobi*, meaning cool waters, even though the place was actually damp and uncomfortable. Like an iron snake the locomotive would twist across the savannah, highlands, and wetlands of southern Kenya, belching fire and smoke. Perpetually hungry and unsatisfied, it would swallow up and spit out passengers newly arrived from foreign lands. After the British soldiers—whom the great Gikuyu sage Chege wa Kibiru foretold as *frog-like people with magic killing sticks*—pacified Kenya, others came, bringing with them wives and children, seeking a new life in the heart of Africa.

By the time the railroad finally linked Mombasa with Luo land, on the shores of Lake Victoria—not far from where my father was born—growing numbers of British settlers were establishing themselves. In the temperate climate of the Aberdare Mountains and the lush Ngong Hills, just a short drive from Nairobi, they started to realize their dreams.

During the years that followed, the settlers' clothes and habits, races and religions would change, but the dream remained the same: to build a new life.

I remember old friends such as Rebecca the Jewish poetess, who believed Africa was her Promised Land. Inspired by Beethoven's *Eroica Symphony*, she left New York for Nairobi. In Kenya she found inspiration for her work. In her dreamy, rapturous poems she described the Africans, in particular the Maasai tribe, as humankind's last hope. She passionately quoted passages from the Torah that described links between Jews and Africans. To these stirring exhortations my stepfather, Simeon, muttered something best left unsaid, and my mother simply smiled politely and gave that familiar look of her that says: *I don't fully understand but I guess you must be right, even though I think it is a little silly.* Kenyans had big dreams, too, just not that many examples of material success.

Electronics were outrageously expensive. There were few cafes worth going to; most were either too dirty or too fancy. There was no television to indulge in. The single TV channel was government-run and transmitted in black and white. I found the food unexceptional. Coming to live in Kenya required a radical readjustment of a Westerner's expectations.

9

Elated to be there at first, ultimately disappointed, Rebecca eventually returned to America. But that is another story.

Perhaps, as my mother may have thought, people like Rebecca were all a little silly to come to Kenya. They were too idealistic, too naive perhaps, and totally unaware that although Kenyans can seem sycophantic in their attention to Germans and Brits on cheap vacations, there was another side to living there, a darker, more cynical side that revealed itself only to those who stayed the longest.

Yes, these foreigners were silly, some might say. Others were harsher and would whisper in Swahili before the unsuspecting new settlers: *Kweli mzungu ni mjinga.* Truly, the white man is stupid.

In the face of Kenya's beauty and ugliness, harshness and tenderness, I was a human receptacle for new experiences and emotions, which one day I would reflect deeply on and finally understand. This is the land in which I was born, a place of darkness and light, warmth and cruelty, decay and renewal, acceptance and rejection, mystery and transcendence, requited and unrequited love, providence and damnation. These contrasts helped to define Kenya's unique blend of African beauty that, for thousands of years, had lured foreigners to its coasts and hinterland, and would one day entice my mother to its shores. It was from such irrationality, from this divine distemper and cauldron of opposites, that my dreams were born.

I took this photo on the Maasai Mara at sunrise. It captures the stark and harsh nature of the savannah and the magnificence and timelessness of Africa.

CHAPTER TWO

My Parents: A Failed Elopement

MUSICAL EVOCATION

Prelude for Piano Op. 23 No. 5: Sergei Rachmaninoff

The first time I heard this slow prelude, the pianist was Sviatoslav Richter, and the performance was magnificent. I think of this work in relation to my parents because of the many dueling melodies within, each speaking a secret, intimate conversation, sometimes in opposition, other times in harmony. The piece is labeled a prelude, but I often think of it as a nocturne, a piece of the night, because of its ABA structure and wide, arpeggio left-hand figurations. The far-ranging arpeggios, in a sense, represent my mother as she persistently, doggedly follows her heart, and the accompanying melodies represent the two men in her life, Barack Obama Sr. and Simeon Ndesandjo.

> *Liebe Marcus,*
> *Funny how so many years ago, I just boarded a plane to Kenya, never thinking I would spend most of my life here. No regrets—[I] have lived and am living a more fulfilling life than I would have in the US, ALTHOUGH I still love America, my friends and relatives there.*
> *Love, Mom*

MY MOTHER RECENTLY MAILED ME THIS BRIEF LETTER, JUST A COUPLE of sentences in ballpoint, scribbled rapidly onto a plain blue card backed by a flower design. Because she mostly uses e-mail, the letter was something of a surprise, and, I suspect, written in a mood of nostalgia.

When my mother stepped off the plane at Jomo Kenyatta International Airport in August 1964, the first thing she saw would have been the Ngong Hills in the distance, shimmering in the noonday heat. She would likely have been dressed too warmly, in clothes suitable for Boston's Logan Airport. She would have walked down the steps from the plane and headed toward the silent group of ash-gray and nondescript single-story buildings. She would have seen more black people in one place than she would ever before have been exposed to in her life. Unaware of her own beauty, she would have passed by the slightly astonished workers, first confidently, then hesitantly, finally stopping, unsure where to go.

At Logan, only one of her close friends had seen her off (her parents, Ida and Joe, having refused to come). Before they hugged for the last time, her friend had exclaimed, "Ruthie, why are you going there? Everyone is black!"

My mother once described her own mother's reaction to her elopement:

> When I decided to leave for Kenya to marry Obama, one of my friends told me that Ida literally started tearing her hair out. She couldn't stand the thought of a black man marrying her Ruthie. Before I left, Ida gathered our neighbors and brought them to our house. They all tried to talk me out of going. For many years she wouldn't even talk to me. After I left she had a nervous breakdown. My father took her out of the country on a three-month trip to help cure her—she was so depressed.

Ruth Beatrice Baker had never even been on a plane before, any plane. Kenya was thousands of miles away. But she was persistent and undeterred, like a bulldog in her tenacity. She felt no regrets for what she was leaving. She wanted only to rejoin the man she loved.

She'd expected my father, Barack Obama Sr., to greet her at the airport. Seeing no one she knew, just a handful of bored or busy employees, she would no doubt have made excuses for him—for that is what lovers do. They excuse the defects of the people they love, for their hearts are full of magnanimity and to them there is no need to explain or justify.*

⌒⌒

My mother, Ruth, was born in 1936 in Brookline, a small town in Norfolk County, Massachusetts, which is surrounded by the horseshoe-shaped conurbation of Boston. Established in 1638 and incorporated in 1705, it has been a magnet for immigrants throughout its history, from the Quakers, Irish, Jews, and Italians to the Eastern Europeans, Israelis, Chinese, and Asians. My mother's father, Joe Maurice Baker, was a street trader who would source goods for companies and individuals and sell them for a small profit. He and his wife, Ida Indursky, were both first-generation immigrants whose families had fled the Russian and Lithuanian pogroms at the turn of the twentieth century. They were proud of their ascent into the middle class, believing they had realized the American Dream.

"They worked hard all their lives," my mother used to say proudly. She always sounded grateful for all that her parents had given her, in spite of their differences and conflicts.

"My father saved enough money to support us and bought us a nice home. Then we moved from Brookline to Newton."

Her parents had doted on the only child born to them, "Ruthie," as they affectionately called her. After Ida had a miscarriage, they decided to adopt a younger sister for Ruth and named her Janet. To all outward appearances they were a normal, successful, middle-class Jewish-American family—right up until Ruth decided to fly to Kenya.

I remember visiting Boston when I was about eleven or twelve. We stayed with Joe and Ida in their home in Newton, an affluent suburb.

"You will love the Reuben sandwiches down the street," my grandmother told me. Together we walked into a small deli down the road. We received a few curious stares from the clientele, mostly elderly Jewish retirees, but she was right. The Reuben was delicious.

---

* In 1998 my mother wrote a memoir of her life, including her experiences with my father. In my novel, *Nairobi to Shenzhen*, many of the letters between the protagonist, David, and his mother are based on this.

My next visit was when I was about to enter Brown University and I stayed with Grandmother Ida for a few weeks. Her longtime renter, Edward, gave me some words of advice. "We all know our place here, Mark. Your mum is Jewish. I'm Irish. You are Jewish . . . and black. I would say stay away from certain parts of Boston, such as Charlestown. They don't like folks like you."

His voice suddenly turned soft so Grandma couldn't hear, as though he was betraying a secret. "I mean . . . some places *you* can go to don't like *me*. It's the same thing, you see?"

I just nodded. I did not visit Charlestown, not because of what Edward said but because Boston had a lot of other more interesting places, like the Faneuil Hall Marketplace, Harvard Square, and the Isabella Stewart Gardner Museum, among others.

Both times I stayed there, everything in Boston seemed so clean and organized. Faneuil Hall, Copley Square, the T Wharf—all seemed to me like places from a fairy tale. Yet in the 1960s, about the time my mother met my father, Barack Obama Sr., the country was in racial meltdown and Boston was in the thick of it. In 1956, a few years before they met, the US Supreme Court had handed down the *Brown v. Board of Education* verdict, which ordered that schools be racially integrated "with all deliberate speed." Yet for years schools were constructed and school district lines intentionally drawn to segregate schools along racial lines. The Civil Rights Act of 1964 and nationwide riots over busing heightened tensions in Boston's already tense racial mix. With perhaps the highest density of schools and colleges in the nation, the city and its citizens experienced tremendous social pressures, including violent and nonviolent protests. Sections of Boston, such as South Boston, stubbornly maintained their ethnic character. It was not unusual for citizens, such as some residents of Quincy or Charlestown, to spend most of their lives without ever coming into contact with a black or Hispanic.

"I didn't know any of these things," my mother told me. "My father had always raised me to value people for what they were, not what their skin color was."

"I always thought I was too fat," she would add, as though this was the reason for the big decisions of her early twenties. "I was so insecure in those days."

In my experience, insecurity derives from an inner sense of imbalance and confusion about the appropriate direction to take in life. While this may have accounted in part for my mother's decision to leave America, I believe there was something else that drove her. Perhaps it was an urge to escape the ennui of her middle-class existence. It could have been the dreary day-after-day reliving of Boston routines, from sharing coffee and boyfriend gossip with girlfriends to doing the laundry, teaching third-graders, boarding the familiar trams that snaked through Brookline. Then there must have been constant pressure on her to get married—from her parents and friends—that weighed her down.

In her memoir she recounts the time just before she met my father. She had graduated from Simmons College and was working and living with two friends, Ann and Annette, in Boston:

[I] was floating around in temporary secretarial jobs. Finally Ann suggested I take a summer course to qualify as a Primary School Teacher, which I did, and then got a job at Brockton Elementary School, as did Annette. Every morning, from September to June, we would trudge off to our jobs—I taught 10–11 year olds and though I basically liked teaching, since I had no experience I was thoroughly exhausted most days, and at the end of the year I was anemic.

By chance, her social life started to involve people who were not from her milieu:

One day during this time, I was coming back to my flat on a streetcar and a black man sat behind me. I guess he thought I was not too threatening so we started to talk. He was from Nigeria and lived almost across the street from my flat. He invited me to a party or perhaps it was just to come and talk, so I did. At that time I was very lonely and insecure. Any friendly face was OK with me. Within a short time I was having an affair with him, and I felt I loved him, but after only one fairly turbulent week he flew back to Nigeria. I was devastated, but a friend of his befriended me and told me he was married anyway. Boy—my eyes were really opening.

Soon afterward, she met my father.

Anyway there was to be another party on the following Sunday, and this new friend said he would like to take me. It was at that party I was to meet my fate—i.e. Barack Obama. He was attracted to me and within a few days he came to my flat with an American friend (older) and asked to take me out. I was on my way to a completely new life.

I can imagine their first meeting. Barack Obama Sr. would have been a force of nature.

My swashbuckling father, perhaps wearing his characteristic black sunglasses, a pipe dangling from his fingers, would have swaggered across the room, his dark, deep voice penetrating every corner of it and charming the impressionable and bored Ruth. When she met him, she would have spotted that he was something different from the usual run of men: mysterious, alluring, and even a little dangerous. She would have seen in Barack Obama Sr., then a graduate student at Harvard, a touchy, sarcastic intellectual whose brilliance overwhelmed those around him and made him admired, sometimes hated, and occasionally, as in her case, loved.

He had a flat in Cambridge with some other African students and I was there almost every day from then on. I felt I loved him very much—he was very charming and there never was a dull moment— but he was not faithful to me, although he told me he loved me too. I am still grateful it was before the days of AIDS, or I would definitely have been a dead duck. He was very promiscuous! I of course was totally innocent and thought I was in love.

After two months of steady romance and fun, he said he had to return to Kenya. He said I should come there and if I liked the country we could marry. I took him at his word. Now I realize this was perhaps a line he gave to every woman/girl he met, but I didn't know that then. So I planned to fly to Kenya in August 1964.

Boston was the only city she had ever known, yet she wanted out. Something made her take the great leap, to leave behind everything that she knew for an African country that was utterly different from America. Ruth Baker was a dreamer in love, and there is no more powerful traveler in the journey of life.

My mother's willful blindness was perhaps something to love. With the insight of a man who played with the emotions of others—possibly because others had always played with his—he knew she trusted him, would forgive him his faults and exaggerate his abilities. Indeed, he would have welcomed her naivete and gullibility, because it allowed him to shirk his own responsibilities and conceal his secrets.

Yet there was one secret he was unable to conceal.

Barack Obama Sr. had married his first wife, Kezia, in 1956, and there were two children from their union, Rita and Bobby. I do not know what made my father tell Ruth the truth. He may just have decided to be honest. He may even have loved her enough to break it gently to her. I tend to think he loved her less than she loved him, and he could bear the prospect of separating from her if she took the revelation badly. So during the spring or summer of 1964, he told her about the two children and asked her if she would be willing to look after them.

He also told her he had a "son by an American woman," in my mother's words. He did not reveal his recent divorce from Stanley Ann Dunham, Barack Jr.'s mother. "I knew he had a son in America but I didn't care," she said. About Dunham herself, she would later tell me, "I did not want to know."

How did my mother react when she learned that the man she loved already had two children in Kenya and an African wife from whom he may or may not have been divorced? Intensely happy and deeply in love, she agreed to become a stepmother.

I sometimes wonder if she knew what she was getting into by deciding to move to Kenya. She not only had to cope with the complexities of Barack Obama Sr. and his culture, but with the opposition of her own family as well.

Ruth's family might have understood had she married a gentile, but Barack Obama Sr. was much more than just a goy.

"Many Jews don't like black people," my mother would sometimes say, almost cutting me off, when I spoke of my admiration for Judaism.

Obama Sr. was foreign and very black. His skin was as dark as ebony, his eyes glinted against it like twin moons, and his teeth shone like pearls. In his terrible magnificence, my father was no mere colored. His blackness went beyond color, like moonless nights or dreams lost in the abyss. He was also from a Muslim family—though personally nonreligious—and from a country and culture thousands of miles distant.

Tie all this in with a somewhat innocent, naive, and lonely Jewish girl from Brookline, and it was remarkable that they managed to stay married for seven years.

But when those two young people shook hands at that party in Boston, their families were not on their minds. They were young, full of life, and just wanted to have a good time.

"Obama was such fun to be around," my mother told me. "Always charming, a great dancer, always something happening. I was young, and I loved it."

About Barack Obama Sr.'s childhood, I know very little. He was born in the scrabbly, sun-baked terrain of Rachuonyo District, located deep in Nyanza Province in western Kenya, in Kanyadhiang village, in 1936. His father, Onyango Obama, a colonial cook, and his mother, Habiba Akumu, who was Onyango's second wife, later moved to settle in Alego-Kogelo, in Siaya District. They had a brief, tumultuous, and violent relationship, exacerbated by Onyango's disciplinarian tendencies. Eventually Habiba would flee, leaving her son, Barack Obama Sr., behind. Although Onyango spent his early life in Rachuonyo, he lived and experienced World War I and II as a road laborer, a cook, and a fighter. Eventually, my grandfather married Sarah Ogwel, the popular Granny Sarah, who cared for him. Obama Sr. was the second-born in a family of nine children. He had his early education at Gendia Primary School, near Kendu Bay, and Ng'iya Intermediate School in Siaya. He then enrolled in the prestigious Maseno School, where teachers described him as an exceptionally bright student. According to reports, he was promoted from class B to A because of good grades.

I visited Alego often as a child and remember it as dirt-poor with dust everywhere. The tropical scrub vegetation, low hills, and red earth seemed ravaged by the cows, chickens, and goats that grazed and trod everywhere and filled the air with the strong smell of dung. Sometimes at night one could look into the distance and see the moonlight dancing like thousands of fairies on the placid surface of Lake Victoria, Africa's largest inland lake, source of the River Nile.

My uncle, Said Obama, recently spoke to me about his father, my grandfather, Onyango Hussein Obama. "He spent his younger, strongest days, fighting in wars in Ethiopia and other places for the British, before returning to Kenya," my uncle told me. "He fathered me when he was very old and lived to the age of one hundred and five. Although many of the older people who could verify it have died, I think he served in some capacity during the First World War, as a laborer or a soldier. He traveled frequently and was extremely strong. He would sometimes walk from South Nyanza Province to Siaya, and then, armed with a whistle to scare off animals, continue by foot to Nairobi in the space of two weeks. He spent much time in Zanzibar before the Second World War, perhaps working small jobs for the Colonial government."

There, in reaction to the Catholicism of his British masters, some say, and in the multicultural environment of this great port, Onyango converted to Islam. He was called George Lucas by his Colonial masters and was glad to henceforth be known as Hussein Onyango. As a cook with a rifle (the British relegated Africans to menial jobs), he also served in the Second World War and traveled extensively to North Africa, Ceylon, Burma, Ethiopia, and the Middle East.

Apart from the horrors of warfare, the World Wars no doubt exposed him to many experiences he would otherwise never have had, such as meeting people from many different cultures. Perhaps the experience awakened in him new dreams for himself, as well as for a better future for his children. Nevertheless, when he returned, the British continued to hire him as a cook, something that he might have regarded as beneath him. In some ways I think my grandfather was a natural intellectual, a man without a formal education but conscious of his own worth and someone who chafed at taking orders from less-talented people. He took the Koran very seriously and also studied books on horticulture.

"He was a very serious man," Paula Schramm née Hagberg once told me in conversation. Onyango Hussein worked for Paula's mother,

Gloria Hagberg, as the family cook during the fifties. Gloria Hagberg was an American teacher, activist, and socialite who, with her husband Gordon, created major multiracial forums for key independence figures such as Mzee Jomo Kenyatta (the first president of Kenya) and the Luo leader Tom Mboya. She later helped my father and many others find ways to study in the States. I was also interested to read further recollections of my grandfather in an article about Gloria, "Cold Warrior for Racial Equality," which appeared in the *East African* newspaper in 2009.

"He never smiled. I was about twelve then," Paula recalled. "He lived in the servants' quarters behind our house. I remember that my mother tried to get electricity for the servants but [was] not able to. He would read the Koran every night in the near darkness. Sometimes your father would knock on the front door, and we would hear his loud and polite British accent: 'Is the Old Man here?'"

"[Onyango Hussein] used to dress in a long Muslim robe," Paula went on, "with a fez on his head. He wore no sandals and worked barefoot. I remember once he stepped on a nail and calmly reached down and pulled it out of his foot. I was shocked. I asked him, 'Doesn't that hurt?' He just shrugged and didn't say anything."

Even now, I imagine this "tall, gray-haired, dignified man," as someone else described him, squatting every evening in his small room, reading the Koran by lamplight, the flame casting a faint glow over his earnest, wizened features. I remember my own *ayah* (maid) Juliana, who helped to raise me. She could easily grasp hot steel pans and pots of boiling water and soup with her bare hands. Juliana also often walked around the house barefoot, as did the other help.

"*Sitaki Maneno!*" ["Don't give me trouble!"] Juliana would just have clicked her tongue had I looked askance at her thick, callused feet. Then she would have smiled, eyes twinkling, her skin shining from the heat of the stove, and perhaps allowed me to try one of her delicious *chapatis*.

When my father was four or five, his mother fled their home to return to her parents' homestead in Kendu Bay. Members of my family tell me that Habiba left Onyango Hussein because he had a violent, authoritarian streak. Yet, I wonder, was the heavy hand of male authority unusual in fiercely traditional and patriarchal Luo society? Here, as in much of

Africa, women were often treated as property. I think there was more to Habiba's story, but most likely I will never know for sure. Some say she visited me when I was a child, but I do not remember it. What is indisputable is that my father, at the age of six or seven, ran away from home with his older sister Zeituni to seek their mother. They were found by their father days later, filthy and lost, on the road to Kendu Bay.

In some ways I see the disintegration of my father's family in his childhood as the forerunner of his own problems with his wives and offspring.

"Losing your mother at a young age," my own mother reminded me, "does things to a young boy."

Yet I also admire, in this early story, his rebelliousness and courage, which sustained him throughout those starry nights spent on the shore, fleeing his father, evading wild animals and the shamans of legend in the heart of Africa.

—◦—

Feet, what do I need you for when I have wings to fly?

In some ways it seems to me these words by the artist Frida Kahlo speak of the longing, pain, and dreams of Habiba, my mother, and even my father as a boy. He, unlike his mother, would eventually resort to an airplane, and not his own feet, to whisk him away in pursuit of his dreams.

I remember seeing a photo of Habiba on the wall of our Alego homestead. She was shown sitting next to her husband, her son Barack on her lap, held tightly in her arms. Her face is proud and beautiful. She had high cheekbones and steeply arched eyebrows that reminded me of pictures I have seen of Kahlo. Like Kahlo, too, there was a flash of anger or else rebelliousness in her eyes, as though she knew she had been wronged. I sensed in Habiba a proud soul that sought her own path, and wanted to fly away and be mistress of her own fate.

"I will fly away, too, and you, old man, will never catch me!" I could imagine her saying.

Photographs like this one of my grandparents are searchlights shone into history. They are also convenient excuses for avoiding the spoken word. The Maasai tribe of Kenya believe that photographic representation captures a man's soul, and it cannot and should not be lightly used. In these past few years, photographs of my parents and of myself in early childhood have helped me unlock memories of my past.

"Bah, photos. I never keep them," my grandmother Ida used to say. "Why keep images of dead people?"

To her they were exercises in vanity and an abnegation of the present. But in these grainy images, I see aspects of people whose genetic code shaped the person I am today. There are, for instance, some photos taken of my father and mother when they were courting in 1964. In one of them my mother is shown seated on a sofa. She looks prim and demure, dressed in a sparkling evening dress. My father lies next to her, in slacks and a plain cotton shirt. His feet are resting on my mother's lap and are closest to the camera. I cannot see his head, which is outside the frame. *This is my mother playing*, I think, almost with shock. Imagining my parents flirting with each other, and being so carefree in each other's company, is unsettling to me because I never saw it for myself, and yet that fun-loving side to them has been passed on.

Particularly striking is a photo of my mother taken while my father was a student at Harvard.

Alone in the black-and-white shot, smiling and looking radiant in an evening dress, she is shown half leaning, half sitting against the edge of a white sofa. The setting is severe, almost spartan. The white wall behind her is bare. She wears makeup, and her hair is coiffed to expose her long neck. Her earrings glimmer. She looks confident and beautiful, far from the insecure young person she believed herself to be. I contrast her smooth, unlined skin with her current wrinkled face. The eyes and that smile have not changed. They are luminous, almost Buddha-like in their warmth and serenity.

I sometimes wonder where the photo was taken. In her parents' home? Or perhaps the place she met my father? Was it taken as she was about to go out for the evening with him to a party? The details of the photo are crystal clear. Everything about it seems perfectly composed: the solid sofa, the stark white wall, the well-designed dress that followed every contour of her body. I see her leaning against the sofa as if for support. Perhaps she was thinking even then of the choices she would have to make, the uncertainty of her future life. I learned later that it is one of three photos taken when they were in Obama's dormitory. In the other two he joins her, and in one he casually places his leg on her lap. They are in love, at ease with each other.

"I was so young and naive then," she would tell me with a hint of sadness in her eyes. Then, with a quick toss of her head, she would turn her attention back to the matter at hand, as though the past had no bearing on the present. My mother, despite her claim of no regrets, would have outbursts of sadness when she recalled something particularly poignant. Her eyes would well up and she would seize my hand tightly then, as though trying to open up a particularly resistant can or soda bottle, and bring her flushed face close to mine.

"Sometimes you're so hard, Mark. I don't know why. But I did so many things for you! Because I loved you so much!"

In early- or mid-1959, when he was twenty-three, Barack Obama Sr. visited the United States Information Services office in Nairobi to get help applying to university in America. He interviewed with Bob Stephens, the Cultural Affairs officer. As Mr. Stephens's wife explained to me in an e-mail:

> . . . *your father was seeking help in getting to the States to go to college. Bob was unable to help him since he had not graduated from high school and therefore lacked a Cambridge School Certificate, not because of academic failure, but apparently for some kind of behavior infraction—not sure what . . . he was helped by Elizabeth Mooney, an American woman who was in Kenya with an adult literacy program and who is now deceased. I believe she did help him financially with travel and later when he was at the university, where he also had a scholarship. He was not chosen for a seat on the 1959 airlift, as others were better qualified. He left sometime after the airlift. Later during his college days he also received some support money from the 1960 Kennedy grant for support of African students from Kenya. We know this from Cora Weiss, who was on the Board at the time of the African American Student Foundation.*

On reading this, I noticed two things in particular. First, my father's persistence. He doggedly sold himself to others, persuading them he was worth helping even without certain educational qualifications. The second is that reference to a behavior infraction. I think of my own infractions later in college, and the fact that I too entered Brown without a high-school diploma. Much can be written of the remarkable coincidences that link fathers and sons.

Just months before my father met my mother, Kenya had obtained independence from Britain. For more than one hundred years, since explorers such as Livingstone, Speke, and Burton started "discovering" Victoria Nyanza—as Kenya, Tanzania, and Uganda were then collectively called—Africans had been struggling for independence. Finally, due to the political leadership of Mzee Jomo Kenyatta, the waning power of Britain, the military resistance of groups such as the Mau Mau, as well as the global shift in attitudes toward colonialism, Britain was forced, even shamed, into granting independence to Kenya. The protests of landed English gentry, who also called themselves Kenyans and who wanted the country to become another minority-ruled South Africa or Rhodesia, became muted and were eventually ignored. However, the bitter dregs of colonialism endured in various forms. The class conflicts the British had used for decades to divide and conquer the inhabitants of their dominion would resurface as nepotism, tribalism, and racism. Kenya would be multiethnic and multiracial, but it would never fully achieve peaceful status. From time to time, such as during elections, the country would spontaneously erupt in outbursts of violence.

The years after independence were heady ones. I can only imagine how happy the Kikuyu, Luo, Kamba, Luhya, and the other forty or so ethnic groups of Kenya were to see the last British soldiers leave their country. Now, they believed, was the time to fill the government and its sprawling bureaucracy with Africans. Barack Obama Sr., a prominent Luo, was a sterling candidate.

My father had first studied in Hawaii (where he met Barack Jr.'s mother, Stanley Ann Dunham). He then transferred to Harvard to continue his studies in econometrics. One of the first Kenyans to study abroad in the United States, he was part of a small and privileged elite, and no doubt well-known to many. He eventually returned to Kenya, and for a time he was on a fast track toward a successful government career, before his life disintegrated and his family broke up.

So now he was back in Kenya, and his new American love had followed him there. Ruth refused to be daunted even when Obama did not turn up to meet her at the airport:

I looked/talked around and met an Airport Supervisor, Mary Radier, who knew Obama (he was well known) and said I should go to her home where she would then get in touch with him. After some hours he appeared and we went off and started living together.

Ruth's perception of my father quickly changed. It was as though he was a different man here from the person she had known in Boston. My mother told me, picking her words carefully, "At that time Africans living in America were held to a certain standard of behavior, particularly if they were dating white women. When they later returned home with these women, it was as though they did not have these restrictions anymore. They also had traditional expectations of family and friends. Many times, the women would pack up and return home."

In her memoir my mother says that he was happy to see her, but:

Right from the beginning he was drinking heavily, staying out to all hours of the night, abusing me (sometimes hitting me and often verbally insulting me) but I was in love and very insecure and somehow managed to hang on. I had come in August, and in December we were married at the Civil Office, with two witnesses.

We were then living in Rosslyn Estate in a big house which was quite lonely and every night I cried for my parents.

Why didn't she take the next plane back to Boston? For his part, if he didn't love her, why didn't he leave her and go back to the other women in his life? I believe both my parents possessed a streak of obstinacy that runs through my own character, an obdurate refusal to recognize failure. It is something deeply conservative, a personality "flaw" that has also, when applied to a worthy goal, been a great source of strength and accomplishment in our family. Although Ruth's love for Obama ran deep, it was also ambivalent, mixed with anger, bitterness, and fear of the unknown.

Obama was actually a very neurotic personality. He would shift moods from very loving to very cruel in a short space of time. Of course, he had a very traumatic background and a very sensitive, highly intelligent nature, so this combination is dynamite. He would often torture me mentally by teasing me, and hitting me. But somehow I hung in there for seven years. I hung in because I loved him a lot—I will never love a man as passionately as I loved him, and I also was very, very insecure. My confidence has been built since the time I left him, but during my stay with him I was very weak. However someone— Mungu—God—Fate—intervened and it was determined I was not to stay with Obama forever.

Of Stanley Ann Dunham, the president's mother, people have wondered if there was domestic violence when they were living in Hawaii. As my mother pointed out to me, African men behaved differently while they were in America. There, particularly in the 1950s and '60s, they would have been sensitive to their minority status. But back home they were surrounded by family and friends and had much more social importance than their significant other, who was generally regarded as property, managed and controlled by the men in her life. White women who married African men, even highly educated ones, were shocked by the change in them once they arrived in Kenya. The consequences were often ugly. The first time my mother's parents visited her from Boston, they were shocked by the squalid circumstances of our home in Woodley. The house was small and dirty, Obama was often out drinking, money was scarce, and Ruth was very unhappy. I remember we didn't have good shoes and I walked barefoot when playing outside. My mother never forgot her father's words to her: "You made your bed. Now you lie in it."

She would lie in it for more than seven years. There were a number of reasons for this.

First, she had burnt many bridges with her family, particularly with her mother, Ida, who for many years could not forgive her for marrying a "colored," though later her attitude mellowed.

Second, my mother loved Kenya and would defend it to the hilt against naive foreign visitors.

"These people," she would scornfully say of visitors' comments about Kenya's corruption and tribalism, "they visit for three days or three weeks, and they think they know everything about us!

"Kenyans are good people," she would insist. "The men have plenty of sex and make things terrible for the women. But," she would add, without hesitation, "Kenyans have always welcomed me. In America, with all that racism, I could never have raised you boys right."

Finally, and above all, there was the love she still felt for my father, and the fear she had of losing her children in a messy divorce.

———

Soon after she arrived in Kenya, my mother became pregnant. I was born November 28, 1965, at the Aga Khan Hospital in Nairobi. It was a Sunday, about two in the morning, and the rain was pelting down outside.

"It's raining, so we will call my son Okoth," my father decreed. My sister Auma was named because she was born facing down. Three years later my brother David would be born quickly and easily, and thus in keeping with Luo tradition was given the name Opiyo.

My mother had another opinion.

"I did not want you only to have a Luo name. I wanted to give you something that would remind you of your Western heritage. I read in the Bible about Mark the Roman. He was very brave and a great hero. So I also called you Mark."

But I was not always wanted by my parents.

"I never wanted a baby. I thought we were moving too fast," said my mother years later. "I was young then, and naive. I would have had an abortion, but I didn't know how! I didn't know about these things!"

She said the last sentence with her eyes flashing, as though someone was about to lash out at her and she was defending herself.

"So we sort of had you by accident. Obama wanted a child."

Then she would turn to face me, now a full-grown man, with something of disbelief in her large hazel-brown eyes.

"You kicked so hard I thought you were going to kill me!" she would exclaim. "But then when you were born I was so happy!"

My wife thinks that my constant sense of insecurity stems from those early months in my mother's womb.

"When she was pregnant she did not want you. You felt you were not loved and have always felt unsafe. Even then your mother's feelings were passed on to you."

Could this be? I received my mother's comments (and later read them in her memoir) with cool objectivity and thought, *I'm here, and that's that. I have no doubt she loves me now.* Yet, I reflect, could those first formative months have sowed the seeds that made my subsequent life a roller-coaster journey, a perennial search for acceptance and love, an eternal battle to come out ahead, no matter what the cost?

Once she had me, motherhood won out.

My mother had great expectations of me. I was her firstborn, and although, in her opinion, I would always be a "difficult" child, she believed I was capable of greatness. In many ways my life would be an attempt to realize her expectations and beliefs.

I don't know if I was kicking to get out or to stay in. Nevertheless, I have always loved the rain, and perhaps it has something to do with that cold, damp Sunday morning in Nairobi, when I emerged kicking and screaming from her body.

But the joy of having a new child could not compensate for the daily fights and arguments between my parents. Ruth was so unhappy in that first year living with Obama that she finally returned to America.

I stuck this out for one year when a friend of Obama told me he would help me get away. I decided to go back to the US. I got a ticket from my parents and flew off . . . with Okoth. My parents found a house for us to stay in—of course I couldn't stay with them as I had a BLACK baby! Nevertheless, they loved me but probably didn't know what to do with me and my baby. However within a few weeks Obama came back after me! I had never expected this and of course I returned to Africa with him as I still loved him. But of course—after moving into a city council house where we were to stay for about four years—he didn't change and in fact was probably even worse.

My earliest memory is of following my mother through a field just outside our house in Woodley. I was wearing diapers and what looked like a dress. She was walking fast and I couldn't keep up with her. The sun was very bright and the grass was tall. It looked like thin golden feathers waving gently in the breeze. I must have been about two or three at the time. I remember the frustration I felt trying to keep up with her. She walked fast. Her legs looked huge to me, and ever out of reach. I wanted to walk faster than she was. Perhaps there is truth in what some say: The clue to understanding a man's life lies in discovering his earliest motivation and desire, the one idea or urge that he, even as an infant, pursued like no other. Perhaps this is why I became so competitive, seeking to move faster than my mother in every way.

In September 1969 my brother David was born. While we lived with Barack Obama Sr., my mother also raised Bobby (now called Malik) and Rita (now called Auma). Bobby was about six, Rita a little younger. Unlike her brother, she was sent by her father to a boarding school at the age of four or five, before returning to live with us. According to my mother, both children, particularly Rita, were devastated at the separation from their mother, Kezia. She and Barack Obama Sr. had been married in a traditional Luo ceremony. Although their marriage had ended in separation, the bridal wealth was never returned to Kezia's family, and thus, according to Luo tradition, they never divorced. Despite reports to the contrary, and according to close family friends who knew my father well, Obama Sr. never returned to Kezia, even after his divorce from my mother. I was Barack Obama Sr.'s third son (after Bobby and Barack Jr.) and fourth child. In all he would have six children: Barack Obama Jr., Bobby, Rita, David, George, and myself.

To me it seemed natural that my mother would take on the responsibility of raising Rita and Bobby. Coupled with her strong will was a devotion to helping others, particularly children. Years later she would set up her own kindergarten, and she always raised money to help local children's charities such as the Thomas Barnardo's Home in Nairobi.

Her belief that she could raise my father's children by Kezia stemmed perhaps from misplaced self-confidence. "I could do it better than others in the family," she convinced herself. "Obama didn't support Bobby and Rita. I did. He used all his money for drinking and going out. I was very sorry for them, because I knew they missed their own mother."

But whatever my mother's hopes might have been for her integrated family, there was always a distance between Bobby, Rita, and myself. It was as though they resented her love for me. I, in turn, was fiercely possessive. To share her, even later with my brother David, was a struggle for me. In retrospect, I see that I was very lonely and needed stability, of which our family knew very little. My siblings required the same, but the only source of stability and safety in our home was my mother. Everyone wanted a piece of her. As her firstborn, I clawed away all competitors.

Bobby used to hit me a lot, and I was quite afraid of him. Barack Obama Sr. must have had high expectations of him as the firstborn son. Nominally the most important child according to Luo tradition, Bobby would have a lifelong struggle with duty, individuality, and understanding his own limitations. There were many times he would run away for days on end. On one occasion, however, he saved my mother's life, and for that I will always be grateful.

Rita was aloof and looked down on me, perhaps because she believed we had stolen her father and taken her away from her mother. Conversely, she loved her father, for she was his only daughter, and may have seen my mother as a competitor. Her sensitivity ran deep, and her anger, like a slow-burning ember, was slow to reveal itself. Then, at a critical moment, it would suddenly burst into flame.

There were times we argued bitterly. I remember once receiving an inflatable swimming pool as a birthday present. I was about five or six then. I don't remember who gave it to me. It was brightly colored, firm, and resilient. The plastic smelled of that opulent newness that beguiles children. I had never received such a valuable present and was very happy. I would fill it with water and play in it for hours on the bright sunny lawn of our small house.

"Okoth, I am visiting some friends. Can I borrow your swimming pool this afternoon?" Rita asked me one day.

I refused. Borrow my swimming pool! It was the equivalent of lending someone your brand-new iPhone today. Such gifts were rare and could easily be damaged.

"Let me borrow it. I'll be very careful. I'll bring you back some sweets."

Rita could be very persuasive. At that time we could afford few toys. For snacks we sometimes ate the often bitter fruit that grew on the thick hedges surrounding our little house. Sweets and snacks, like cheese, ice cream, and mangoes, were luxuries.

"Okay, if you're very careful," I told her reluctantly.

She skipped off happily. When she returned hours later, the pool had been badly damaged and would not inflate. I cried for hours, hating Rita for what she had done.

I remember that day even now, almost forty years later. When I recalled this incident recently, my wife laughed.

"Why did you remember that for so long? I guess you must like swimming pools and water very much."

It was my father, of course, who gave me the memory and fixed sense of purpose of an elephant. These characteristics helped me study for hours a day during exam preparations, but they would also produce a rigidity in my approach that often prevented me from seeking alternate routes.

"A brilliant man, but a social failure," my mother would often say of Obama Sr.

She would say it judiciously—as though balancing oranges on a scale, making sure nothing tipped over. This was neither defense nor attack. She no doubt did not want to prejudice me against him, but when pressed she would reveal details of their relationship in a dry, and mostly unemotional, way.

We would often accompany him to pubs and hotels, particularly the Starlight Club and the Panafric Hotel, two popular Nairobi nightspots. We would wait in the car or hang around until he'd finished having drinks with his friends. I was very young then, and the images in my mind are now like out-of-focus color photos: a hotel room here, a wet tabletop there, a white Datsun that seemed to creak along the bumpy roads . . . and always the inquisitive stares of strangers. I remember my mother and me waiting for him to come back to the car once.

"Where's Daddy?" I asked

"He's coming," she said.

I saw him standing near some bushes, not moving. "There he is! What is he doing?"

"Just watering the flowers."

I wanted to water the flowers but was too reserved to do so.

This is the one memory of my father that makes me want to laugh a little, and even want to be like him. If there was one thing I wanted that he possessed, it was the ability to be free, uninhibited, even blatantly so. However, my father's freedom of expression came at a high cost, with consequences that deeply affected his children. It would ultimately take a terrible toll on all of us.

Barack Obama Sr. at a friend's family event in Nairobi, next to an unidentified friend and her baby. Until someone pointed it out, I did not realize it is one of the rare photos I have of him smiling. At the time, he had a good job, a house, and a beautiful wife. c. 1965

Obama Sr. was an outstanding student at the University of Hawaii, where he met Stanley Ann Dunham, the mother of President Barack Obama. While at Harvard, he met my mother, Ruth.

My parents shortly after they married in Kenya. I love this photo because of the evening shadows that hover over the scene, like bold and anonymous phantoms. c. 1964

My mother, Ruth Ndesandjo, née Ruth Beatrice Baker, is still an avid tennis player. Here she is in Boston, while in high school. c. 1952

Barack Obama Sr. on the University of Hawaii campus, shortly before he transferred to Harvard University, where he met my mother. c. 1963

Ruth at the time she met Barack Obama Sr. in Boston. She was then working as a teacher c. 1964

My mother and me. I was born November 28, 1965. Our bond was inseparable, and remained so.

CHAPTER THREE

Dissolution: Johnnie Walker Black Label

MUSICAL EVOCATION

"Jerusalem the Golden" Band Variations: Charles Ives

Charles Ives was an insurance salesman who happened to be also one of America's great composers. His works were often atonal and unpleasing to the musically untrained, who often think his music has no melody. While listening to a stonemason's off-key singing, Ives's father once said to him, "Look into his face and hear the music of the ages. Don't pay too much attention to the sounds—for, if you do, you may miss the music. You won't get a wild, heroic ride to heaven on pretty little sounds." This work was written to evoke various marching bands, each playing different tunes, passing by each other in a town square. There is an emotionally wrenching quality to the music that makes me think of the final years of my parents' marriage and the wreckage left of their wild, heroic ride.

"THIS IS NOT GOOD," ONE OF MY BROTHERS E-MAILED ME AFTER I'D published *Nairobi to Shenzhen*, a novel that alluded to domestic violence in our family. "There are things best left unsaid."

My brother Malik, known as Bobby when he was a child, is a huge, powerful bear of a man. His skin is very dark, and when he smiles his brilliant white teeth seem to glow. Occasionally he wears a Muslim fez over his short kinky hair. He walks with a slight stoop, sometimes giving one the impression that he is embarrassed by his height. His eyes are always a little red, as though he is still recovering from a slightly tipsy evening and befuddled dreams. Malik's dreams do not seem to be happy ones. His mood and his words are colored and weighed down by the past, and guilt for his role in a family tragedy hangs like a necklace around his thick, stocky neck.

"Where have you been, Mark? You were away so long," he told me after we had hugged in greeting. "Where is your wife? Have you any children?"

His voice was deep and gentle. With his large hands and feet he seemed to dwarf the overstuffed sofa on which he sat. The family had gathered at the Mayflower Hotel in Washington, DC, reunited for my brother Barack's inauguration.

"You know we call you the 'crazy one,' over there in China?" Malik's somber expression faded to be replaced by a big smile. "But we knew you would be back one day," he told me.

It had been more than thirty years since I'd last seen him. The plot of my novel, *Nairobi to Shenzhen*, though fictional, had many parallels with my own life. Writing it had been one of the most difficult things I had ever done because I knew it would hurt others in my family. Nevertheless, I would come to see the completion of the book as part of the process of reaching an understanding of my own character and motivations.

I have few happy memories of my early life. I felt I had no real friends then and remember being mostly alone. Those who think that childhood is always a time of innocent, carefree pleasures are fooling themselves. My own early years were tainted by a sense of looming conflict, even danger. It was as though I existed on an island perpetually shrouded in the gloom and anxiety of night, in which, now and again, my mother's ivory-white skin shone like the only beacon of hope and love. During subsequent years the threats that loomed within this dreamscape have mostly stayed at bay, lurking in the hidden corners of my memory. At times, in an occasional nightmare or a forced recollection, they jump out at me still. Troubling details become more clearly defined: the face of a dark man wearing glasses, the sound of angry shouting, blades of tall grass, a black bottle shattered to pieces on the ground.

Though I know of his many accomplishments, my father remains largely an enigma to me. I remember him the way I saw him when I was a child: a hulking, brooding man with very black skin, an often angry and scathing voice, and permanently bloodshot eyes. Doctorates and diplomas have little currency to children. Much more important is what they witness at close hand, the forces that tear apart or bring together their family. Early memories endure inside a maturing mind like coals glowing in a grate: searing hot, poorly defined, still dangerous. As an adult it's possible to make more sense of them, but they always burn.

To this day I do not know whether he loved any of us, but somewhere I think my father felt obliged, in the back of his mind, to keep the family together. I sensed a mix of anger, bitterness, and regret in him, as though he always wanted to be somewhere else when he was with us. I cannot help but think that he was perhaps seeking a return to his college days. He associated my mother, and perhaps Stanley Ann Dunham and her son Barack even more, with the sparkling promise of his early days in America, a time when it must have seemed to him that anything was possible.

The words of the poet Xu Zhimo sing through my mind:

The pool beneath the elm,
Is not a clear spring, but a heavenly rainbow:
Shattered by the floating greenery
It settles into a colorful dream . . .

Every day that he saw my mother, Barack Obama Sr. must have been reminded of those younger days and wondered if the past was irretrievable: the rainbows he remembered now just pools of water and silt.

Yet he still infused the lives of his family with more than intoxicating dreams and a bittersweet sense of melancholy.

My mother says Barack Obama Sr. beat her as well as my brother David. "I don't remember him beating you," she once said. "I think he wanted to keep away from you."

My father did beat me, though infrequently. There was never anyone around to help me then, and the images I retain of these incidents are fragmentary: a raised hand, the smell of Scotch, a momentary furtive blow—and always that large, dark raised hand. I try to dig deeper in my mind, but something stops me, as though there is a place I do not want to go. Things, as Malik chastised me, *best left unsaid.*

To admit "my father beat us" even now feels shameful to me, like an admission of weakness. For a long time I hated the memory of my powerlessness then and dismissed it from my mind. Yet the consequences for all of us have become ever clearer, like ghostly images that gradually come into focus over time.

———

Most of our life with Barack Obama Sr. was spent in Woodley, on the outskirts of Nairobi. Not far from our street was a large grassy field. These days squatters in makeshift canvas-and-wood tents camp there, selling soft drinks, pirated DVDs, and drugs. In Adams Arcade, a small commercial strip of mom-and-pop grocery stores, the local bank and butcher are still there, though a little more grimy and crowded. Not far away our home, an unexceptional, single-story, brown-brick house with grilles over the windows, was sequestered in a small warren of similar residences. Tall shrubberies enclosed our little archipelago, cutting off the house from everything except the sky above our heads.

Our life there was characterized by continuous conflict and domination. My elder brother and sister dominated me as I tried to dominate my younger brother. The man who looked after me when my mother was away would lock me in the kitchen closet for hours while he worked. I don't remember how my mother found out, but I remember one day he was no longer in our employ. There was always fear and tension in the air, particularly at night. My mother once shouted out in fear when she bumped into Bobby in the dark. He was carrying a large kitchen knife, and she thought he was a burglar. I rushed out to her, screaming and terrified. I can still see those two faces in my mind's eye: my young mother and my large, loping African brother, frozen and silhouetted against the silvery moon, like Janus faces.

Our father loved Johnnie Walker Scotch whisky. Even today the words *Johnnie Walker Black Label* float out of my mouth, unprompted and fluid, like an Irish ditty without the brogue, or like the Lord's Prayer, which was drummed into us day after day in my Roman Catholic high school. I knew whenever my father was present by the sweet, pungent, and heady smell of whisky. Johnnie Walker Black Label, and later the cheaper Red Label, added a physical component to his verbal abuse from which there was no protection.

For me the blackness of the night, of my father's face, of my African siblings, even of my own skin, came to be associated with everything that was hateful, menacing, and destructive. The only solace I found was in the unconditional love of the woman who had borne me. With her I shared an unspoken bond forged out of equal parts of self-preservation and loyalty.

Memories are strange things. When combined with the wisdom of maturity, incidents that once seemed normal appear in a completely different light. They reveal themselves, like a palimpsest, or the hidden sketches beneath an Old Master, and become a fresh portrait of a life. I now know why my mother sometimes seemed reluctant to take off her dark glasses (although she said Barack Sr. mostly pummeled her body). I now know why in photos taken of me with my father, I always seem to flinch away from his hands. We Obamas have big hands. They can be used to create or to debase. My hands enable me to comfortably reach across twelve keys and play piano well. My father would use his big hands to knock my mother down when he came home from a night of drinking. I would move protectively toward her and clutch her legs, crying. I know now why I mostly remember her legs, not her torso, or even her face.

"You take care of him too much!" my father would yell at her, his loud voice booming from the living room and easily reaching our bedrooms.

Other times I would be woken up in the middle of the night or early morning by strange sounds coming from outside my room. I was afraid of the dark and would always wait for my mother to tuck me in. I would carry my security blanket and suck my finger everywhere I went. She would tenderly place the blanket next to me before she switched off the light.

"Don't close the door! Leave the light on outside!" I would shout.

When I was abruptly woken up, I would see light streaming in around the sides of the door. There would be thumps and yells, often followed by the sound of my mother screaming in pain or anger. Once I heard a loud crash and rushed to the door of the living room. By the orange light I saw my mother on the floor and my father standing over her, his hands clenched. Now, as an adult, when I try to remember more, it becomes painful for me and I close my mind. I can only imagine how it must have felt for a child, any child, to have been unable to protect the one he loved the most. Every blow my father gave my mother I felt, and each time it seemed to shatter the safe world I was trying to construct for myself, through refuge in study or play.

Sometimes I would hear slamming doors and the sobbing sounds of my mother in the street. Left in the house with just him, I cried because I did not know why she had left me. However, she always returned a few hours later, and then the shouting would begin again. My mother later recounted these experiences in her memoir:

> *I can remember running out into the night several times when he was after me to beat me, and screaming for help . . . These memories are very painful for me to write about but I think I might as well once and for all. I can remember a neighbor coming out of his house trying to help me as I went screaming down the street, but I think I eventually stayed in a friend's home and then begged Obama to let me come back because of course I couldn't bear to be away from my baby. EVER!*

I also remember the night I was woken up by a terrible pounding on the door to the house and my father's voice yelling outside. I remained in my room, frozen with fear. Then there was an abrupt silence, which was broken by the sound of the front door slamming open followed by my mother's terrible screams. And my mother did not scream like normal people or the way one hears actors do it in the movies. Her scream was terrifying, like an animal's, high-pitched and flat, repeated again and again. Every time I heard it, it tore into my heart like a lance. I was too afraid to go to the living room. I heard Bobby and Rita crying, and my father yelling at my mother. It went on like this for several minutes, the voices intercut with thuds, slapping sounds, and screeching furniture being shoved aside. Then I heard someone else talking to my father in Luo. When I eventually walked into the living room, my mother was on the couch, sobbing, and my father was being restrained by another African. A long knife lay on the floor. My mother later filled in the gaps in my recollection:

> *I had obtained a restraining order against [your father]. Then he came home one night, drunk. He pounded on the locked door. I refused to let him in, but Rita then opened the door for him. He rushed in, extremely angry. He threw me on the couch and held a knife to my throat.*
>
> *Bobby saved me. He ran across the street to get the neighbor. I would be dead if it wasn't for him.*

When I was six or seven, I had my first sexual experience. A boy who lived across from our house sometimes used to play with us. He was much older than me, perhaps ten or eleven. One day he came up to me while I was playing alone in the garden. He was accompanied by another boy I did not recognize.

"Okoth, do you want to see something interesting?"

I nodded.

"Over there." He pointed out a spot some distance from our house.

Expecting some fun, I ran with them to the hedge bordering our garden. The grass grew tall and green there, concealing our activities.

"Look at this," he said, and drew down his pants.

His penis looked strange. It was covered with something that looked like green mold. I did not know what to make of it.

"What's wrong with your willy?" I asked. The other boy laughed.

"He's sick."

"Big people put these between your bottom. I can show you, if you like?" the older boy quickly said.

I don't remember how I answered. Perhaps I nodded. I remember lying on my stomach on the grass while he lay on me. It was painful. Then he got up and he and his friend ran away. I did not know the significance of what had happened, but I never told anyone this story at the time. I wondered for many months if my penis would turn green like his.

I sometimes wonder why I did not talk about these things to my mother. I believe it was because I had been hardened by my early

43

experiences to say to myself, "So what?" as though wife and child abuse, and homosexual rape, were everyday occurrences.

Like Malik said later, it was normal for *some things to be left unsaid*.

Only recently when a reviewer of my novel referred to the scene in the garden *as a rape* did I actually start to see it as such. Then, my mother told me my stepfather, Simeon, was shocked to read about it in the manuscript draft I had sent both of them. Up until then, I had thought it was just some kids playing around.

———

By the end of his third marriage, Barack Obama Sr.'s once-bright spark had decayed into smoldering ashes. Under normal circumstances, my father's brilliance would have propelled him to a magnificent, perhaps glorious, career. However, the nepotism and tribalism that were rife in the young republic of Kenya combined to raise obstacles in his path; his tactlessness and flamboyant behavior, plus the scars left behind by his own traumatic upbringing, did the rest. The government jobs he was offered became more and more inconsequential. Kenyan politics drew a vise around his ambitious nature, and his steady consumption of alcohol gradually dulled his intelligence with a terrible thoroughness.

His self-hatred and tendency toward self-sabotage was passed down and became part of my identity. My mother's lily-white skin and my father's ebony-black visage came to symbolize an eternal incompatibility in my mind's eye. For a long time I hated to have anything to do with what my father represented, whether it was him personally or even the positive aspects of African culture. In violent reaction against him, I turned passionately toward Western culture and music, which brought me a measure of solace.

At the time of my mother's marriage to Barack Obama Sr., his relatives would often arrive unannounced and live with us for extended periods. There was Aunt Zeituni, who stayed with us for about a year, always dressed in hippie clothes and immensely proud of her huge afro. Then there was Uncle Ogosa, who may even have loved my mother in an innocent, adolescent way, but that shifted eventually into unthreatening admiration. Others came and went, eventually returning to the amorphous hinterland from which my father originated, like phantoms in the night. My mother couldn't stand the upheaval and, before she remarried, made her new husband promise her they would maintain their privacy. Western and African cultures have diametrically opposite notions of privacy and of one's duty to his or her extended family. The conflict between them would later cause repercussions in my own adult life.

Every now and again we would visit Alego-Kogelo. We would set off by car early in the morning and after a daylong drive arrive at our ancestral home. There was a time when the roads to Kisumu were too dangerous for many travelers to use, with a driver having every likelihood of smashing into a parked or broken-down bus, of falling into a huge pothole, or of veering off an unsurfaced track. The police might ask for bribes, and robbers wouldn't bother asking. These days the roads are considerably better, and tourists can cut across the fine Mara Road and bypass Kericho and Nakuru.

Our car would pass by the Great Rift Valley and mystic Mount Longonot. I remember spotting by the side of the road, almost hidden behind thick bushes, the remains of the old chapel built by Italian POWs during the Second World War, which is now a refurbished tourist attraction. The land would turn richer and fields of sugarcane, wheat, sorghum, millet, pyrethrum, and *sukuma wiki* (collard greens) would appear in shimmering waves of green and gold. We'd see tea pickers and their children in the emerald fields of Kericho—where white colonial farmers once usurped the land from the Kikuyu and Kamba—develop an industry that produced the best tea in the world.

We would pass Kericho on our way to Ahero, finally arriving in Kisumu late in the evening. If we were lucky we would see the sun set over the equator as we passed the magnificent rocks and boulders of Maseno. These days there are acres and acres of rice fields visible, reclaimed from the Yala River when it was joined to Lake Victoria. Thousands upon thousands of herons, pigeons, kingfishers, hammerkops, and egrets alight on the white husks like trembling clouds of ash and are promptly driven away by legions of women clashing pans, making enough noise to drive away devils and demons.

I was about five or six years old then. My brother David was just a baby, and I do not think he came with us on these long trips, except for once when he got very sick with malaria. In general someone would care for him back home, and my mother would count the days until she could hold him in her arms again. I never understood why we had to leave our home in Nairobi to travel to this poor set of thatched huts, where people in cheap clothes and sandals spoke a language I couldn't understand.

Not speaking Luo, I was never accepted by the African children. My air of reserve was taken for aloofness and met with disdain and taunting. It was all very strange, difficult, and intimidating.

However, there were lighter, more surreal moments. Most nights we would go to the local bar, a one-room house with a single bare lightbulb and rows of benches lined against the wall. Outside there were flimsy chairs and tables, with lots of beer in huge vats and men talking and yelling in Luo.

The air was thick with the voluptuous, oily smell of fermented maize *kong'o*, and people fought to be heard over the sound of rock and roll playing on the local radio station. My father would forget us as he drank with the villagers into the night. My mother and I would regularly sneak away to a small storage room, where there was a tiny iron-framed bed. We would try to talk over the din until, tired from the effort, she would get up to leave me.

"Mum, let's go home," I pleaded sometimes, when I heard the shouts of men, the clinking of beer bottles, and the beat of Benga music from the radio.

"Hush. You can sleep here a bit, and when we leave I'll wake you."

She would gently tuck me in. I did not want to go back to where we were staying. I wanted to return to Nairobi, which I knew and was used to. I would try to sleep but the noise of the partying was deafening. Unfazed by the harsh glare of the overhead lightbulb, the mosquitoes would bite me when I dozed off.

One night the clamor was so loud I had no choice but to come out of the storage room into the bar. I stood glumly next to my father and mother and the women and men who sat happily gossiping and chattering. Wet wooden tables filled with beer bottles and glasses loomed around me.

"AAAAAAAAAAAAAAAYOOOOOOOOOOOOOOOOO!!!!!!!!!!!"

The sound seemed to rise like a ghostly wail from the alien landscape that surrounded me. I looked around and saw the source of the sound, a strange musician, the bugler of Alego. Dressed in a straw loincloth, long bead necklaces, and a traditional Luo hat, his distended, bare potbelly and jolly face were a terrifying sight. He was weaving between the revelers like a black Santa without reindeer.

"AAAAAAAAAAAAAAAYOOOOOOOOOOOOOOOOO!!!!!!!!!!!"

I heard that sound again. When he lifted his wooden clarinetlike horn to his fleshy lips, his cheeks blew up, Dizzy Gillespie fashion, to an incredible size. It was as though both sides of his face had been hijacked by shining, coffee-colored soccer balls. I looked in amazement at the two glistening orbs, afraid they would burst, so tight was the bulging skin. Above those bulbous cheeks his small eyes were narrowed to slits that shone with a maniacal intensity. And then that sound issued forth: high-pitched and yodeling, as if to the very gates of heaven or hell. It was deep, throaty, feminine and masculine all at once, as it flowed from the pub and out toward the gorges and valleys, thrusting through the streets of night-time Alego like a hell-driven banshee. Then, just as suddenly, the sound would cease and the distended face would shrink back to the jovial, blubbery visage of the old bugler.

"Mum, what is wrong with that man's face?" I gasped in horror.

"It's nothing to get upset about. The muscles in his cheeks are worn out. It's normal for him," she murmured, smiling at me.

I identified in some strange way with this old bugler. I wanted to be as free as the sound he made, free like Habiba, to fly away over the hills, away from this confusing place.

I would wake up early in the morning to the clanking of pots outside, the constant singsong murmur of women, and the sound of roosters crowing across the wet green hills. The smell of milk and dung would be everywhere, almost overpowering.

Although I played with the other children, we rarely understood one another.

"There was always a language barrier between us," my uncle Said told me years later. Said was my father's youngest brother, born late in life to

Onyango Hussein Obama and his third wife, Sarah, and was about my age.

During the day I would sometimes follow Said and his friends as they led the cows to pasture. I can still see the other boys running before me, swishing their sticks with stopwatch regularity against the loping, hulking hindquarters of the steers and cows. Emerald-green vegetation surrounded us, still wet from the night's dew, and the narrow path would run between the shallow hills like a swab of brown paint, squelching under our feet.

When we returned to the compound hours later, I asked for the toilet.

"Behind the bushes." Said pointed out a small patch of vegetation not far from the house.

"Is there toilet paper?" I asked.

"You can use this." Said tore some leaves off a large bush and handed them to me, smiling naturally, as though it was the most normal thing in the world.

The games we played included trapping and shooting birds with makeshift arrows. I do not remember how we actually caught the birds, but it was difficult and took a long time. When we finally caught a small, scraggly brown one, everyone was excited and rushed back to the homestead.

I wanted to ask what they were going to do with it, but I did not know how.

I followed the other boys to a hut and was shocked when they pulled out its feathers and prepared to cook and eat it. It had been such a small bird, and so weak and helpless. I hated the taste but tried to eat a little.

I was eager to leave this place with its strange people, funny smells, and unfamiliar foods. Most of all, not understanding poverty, I could not accept its harshness and indifference. Granny Sarah, my father's step-mother who had replaced Habiba, was the only person who seemed to understand. I remember her kindly face, deeply wrinkled with smile lines, and bright eyes that were curious, welcoming, and shrewd. Even when she was busy, she would take time to give me a hug or two or point me out and shout, "Okoth likes playing with the dogs and chickens!"

Then she would give a huge bellow of laughter that could have come from the lips of Zarathustra himself, proud, deep, and resonant.

I pronounced laughter holy; you higher men, learn—to laugh!

When we returned to Nairobi, the violence would continue. My father turned his anger on David, the baby of the family, which my mother could not ignore. Even then it took a chance meeting and a few thoughtless words from someone else to wake her up to the true gravity of her situation.

"My God, Ruth! Are you okay?" a friend told her. "Your face looks so old these days!"

It was as though the reasons for the eventual divorce had always been around, but now, at last, she could see them clearly, in her own changed face.

My mother wrote about it in her memoir:

One day as I was driving back to my home in Woodley . . . I saw a white girl, carrying a portfolio, walking on the road. I decided to pick her up and thus started a fateful relationship. Her name was Anna and she was a writer and artist.

At any rate, she was a good friend to me and [she] encouraged me to leave Obama. He sensed she was his adversary and literally threw her out of the house. However she had lit a fire in me and I went ahead with the idea of leaving him. She made a statement which was witnessed so I could use it in court . . . [It] explained how she had seen him abusing me, had seen him drunk, etc. Also about that time my cousin Lois, to whom I'm still very close, visited me. She too was on safari to Africa. She stayed with me awhile and told me she couldn't understand why I put up with such abuse.

These two girls were my support—it had been long since I had had support from women of my cultural background—and I found the strength to go ahead with a divorce from Obama. I was also lucky because just at that time Obama decided to take a trip around the world . . . he had the money for a three-month-long trip.

Unknown to my mother, during this trip Barack Obama Sr. also included a stopover in Hawaii, when he visited Stanley Ann Dunham and the young Barack, then ten years old. To this day I wonder if he and Dunham talked about us. Did he tell her he had married another white woman and had two children by her? I would guess that she would have not wanted to know. Nevertheless, she must have understood Obama needed to see her and their son. I believe my father loved and was very proud of Barack, and in seeing his son, he could temporarily escape the friction and sadness of his Kenyan life. He would not have discussed the car accidents his drinking had led to and that had resulted in severe fractures to his legs, his failing third marriage, and his disintegrating career. Instead he would have dressed sharply for the occasion, perhaps whipped out a pipe, delicately arranged his broken legs and cane, and talked about how wonderfully things were going.

It was easy for my father to love Barack and Ann. They were far away and he could idealize them. He hated to see the reality, the defects in people close to him. The problems of strangers by contrast were distant things, of little real import and easier to handle. Charity to distant family members who needed money or drinking buddies could be easily dispensed and then ignored. However, when his immediate family needed something urgently, like medicine or food, he would realize it was his duty to respond even though he was often unable to rise to the challenge. This would leave him laboring under a tremendous sense of injustice, as though it was he who had been wronged. Those who needed him would have shamed him by exposing his vulnerabilities. Forced into action, he would conclude the unlucky whims and caprices of fate were no longer indifferent but actively hostile to him. He would then blame the family member asking him for help, or for love.

The women in his life would naturally have been bewildered by this and would not have understood why even their thanks made him feel so guilty, so angry. Their meekness and gratitude would be perceived by him as weakness. My father was a man who only respected toughness, and until he saw it, he would push and berate, probe and maul. It was as though his heart was a bank account in perpetual deficit, and his wives were perennial debtors. And all of this, all this waste of talent and energy and love, would never be understood by my father himself, who was never one to reflect on his own character and behavior.

My mother had finally found the courage to take the fateful step. While my father was abroad in 1972, she started divorce proceedings with the help of a very supportive lawyer, Michael Shaw of Daly & Figgis.

And then Obama came back. He begged me to drop the divorce case . . . Mr Shaw convinced me to go ahead with the divorce . . . because if Obama did change, it wouldn't matter. I could still live with him.

During the final [hearing] I remember being more undecided in my mind than at any other time in my life . . . finally I went through with it and we were legally divorced. I continued to live with Obama but told him that he had no hold over me anymore, but of course he didn't really listen to me and thought I would always stay with him. He was mistaken.

I got so fed up with his abuse and cruelty that I found an Indian male friend who brought a pickup to our house one day. I loaded whatever I could into it, and fled to a flat in Westlands on East Church Road with my two babies.

I still remember the day we left. The sky was bright and clear, the pickup truck stacked high with boxes, and my mother breathless but determined. I mostly remember the sound of her voice, filled with newfound confidence and determination.

"Hurry up, we have to go someplace before your father comes back."

It was indeed a sudden move. Obama had no assets (and a house he had bought would soon be foreclosed on), so my mother had only her salary to support us.

Juliana, our maid, called her a few days later. "Memsahib, can I come and join you?" She did and brought along with her a pressure cooker and a carpet. I was glad to leave my elder brother and sister. It was as though they, my father, and the little Woodley house were a noxious brew of violence and unfulfilled dreams. I remember their faces, Rita's in particular, as I looked out the window of our departing car. She was standing in the doorway, her face kept carefully blank but with a trace of wistfulness. Her dark eyes looked back at me with an expression I will never forget. It was as though she was saying, *Are you leaving us, Okoth? Going away with your mother, who was once my mother, Bobby's mother? Well, you have won. But I will give you back a gift. My gift is the gift of regret that says you will never know us, you will never be a part of us again.*

I was happy to leave those iron-grilled windows that shut me in and that somber interior filled with dark memories. But I still see Rita's eyes staring after me, peering into the interior where I huddled in my seat. Beside me, David also looked out the window. I vaguely recall him saying, "Where are we going? Is Rita coming?" Then he started to cry.

But Rita and Bobby were not coming. It would be years before we saw them again, and that precious, fragile era of childhood would be experienced differently by each of us, in different worlds. We would be linked only by memories and genes.

Of course I wondered what would happen to them. We had lived together for seven years. Yet for some reason it seemed natural that my mother would take only David and me, for we were her own children. Only years later did I think of the pain they must have felt at being abandoned. After all, they had lived with us for most of their young lives. Rita had been about four when her father married my mother. She was now eleven years old, and Bobby was already in his early teens. We had been physically together but often spiritually apart. I had never developed a close bond with them, perhaps because they were much older than me, perhaps because they were too close to my father. Yet for me our final departure meant I would no longer have to share my mother with them, no longer have to battle the two universes within me, black and white, nurturing love versus violent rejection.

"I wanted to take them but Obama wouldn't let me," Ruth confessed to me years later, "and I couldn't stay with him."

Rita was not Ruth's child. Nor was Bobby. But was there not love between the three of them? Did they not need a mother's guiding hand and soft touch? My mother's face was torn, as though pummeled within by a rolling ball of pain and regret. In the end my brother and sister were left behind, tumbleweeds tossed beneath Africa's unsympathetic sky.

I attended Mrs. Taylor's Nursery School. One day Obama Sr. gave me a haircut and almost shaved my head clean. I felt all the children in the photo were laughing at me! I am in the top row, fourth from the left. c. 1970

Auma (then called Rita), Malik (then called Bobby), David, and me on a swimming outing at the Panafric Hotel around 1970.

This photo of Barack Obama Sr., my mother holding David, and myself was taken around 1968 at our home in Woodley, a Nairobi suburb. At this time our family suffered domestic violence almost daily, amplified by my father's drinking. I clung to my mother and, unable to protect her, feared and hated my father. In this photo I seem to shrink away from his touch. It took decades for me to come to terms with our history and accept the Obama name again.

In 1970 my maternal grandparents, Ida and Joe Baker, visited Kenya. Rita is standing, and two unidentified friends are next to David and me. c. 1970

CHAPTER FOUR

Cleansing

MUSICAL EVOCATION

"Puppy Love": Written by Paul Anka (recorded by the Jackson 5)
While I was growing up in Kenya, the Jackson 5 was the coolest fad to hit
Nairobi for a long time. I found an LP of this song in Simeon Ndesandjo's
drawer one day. Frizzy-haired Michael and his brothers and sister had the
coolest dance moves, and every Kenyan between the ages of ten and sixteen
wanted to wear bell-bottoms and dance like them to "Puppy Love." I like to
think that even adults like my father could fall crazily in love.

IT WAS IN WATER THAT I FIRST GREW TO LOVE MY STEPFATHER, SIMEON
Ndesandjo. The surname comes from his father's Chagga tribe and means
cleansing. Little did I know that Simeon Ndesandjo, as his name promised, would cleanse much that was troubling from our lives.

But when he first met my mother, he represented something terrifying:
David and I feared he would steal her away. The filched kisses, the private
embraces, the sounds of love—our new security had been hard won. It was
no wonder we did not welcome the prospect of a new man in our lives.

Yet Simeon seemed to have a method that worked. "I did not love
him at first," my mother confided in me.

"Then why did you marry him?"

"Because I knew you two boys needed a father, and Simeon was a
good man. He could also support us."

After we fled from Woodley, the three of us settled into a small bungalow community on East Church Road. The brick-and-wood duplexes perched like white-painted birdcages on top of a small hill. Thick green grass ran down a slope toward a narrow brook. It was a beautiful place to start afresh. We thought we were free at last, but that was not quite the case.

Sometimes my father came to our home, pounding on the locked doors as we cowered behind the long white table of the small kitchen. "Give me back my children! Or I will take them myself" his voice thundered. Cold waves of fear washed over me and David. We clung to our mother, who hugged us and looked silently at the naked floor. We would remain in that position, sometimes for hours, until the voice was no longer there. My mother slowly found protection and courage with the help of new female friends. "If that bastard comes, I'll cut his balls off!" one of them said to her.

One of these friends, Lillian, introduced her to Simeon Ndesandjo.

"Your mother was looking for a better job," Lillian told me years later. Lillian was a tall woman, her hair pulled back tightly in a bun. Lighter-skinned than her African sisters, she sometimes seemed more African than they did, so often did she mix Swahili into her sentences.

"She was also afraid of Obama. He would come to her little house and shout through the door at her. His voice was so deep, so strange. We were all afraid of him. *Everybody* was afraid of Obama."

Lillian knew Simeon had wealthy real estate tenants who might offer Ruth a job. When Ruth first walked into Simeon's office, he was entranced. "What a good and decent woman," he confided to Lillian afterward. "How could such a woman be married to Barack Obama? How could such a beautiful woman be treated that way?"

Shortly afterward, Lillian arranged a birthday party for Simeon and invited Ruth. They hit it off. "Simeon came on very strong," my mother wrote. "He had known me from my days with Obama—they had been friends—and we began dating . . . Simeon was very serious, and from the beginning I knew he would soon be in love with me. He didn't know this, but I did."

To help ease her constant fear of meeting Obama, friends would take my mother out partying almost daily, often to the Grosvenor Hotel. Because Obama could not find her there, they called it "The Hideout."

When Simeon and Ruth entered, the DJ would put on the same song—Michael Jackson's "Puppy Love." How strange their dancing must have appeared. Simeon would have been short and stocky, his tubby face wreathed with beads of sweat under the flashing lights. Ruth would have towered over him. As she danced she couldn't reach his lips, so she would bend down and kiss him on his luminescent, bald head.

Simeon Ndesandjo was half Chagga and half Kikuyu, and because he purposely avoided politics, he managed to stay removed from the tribal strife that consumed his Luo and Kikuyu drinking buddies, including Barack Obama Sr.

Simeon had visited our home in Woodley a few times.

"You and your brother David were always eating bananas with tea. I thought it was a little strange," he would tell me many years later.

Compared to Obama Sr., Simeon was all gentleness and light. He would announce himself night after night with a timid knock on the door of our little bungalow, a pudgy, stocky man who held himself very straight, as though sensitive to remarks about his height. We'd smell a whiff of his cologne and catch a brief glimpse of his bald pate surrounded by a neat ring of brown fuzz, and then he would whisk our mother out to a good restaurant or to see a play.

Simeon knew that he not only had to win over my mother, he also had to win over David and me. Whether it was planned or spontaneous I do not know, but whatever he did worked. For the first time in a long while, I realized my mother was happy.

She had forged ahead with the divorce, bearing the stigma of being a single white mother living and working among people who mostly looked down on mixed marriages. She had been like a mountain climber, hauling herself up the side of an ascent that nearly broke her, but whose summit she had to reach.

She started to laugh again. To hear my mother laugh was a powerful thing. Laughing and crying can sound the same. My mother made them sound different.

"I want to marry him," she told us one day. To her surprise we were overjoyed.

For me it was Simeon's affinity with water that was the clincher. David and I were strong swimmers. When we went to swimming pools in Nairobi or Mombasa, Simeon would swim with us, and he did not swim in any normal or accepted style.

Most likely he'd taught himself, and he had never properly mastered the art of breathing while in motion. So he would lurch into the water from the side of the pool, dip his head beneath the surface, and, without once bringing his face up for breath, thrash his thick, beefy arms and do the breaststroke to the other side. Finally, like a brown humpback whale, he would surge out of the water with a tremendous exhalation of air and water. David and I would hold on to his shoulders as he dragged us along just under the surface. I remember the feel of his firm, slippery skin. When he lunged upright we would be tossed aside like sardines.

Occasionally, in a coup de grâce, he would grab us by the waist and throw us into the middle of the pool while we screamed with laughter. It was this simple camaraderie, not the nice hotels and restaurants, the Mercedes or the toys, that drew us to him.

"I do not think I loved him when I married him," my mother said to me once. "But I grew to love him."

My large, pink-skinned mother loomed over baby-faced Simeon when they walked together, and the couple attracted curious stares. He would need to trot to keep up with her, while she would try to slow her steps and hunch herself down in an attempt to make him more comfortable.

Simeon had worked for the Voice of Kenya, the government television and radio station, making a reputation for himself as a talented producer and radio announcer. He even acted in some of his own commercials. In one of his most famous, the camera focuses on Simeon in a nice suit, seated and reading a newspaper. An unseen woman's hands start snaking around his neck. He continues to read, serious and unflappable. Then a fly starts buzzing around his head. In one smooth, mellifluous motion, a can of insecticide suddenly appears and zaps the unfortunate fly.

"Kill it with It!" the announcer declares in a ringing voice.

The image of those brown arms curving up and over his bald brown head, his face, and his shoulders is still etched in my mind.

Simeon was well respected in town; he had a stable income and a nice car, but to my mind he had no sex appeal, which I was old enough to consider important. After seeing that commercial, I remember thinking, *He's bald and short, even a little fat. Why would a woman grab him like that?*

Yet my mother saw in him things that I did not see.

"I made Simeon promise me a number of things when I married him: one, that he would never beat me; two, that he would never allow relatives to live with us; and three, that he would enable my boys to go to St. Mary's High School."

"Oh!" she added. "And I said he would have to get us a piano."

Simeon had grown to dislike Obama Sr. "He was a drunkard who beat your mother," he told me. "And he couldn't drive. He drove like a crazy man, always talking and waving his hands while driving, never keeping his eyes on the road. We used to drink together, and the one time I let him drive, I thought he would kill us both. I never went in a car with him again."

Perhaps to Simeon the erratic driving was symbolic of what happens when a man loses control of his life—something he could not respect.

—⁓—

The courtship was rocky at first. Simeon had his own romantic complications, which threatened to intrude on our immediate family. He had just ended a long relationship, and he had children from a previous marriage.

The engagement party was held on the broad grassy lawn of Simeon's old house. His son Kenneth, a small wiry lad with a cute upturned nose that resembled his father's, scrambled between the legs of the guests like an African Mercury. Laughter and the smell of roasted goat and beer filled the thick, humid air. Beneath the spreading branches of a magnificent tree, Simeon and my mother greeted their guests and smiled constantly.

"Friends," he roared eventually, "I have an announcement to make." He raised his glass and smiled broadly, gesturing to the partygoers with his other hand.

"Friends, I want you to meet the woman who has brought love to my life, and who will be my future bride."

My mother blushed, happy but a little taken aback, and David and I stood openmouthed at the announcement.

"I met Ruthie not long ago, and I love this woman. She will be my wife."

Then there was a sudden commotion. A large African woman in a colorful sari swiftly grabbed my mother's hair.

"You bastard! You bitch! Coming between the two of us . . . You came here to take away my family!" she screamed.

The assailant's eyes were wide with rage. My mother shrank away in the face of this woman's fury. It was Simeon's former partner.

The other woman continued screaming, yanking at my mother's hair and clawing at her face. Shocked, Simeon and some other men pulled her away and held her off with difficulty. My mother, David, and I were piled into a car and quickly driven away.

Several hours later there was a very timid knock on the door and Simeon walked in. "I am so sorry, Ruth. Please forgive me."

My mother told the two of us to go upstairs to bed. As I rested my head on the soft pillow and sank into sleep, I heard them whisper together, slowly and urgently, long into the night.

Soon afterward, in early 1973, they were married in Malindi, on the shores of the Indian Ocean. Of the ruckus at the engagement party, my mother said dismissively, "That crazy woman . . . what a *mkorah*,* attacking me like that!"

———

My Luo names always sat uneasily with me, and in time it seemed very natural to use Simeon's surname Ndesandjo, which I accepted unquestioningly. Later, when people asked me where Okoth came from, I would remember Barack Obama Sr. and try to forget its provenance. My mother tried to convince me otherwise: "It's the name Obama gave you. It is part of you. You should keep it."

———

* Troublemaker.

It would be years before I called myself Obama again, and then only under extraordinary circumstances. In the meantime, I was getting used to having a new father.

After the wedding we moved out of the bungalow on East Church Road and into a house in Westlands, a prosperous suburb of Nairobi, where my mother eventually bore two more sons, Richard and Joseph.

One day I returned home to our new house and heard the sound of music wafting through an open door. Walking into the living room, I saw my mother behind a huge brown piano. I was entranced.

"What is this?" I asked.

"It's the piano from Simeon's studio. He brought it home for us." A few weeks later, under my mother's guidance, I started to play it. Only years later would I realize that Simeon had been responsible for introducing me to one of my greatest loves in life, something that will always sustain me. He gave me the gift of music, and for that I will always be grateful to him.

In my adolescent years there were difficulties between my stepfather and me. I sensed that he loved Joseph and Richard more than he did David and me, and I was too proud to admit that I wanted his love, or even just his liking. Simeon could be intimidating too. I was too young, perhaps too naive, to realize that parents can love their children in many different ways, without necessarily being demonstrative. Simeon would hardly ever smile as he munched through his dinner or breakfast, and he'd hold his newspaper in front of his face while he read. Naturally introverted and quiet, he cared little for conversation, only demanding punctual meals, his newspapers, a quiet house, and a seat in the living room that no one else dared to sit in.

We would not speak to each other for long periods of time. I began to avoid him, and it was easy enough because his schedule was so predictable and he was only around in the evenings. I'd see him at dinner and on our weekly outing.

Every Sunday the family would go to lunch at a nearby sports club. We would then bundle into Simeon's car and head off for the afternoon.

I enjoyed the outings, because our favorite destinations, Parklands and Karen, were beautiful places with plenty of diversions to occupy visitors: sporting events, bars, snooker halls, restaurants.

However, at some point the tension between Simeon and me grew so strong that we could not even go on these together.

"I hate him!" I told my mother. "What do you see in him?" She would just shrug.

One day, after David had already moved out, I entered the car after Joseph and Richard and Simeon exploded.

"It's best you don't come," he told me.

I was too proud to ask why. In fact, I knew he just did not want me around. My mother sensed our antagonism and would tell me, "He does love you. He just doesn't know how to show it. You should talk to him more."

Talk to him? Talk to the robot! I was incredulous. He never wanted to be around me, let alone talk to me.

"I married Simeon because you and David needed a father. You should understand that," she told me gently.

A few weeks after that incident, I went out with all of them one last time. Simeon didn't talk all the way to the club. As we were having lunch, my mother suddenly stood up.

"You only think about yourself. I refuse to eat with you! Come with me, Mark."

Instinctively, I knew I was the source of this flare-up. I meekly followed her, while everyone else carried on eating.

"Where are you going?" I asked.

"Home."

"How are we going to get there?" I asked as she marched in front of me out of the door. The club was almost ten miles from our home.

"We'll walk!"

I followed my mother along the long *murram* (claylike material made from rock decay) roads as cars whizzed by and the few pedestrians in the suburban area looked curiously at us. The sun beat down on her bare head, and her blue dress shimmered in the heat. I remember the *tok-tok* of her high heels as she walked proudly down the center of the road, her back straight and stiff. I could not see her face, but I knew she was furious with Simeon, more furious than I had ever seen her.

She would never explain why. I don't remember asking her about it. I knew there was a bond between us that could not be broken, the bond that made her take my side against her husband and that obliged me to follow her on foot those ten dreary miles home. That walk was as poignant as my first childhood memory, when, as an infant, I had run after my mother's fat legs, linked by a timeless, invisible, and magical thread.

Eventually I took my mother's advice and talked to my stepfather more often. It was as though a dam had been broken. We started to discuss politics, television, and even football. But although the tension abated, there was always that degree of formality between us, perhaps because I wanted it that way.

Simeon seemed to mellow with the years. We didn't argue but instead would chat easily about America, politics, and business. The Mercedes was replaced by a Fiat; the Rolex gave way to a Timex. His growing family made demands that he shouldered quietly and without protest. I remember only one time when he seemed to chafe at the constraints placed on him.

"You don't understand," he said, irritated by something Mum had said. "It's a hard world out there. None of you know how hard!"

Then, many years later, I returned to Kenya from the United States after years of absence for a brief visit.

On first seeing my stepfather, I noticed how much he had changed. He was thinner. Where his turtlenecks and suits had once been bulging, his clothes now seemed to hang off his skinny frame. His cheeks used to glimmer with moisture, and his fleshy lips and rotund body used to indicate a man who enjoyed eating and drinking. Now I saw wrinkles and the first waves of white hair.

"We haven't heard from you for so long," Simeon said to me as he and my mother watched me unpack. "What happened?"

I evaded the question and told them I had been busy working, but my bosses had not appreciated my efforts as much as I deserved. When I got a great offer elsewhere, I took it. They bought my house, gave me a better job. So here I was . . .

I didn't want to say it, but now that I had money I had enough confidence to come home.

Simeon listened to me quietly.

"You know, Mark . . ." He seemed to hesitate.

I was half afraid of what he would say next. I was confident in my own success, but Simeon's deliberation, his strong, calm voice, frightened me.

My younger brother Richard interrupted then, and Simeon did not finish what he wanted to say. With relief, we turned to discussing politics and corruption in the Kenyan government.

A few days later Mum was at work and I was at home with Simeon. We were alone in the living room. Outside there was the incessant clatter of the ayahs cleaning pots and pans. A radio was playing some Congolese music, and every so often the wind passed though the trees with a sound like a sigh.

"Mark, perhaps we can go and have a drink at Parklands," Simeon said.

"Okay. Should we wait for Mum?"

"Your mother and her friends, always go mattering, nattering. Always talking, never quiet," he said. "Me, I can't be bothered with that *maneno.**"

I expected him to laugh then. Simeon could laugh with great abandon, and easily.

But today he didn't so much as smile. What was up? He had never taken me out for a drink alone. What could he possibly want to discuss?

At the Parklands Sports Club, we walked into the bar. Apart from the bartender, it was empty. Simeon gestured to the barman.

"Yes, Mr. Ndesandjo, what can I do for you, sir?" Simeon always commanded respect. Often he was called *Bwana* Simeon, or the *Mzee*, and would accept it as his due. But this time he nodded, looking a little abashed.

"This is my son, have you met him?" And he waved his hand toward me.

"No, Mzee."

The bartender shook my hand. "Welcome."

---

* Nonsense.

"He is here from America," Simeon said. "He is working there and ..." His voice trailed off. We got our drinks, some red wine, and fell silent for a few minutes. I was a little uncomfortable. It seemed as if Simeon wanted to say something to me but was waiting for the right moment.

"I'm glad to be here, Dad," I said encouragingly. He looked at me pensively.

"You know, Mark, all those years you were away, we were thinking of you ..."

"I know," I said.

"I wanted to say ..." And he looked me directly in the eye. I waited.

"I read the story you wrote about the swimming pool," he said softly.

With a start I remembered how, in one of my earlier attempts at writing a memoir, I'd described something that had happened while we were swimming together. Once, perhaps because I was being too boisterous, I had jumped on Simeon in the water. Normally, he would have playfully tossed me aside or merely ignored it. But this time I'd jumped too hard, and he swatted me angrily with his fist. It was the first time he had ever hit me. Stunned, I sank back into the water, which suddenly felt very cold.

He didn't say anything about it afterward, but from that moment on our relationship was not the same in my eyes.

The passage I had written was only brief, and part of something I had abandoned by then. I had not expected such a reaction.

"I never realized I had hit you ... I was shocked to think I had ever done that."

I realized then how hurt he was. He had never touched my mother in anger throughout their many years of marriage. That, and the fact that the relatively minor incident in the swimming pool had caused him so much distress, spoke a great deal about his innate decency.

We chatted a little about my work.

"We are so very proud of you. I am so proud of you. You are my son, and I am very happy you have done so much. You have done your own thing."

At last Simeon smiled. He had a gap in the center of his upper-front teeth and had always been a little shy about exposing it. In that moment, with his slightly self-effacing smile, his bald dome of a head shining dully, his bright sparkling eyes and the eternal gap between his front teeth, he was beautiful to me and I realized I loved him.

I was almost overwhelmed by a surge of memories then, all of Simeon, all of them good: the times he had tossed David and me into the water, the encouragement he had given me when I had bought my first house, the times we had played chess and he had playfully chided me for check-mating him, the gold watch he gave me on my thirteenth birthday (which I carelessly lost), the uncomplaining financial support that had gotten me through St. Mary's, Brown, and Stanford. And, above all, that battle-scarred grand piano he'd brought home from the studio.

I knew then that Simeon Ndesandjo did indeed love me, though he had never directly told me so. This man had raised me, supported me through college, loved and cherished my mother in thousands of small but profound ways. I had thought of him as a mere supporting character in the theater of my life.

How ungrateful I had been. No longer.

He had become the father I loved.

A peal of thunder could be heard through the half-open door. Soon it would rain. Outside, a few drops fell on the red soil and were absorbed into the rich loam.

"Yes, Dad, I know," I replied to his unspoken words.

Simeon Ndesandjo passed away in 2011 after a brief illness during which my mother tended to him in our home in Nairobi. They had been together for thirty-six years and it was an abrupt separation, hardest on the widow left behind.

Theirs was a slow-burning love, the sort that develops over years. He always took care of all the finances, held her hand when she needed it, dealt with the thousands of little things that caused her stress. He kept his promises to my mother. Not once did he lift a hand to her, and no relatives of his ever lived with us, although we were courteous to them.

His love for her went beyond words, expressed in what he did, not what might have been said. It reminded me of these words of the poet Xu Zhimo:

You see, or don't see me, I am still there, neither happy nor sad.
You understand, or don't understand me, the emotion is still there,
neither coming nor going.
You love, or don't love me, love is yet there, neither more nor less.
You are with me, or not with me, my hand is still in your hand, not aban-
doned, not forsaken.

Simeon Ndesandjo with David and me. Simeon brought stability and love to our family, and it was like a new, happy life began for us. In this photo I hold his hand very tightly. c. 1973

Simeon Ndesandjo was a well-known announcer for the Voice of Kenya, and he went on to make a career in marketing and the music industry.

This is a 2006 photo of Simeon and Ruth Ndesandjo. They were married for thirty-six years. Simeon passed away in 2011.

CHAPTER FIVE

My Brother David: A Tragedy

MUSICAL EVOCATION

"Reconnaissance" (from **Carnaval***): Robert Schumann*
When an interviewer asked pianist Arturo Benedetti Michelangeli what he thought of his recordings, he said something like, "I never listen to my recordings. They are all abortions!" Whenever I hear or play this piece, but particularly when I hear Michelangeli's recording, I think of a person who treasures every moment. I also think of the happy-go-lucky, vivacious, intense, and tragic life of my brother David. There is a bittersweet quality in this short work that, in an instant, turns from sadness to happiness, and vice versa. Above all it evokes a free-spirited person, one who would gladly sacrifice his or her future to the present.

"YES, BWANA MARK AND BWANA DAVID, YOU OUGHT TO BE CAREFUL. There's no telling what could happen on dark nights to young boys such as you."

The watchman peered at us through the flames of his fire. He was old, lean, and wiry, with strong, sinewy limbs developed by many years of manual labor. His face was dense with wrinkles that mapped his history as surely as a turtle's shell, some sages say, charts its destiny. He always dressed in a huge black coat that made him one with the night. When we drove up in Simeon's big car, he would open the gate with a grand Nosferatu-like sweep and clatter of chains. With another sweep of his voluminous coat, he would shut the gate behind us and retreat to the fire he stoked each night.

Although that night we felt safe and warm, the words of the watchman were strangely prescient.

Unlike me, David, my only brother born of Ruth Ndesandjo and Barack Obama Sr., was never afraid of the dark. He had his demons, but they did not include my father, with whom he reconciled later in life.

A photo of David still hangs in my old room in the Westlands house. It is like a passport photo, head and shoulders only. His face is round and pudgy and a huge mass of hair sticks up around his head like a helmet. There is a formal red background and a huge '70s-style collar sprouting up on either side of his face, like a second set of ears. He smiles and looks animated, but there is a touch of irritation, even anger, about his expression. He might have been thinking of all the other things he could be doing, rather than finding himself stuck in a room with his mother and an old Indian photographer.

A welter of emotions runs through me as I remember this young boy who had such potential and was so full of life. I loved David, but in the blindness of youth I realized it too late. Although there were intimate moments, we were too busy duking it out as sibling rivals to ever truly square with each other. Our relationship was characterized primarily by conflict. Every Saturday afternoon the single government television station showed wrestling programs from the UK, which David and I often watched. We would have preferred American wrestling. Brits were too polite. They obeyed the referees, didn't bite, and never yelled obscenities. American wrestling was the "in" thing, with its gory spectacles of steroid-popping jocks breaking teeth and bones. Next to them, this was just tea and diet crumpets, served promptly at five o'clock. "Let's wrestle," I used to taunt him.

David would always oblige. We would stake out our corners, clear the furniture, and go for it. We grappled and swung each other onto the floor, again and again. I always won, which was perhaps why I wanted to continue. David eventually would concede, although he never did so easily. These matches mirrored our desire to best each other in every way. Yet our respective playgrounds were vastly unequal. David lived in the broad, heady air of Nairobi's nightlife, and Africans were his true siblings. I waged most of my battles within the classrooms and libraries of St. Mary's High School.

That night with the watchman, however, there was peace between us. David and I sat by the glowing fire, its orange flames cutting into the darkness. We looked into the wrinkled face regarding us so solemnly.

"Why should we be careful? What will happen to us?" I challenged the watchman.

"Why, the thieves will catch you and cut your throats," he answered, and then he launched into a stream of Kiswahili and Kamba phrases that I barely understood.

David, however, knew Swahili better than I did and sat absorbed by the unfolding narrative.

"Yes, there was a time when I was young like you, and things were much simpler. There were the Mau Mau and the whites. And they hated each other. And Kenyatta was in prison . . ."

Although I did not understand most of what he said, there was a kind of poetry in the watchman's rhythmic voice. The cool night air of Nairobi brushed our skin. I saw my brother's rapt face, felt the fire's warmth. Above all, I was enjoying the openness and freedom with which this old man had welcomed us into his reminiscences. No distrust of the young half-castes. No chafing at the company of part-*mzungus*.

"I was one of the Mau Mau. We used to hide in the trees when the British came after us. If they brought their dogs, we were goners. The British were very cruel. Much blood, much blood . . ."

The watchman's voice trailed off and his face turned pensively toward the fire, remembering things he did not want to remember, seeing things he did not want to see. He looked into the flames with a half smile, as though it was a friend that would burn away those nightmares of long ago.

David was a child full of the fire of life. He was a true existentialist and did not care about the past or the future. For him it was all about the moment. And, on those rare occasions in which we enjoyed each other's company, such as when he was away from the pull and tug of family, and I was away from my studies or even my music, I always sensed in him something deep, a rich place without a name, impossible to ignore.

I remember how he and I visited Mombasa in the halcyon days of our youth. It was a particularly hot summer. Even in the shade the stones seemed to burn through the soles of our thin plastic sandals. We dreamt of cool water, white beaches, and pounding waves. Simeon had been against us going, until our mother convinced him otherwise.

"They cannot look after themselves. They are too young," he said.

"You crabby man!" my mother furiously retorted. "Here are our children wanting to have some fun for a few days, and you are worrying about money. You go off to Kariokor with your friends and spend hundreds of shillings on your beer and cigars. And you won't let them have some fun!"

"You don't know what you're talking about," Simeon muttered. He always said this when he was on the losing end of an argument with my mother, which was often.

"Yes, that's all you think about, your beer and cigars. My goodness gracious!"

There was an uncomfortable silence.

"And to top it off you look at all those pretty women. You're a *mkorah*." And she winked at him.

Simeon muttered something inaudible at this Swahili reference to his being a troublemaker, but a smile lurked beneath his scowl.

"Women, huhhh!" And with that the trip was settled, though he insisted we take the bus. No expensive plane flights.

I was about thirteen or fourteen the summer we left Nairobi for Malindi. It would be the first time we had taken such a long trip without our parents, but we were happy at the prospect of a two-week vacation away from school and without supervision.

So one sweltering afternoon we were seen off from the Nairobi bus station. From a distance the huge parking lot seemed like a cemetery of abandoned rusting vehicles, stretching their metal corpses for hundreds of yards in every direction. Around each vehicle were piles of what seemed like black ash. As we drove closer I realized the "piles of black ash" were actually groups of people, mostly families, some dressed in traditional black Muslim hijabs, squatting and chatting among themselves while they waited to board. It was the first time I had taken a long-distance bus. In the past we had always used cars or the train. Here—without the comfortable buffers of privacy or distance—everything and everyone seemed so close. The strong odors of unwashed bodies and cheap soap flowed over us. I looked forward to reaching the room at Lawford's Hotel, where we were headed.

Crammed into the rickety old bus, I couldn't sleep a wink during the eight-hour night trip. Next to me was a young Arab boy. He was olive-skinned, with beautiful doelike eyes. Late in the night, as we struggled over bumpy roads, he fell asleep and laid his head on my shoulder. His face was so angelic that for a moment I had an urge to touch it. I kept still until he dreamily awoke and jerked his head away. On the other side of me, David was already asleep.

Outside, barely visible shapes loomed out of the darkness. Through the open window, the sultry night air caressed my cheeks. As I moved in and out of consciousness, I forgot the grime of the surroundings, and the loud snores of the man behind me, and imagined the warm sun of Malindi beating on my back, the glistening water of the Indian Ocean rolling on to the shore.

When we arrived at Mombasa, we took a *matatu*—a cross between a bus and a taxi—to Malindi, approximately a hundred miles away. Mombasa and Malindi are two of Kenya's largest and most historic seaside towns. The Kenyan coast has a rich and tumultuous history. Around AD 1000, foreigners from Arab lands developed a flourishing trade in slaves and ivory here. Today the coastal towns still abound with a rich diversity of cultures.

Tourists, particularly the Italians, Germans, French, and Americans, are the toast of these towns. They cavort in the blue waters and are treated like royalty for the color of their skin, and more particularly their money. If alone, they frequently seek out native prostitutes and gigolos. Centuries of racial and commercial interaction have resulted in a colorful kaleido-scope of skin colors, from ebony-black to pale brown and everything in between. Indians, both recently arrived or, what is more likely, descendants of the coolies imported by the British from India to build the great rail-way, manage innumerable small businesses. The darker-skinned, majority Bantus live in the many villages dotting the shoreline.

The urban heat of the shorelands is much more intense than in Nairobi. At sea level the air seems to stick to one's skin like oil on a hot grate, and the worst torture is to sit bare-skinned on a car's plastic seats. The roads tremble with mirages, and the lofty palm trees appear to dance in the hazy, trembling light. Looking out the windows of the bus, we saw palm trees waving their green fingers at the sky, and then, in a few moments, turning a corner, the azure surface of the Indian Ocean came into view.

Ratnakara, the Sanskrit name for the Indian Ocean, means the creator of pearls, and it evokes the glimmering white sheen of the water in the early morning. For centuries the monsoon winds powered the dhows of Arab slave traders who trafficked in this area. They came from such places as Saudi Arabia and Oman to the coasts of East Africa, bearing incense and myrrh and cheap trinkets in exchange for slaves and ivory. The olive-hued natives are living proof of miscegenation between the traders and the native Bantus. They speak classical Swahili, the Arab-Bantu lingua franca of sub-Saharan Africa, and dominate the social and municipal life of the coastal strip.

More than a thousand years later, there is evidence of the social hierarchies between the lighter- and darker-skinned inhabitants. Throughout Kenya entrenched divisions exist based on religious, social, and tribal groupings. As in most places where races mixed through force of circumstance, the coastal people were long ago graded according to the shade of their skin. David and I were then too young to fully comprehend this. We were innocent, unheeding children. On that holiday morning, all that mattered was the sweet smell of saltwater, the sight of coconuts on palm trees, and the magnificent blue-and-white sky above us. That and the warm water that would surge over our brown shoulders as we leapt and frolicked in the waves of the great ocean.

Pushing past the necks and arms of other passengers squeezed into the *matatu* with us, we craned our necks out the window and eventually saw the familiar elephant tusks leaning over the entrance of Lawford's Hotel like crossed swords. We jumped out onto the dirt road and entered the lobby relieved. We quickly checked in and settled into our rooms before heading to the white-sand beach. The next few days would be spent swimming, eating, and walking around the small, ancient town.

We were staying in a row of cottages that lined the beach. Each had one room with a small bathroom and patio. I was always reading and, because I had no money to buy books, would spend part of every afternoon immersed in a huge volume of Shakespeare's collected works brought from home. Thus engaged, I heard my brother call to me excitedly from outside.

"Come and take a look. They're doing it!" David yelped. "Mark, Mark, come and see!"

His tone was not loud but anxious, as though he did not want to be overheard. He was standing on the patio and pointing wildly at the cottage next door. He urged me to follow him and led me toward the door of an adjacent building. Although it was shut, we could hear a slow methodical thumping, and little screams and yells, coming from behind it.

"Look, look!" David pointed at the keyhole.

"What the hell are you talking about?" I muttered, but quickly bent down and peered through the keyhole.

A few days ago I had seen a very pretty young European woman jumping in the pool. She was blonde, petite, wholesome, and cute, like the heroine of *The Farmer's Daughter*, then a popular TV show. David and I had watched her in fascination, minds filled with teenage fantasies.

She lay stark naked on the bed. A man with a huge belly, his flaccid arse turned partly toward us, was rammed between her legs, pushing against her methodically with hoarse grunts. Huge beads of sweat rolled down his broad, oily, pink back. He went on like this for several minutes as I stood there glued to the hole in the green door. David would push me aside occasionally to take a look himself, but mostly he seemed happy to see me having fun. Other than in the blue movies Simeon constantly tried to hide from us, it was the first time we had ever seen anyone making love. The woman was uttering little moans and yelps. A few times he laid himself flat on top of her and I wondered how she managed to breathe. He was so huge and slippery and gross, she so small and dainty.

"Go on, darling! Yes, darling. Keep it up! Keep on!" she kept yelling from under the mass of pink flesh, in a mix of English and German. Finally, after a particularly desperate bout, he pulled back. They both smiled sheepishly.

"Baby, that was wonderful," she moaned.

"UUUUrgg." He nodded his head, turned toward the door. David and I bolted.

I remember our Malindi adventure because it was one of the few times David and I bonded. Eventually, however, we drifted apart. I tended toward school and studied hard, unlike David who considered school a prison. My mother took pride in my achievements, further amplifying the contrast.

"I love both of you," she would tell me, her eyes red after she had seen David leave yet another school, either because his grades were poor or because he'd fought with other students or fought with me.

I did not care. It was as though I had a lever I could pull to keep my mother close to me. She sensed this and would later blame me for pushing David away:

> [Mark] was always outstanding in school and very charming to all and sundry EXCEPT to David with whom he fought almost constantly. This was the bane of my life for about 10 years until Mark went to university in America. He and David fought so much, sometimes even damaging furniture and/or windows in the house. I now realize that Mark wanted to dominate David and David was refusing to be dominated. It was a very difficult situation and eventually caused David to spend a lot of time away from home—at friends, or at Bobby's (his half-brother), or at a surrogate uncle's place in Eastleigh.

"When David was born, you used to hit him," she once told me. My mother was right. I wanted to control my brother, as I wanted to control everything else in my life. And I did not know it, or, even if I had, I wouldn't have known why.

David did not care about rules. He would not let any authority restrain him, and my mother held little sway with him. There were times he reached out to me for guidance, but I would be busy with my studies or something else and would just ignore him. Eventually he gave up and pursued his own counsel with either Bobby or Rita or others in Obama Sr.'s extended family.

We had no girlfriends. To us, women were an unknown species. I was awkward in society, too white for many black girls, too black for most white girls. David lost his virginity well before I did, and he let me know about it in his unique way. He probably realized I was lonely and wanted to help.

One evening I heard a tap at the window. "Mark, come out here. You won't believe it!"

"What . . . what is it?" I shouted, peeved at being woken from my afternoon nap.

"I just laid this prostitute. She's here in my room!" At that time David was living in the servants' quarters. He wanted his independence and freedom, and our parents were happy to oblige for the peace it gave them. His room was in a small annex separate from the main house and just a few feet from my window.

I had a sick feeling. David had beaten me to it. Now I was the only virgin.

"You're fucking crazy!"

"Honest!" He sounded flustered but happy.

"She's out here, Mark. Come on in. You can try too!" I could tell from the tone of his voice he was serious. I flinched. Part of me wanted to take him up on his offer. But the more conservative part of me prevailed. Suddenly I was no longer angry at David. He didn't consider it a trump card against his supercompetitive brother to have lost his virginity first. Instead, he realized I was lonely, and he wanted to share his happiness with me.

"No way, are you crazy?" I was trembling and didn't know what to do. Anger seemed my best defense.

"Come on, try it out. It's free!" He was half giggling, half pleading, discretion and propriety be damned. In a young boy's life, there are few things more precious than that first time. He had no one to share his moment with except me. He continued pleading, but I held firm from behind my glass barrier. Soon I heard muffled sounds, a woman's voice in Swahili, and the crisp tinkling of bracelets and coins. I relented and half moved toward the door, but it was too late. There was only silence.

David loved my mother but instinctively rebelled against her. I believe he felt unloved, as though he had been damaged by the violence he had witnessed as an infant.

But there was more to David's disaffection than our father's baleful influence. He never did well in school and was always being compared to his "brilliant" older brother, who never supported him as he should have. I remember one evening, back when he lived in the main house, after he had been in a furious argument with my mother and Simeon. From behind his closed door, I heard the sound of sobbing, loud, deep, and prolonged. I knocked and opened the door. He was lying on his bed, his face turned away from me, toward the wall.

I sat beside him. "What's up, man?"

"Why do they hate me so much?" David cried, his face still turned away.

"Don't worry, David. You have a lot of potential. Don't cry." I pitied him, perhaps because I had rarely seen him in tears. It was as though he always wanted to show me he was tougher than me. That day he was exposed, vulnerable even.

I gently held his hand. It was rough and calloused, wet with tears. "You don't really care," he said, trying to pull away, but I held on.

"Really, man, you have amazing gifts. I'm envious of you."

He didn't say anything, but his sobbing died down.

"What do you mean? You're smarter than me. You're always first in class." His eyes were so red they seemed invisible against his dark skin in the gloom of the poorly lit room.

"You have an amazing way with people, David. You are very social."

I used the word social as though it was a hallowed thing. To schoolkids, the word had a special significance, like sweet or cool or tripping. It evoked success, someone who partied hard, was slick with the girls, always the man of the hour. The word signified the difference between mediocrity and greatness.

"Really?" He stopped crying and looked at me. At the sight of his puffy face, a wave of sadness passed over me.

Once, after I had complained to my mother about some annoying habit of David's, she said, "He's your only real brother, in all the world."

About that time I had found a book about IQ tests and out of curiosity tested David, my youngest brother Richard, and myself. Richard, who was only about six, had scored the highest, about 143 on the Terman Index, which was truly outstanding. I had developed an average score of about 120, which I felt was too low. (I subsequently spent days trying to doctor the results.) David's was below average, at about 90. Embarrassed, I had not told him his result. Now, wanting to make him feel better, I lied.

He didn't say anything, but I knew he was touched.

Several months later we had a huge argument and fought about something so trivial I forget what it was. In the heat of the moment I lashed out at him.

"You're such a fucking lowlife. You'll never be anything."

"Look who's talking. You told me that I was superintelligent. So fuck you!"

"I was lying, you asshole," I said before I could stop myself.

He was silent for a split second. I saw the doubt in his eyes. I hated myself at that moment, but I went on.

"I lied to you just to make you feel better. In fact you got ninety . . . below average. You're a pervert and a retard!" He shook his head.

"I don't believe you." But I knew he believed me and it was too late to take back my words. How can I describe the look I saw on his face then? To see anger turn into disbelief and then despair, in less than a second, like the fast-forwarded video of a wilting flower, is something one never forgets, particularly when it is so nakedly obvious. To this day I regret it.

David had some remarkable gifts. He had street sense and an ability to connect with others that put me to shame. He was particularly adept at reaching out to his Kenyan brethren. He could be more of an African than the Africans. He would mingle with crowds of his dark brothers with grace and ease. He spoke Swahili well, and he fearlessly spoke his mind. In the warm way of Africans, they would respect him for his outspokenness, welcome him into their midst, and laugh with him easily. With me it was always cold stares. I was the other brother, the humorless, reserved one who wanted to be liked but somehow never was.

When my brother died some years later, it took me a long time to realize that I had lost something precious. David could have taught me much. He could have been my bridge to the other side. He could have made me realize much sooner just what it meant to be a citizen of two worlds. He would probably have jeered at my stumbling attempts to become more African, had he lived to see me try. Yet he would eventually have supported me, as only brothers can.

"You are not just citizens of one culture," my mother used to say to us, "you are citizens of two races, and in that you are incredibly rich."

David took this as his modus vivendi, and in his quest for acceptance and love, wherever they might be found, he instinctively lurched into our father's orbit. He wanted me to accept Obama Sr. as he was able to do.

He used to leave the house for days at a time, often sleeping at Bobby's and visiting relatives from Kisumu. Once, after an absence of a few days, he turned up at the house. Finding me alone, he said, "I've seen our father. He wants to see you too. Why don't you come with me? I can take you."

I hesitated. I hadn't thought of Barack Obama Sr. for a long time. It was so unexpected, I did not know what to say. Emotions warred within me. David, sensing my indecision, said, "He really wants to see you. Why not come and take a look?"

Perhaps because I did not want to appear weak, I assented. Inside, I was afraid. It was a slow but mounting fear that seemed to start somewhere in my belly and move outward like a misty fog, enveloping the rest of my body.

We left the house together. With David leading, we hopped onto a *matatu* and got off the minibus somewhere in the Industrial Area. I remember seeing David's back receding before me as he darted his way through the ever-thicker crowds of people. We jumped on to another *matatu*. As we alternately walked and rode through mazes of ever-poorer neighborhoods, the smell of desperation and the closeness of strangers almost stifled me. The fear inside me grew stronger and stronger.

At the last stop, on the outskirts of Nairobi, we walked into a grassy field strewn with litter and stubs of trees. In the distance, white high-rises with windows that looked like thousands of watchful eyes stood out against the blue sky. We followed a small path and came to a barbed-wire fence. Just past a shallow hill, one of the high-rises loomed over us like an omen.

David lifted up the barbed wire and crawled under.

I stopped short. It was as though the wire fence was something I could not cross, like a place in my mind where I did not want to go. David turned back and, seeing the expression on my face, urged me on.

"Don't worry, Mark. He wants to see you. Don't be afraid."

Don't be afraid. Why would I be afraid? I thought. But I could not cross the final barrier. The ground was dirty. The place desolate. *My father is here*, I said to myself.

There is a line by T. S. Eliot: *I will show you fear in a handful of dust.*

There was something about the desperation of this place, the wasteland without and within, that prevented me from crossing the stony ground to my father's home. For several minutes David pleaded with me, as though I was a part of him that he could not leave behind. Finally we parted ways. He went on to see our father and I returned home.

Decades later I would learn more about that visit.

David may have been reconciled with our father, but on the broader path of life he never made much progress. To David our middle-class existence was a painful pretense, without shelter or relief, something that symbolized all his own failures, self-doubt, and loathing. He started to stay away more and more. At age fifteen he was begging passersby for money. Bobby found him on Harambee Avenue one day and took him in to live with him in his small apartment. Afterward David wanted nothing to do with our side of the family. I, too, wanted nothing to do with him or that side of the family. Yet there was a time when I had an inexplicable urge to be with my brother. On one of his rare visits back to our home, we chatted and he took me to visit Bobby's apartment.

It was a single-room rental, in a back alley somewhere near Mathare Valley. A pale pink sheet suspended from a clothesline hung across the center of it. A radio and a cooking pan lay next to some mattresses and a bunch of old clothes.

"This is where I live now," David said to me.

A few months later, on a rainy night, David borrowed Bobby's motorcycle and was hit by a truck. He died instantly.

I still remember the words of the letter I received from Mum while I was studying at Brown University.

DAVID IS DEAD!

This was the single sentence the blue aerogram contained, written in capitals. No poet, this was the best my mother could do. Even Camus could only write: *Mother died today. Or maybe yesterday, I don't know . . .*

What more was there? I was mute as I read her words. Not a tear ran down my face. I had thought myself so far apart from David that we had become strangers. Yet images and memories of our times together, good and bad, washed over me then. Before I could be pierced by regret, I pushed them away.

Years later, during a personal crisis at Stanford, the sadness finally hit me. I remembered those days we had played together on the beach at Malindi, racing the waves, our brown bodies glistening in the surf with the sheen of brown berries. I saw him smiling and laughing as the sun poured over his wet, skinny body. Then the tears started to flow, uninterrupted.

To this day everyone who knew David feels some measure of guilt for what happened. During the celebrations for Barack's inauguration week I met Bobby, who now calls himself Malik, and gathered some more details.

"The day he died, Mark, I had been arrested for fighting," Malik told me. "At the police station I asked David to head home to pick up some things for me. He asked me for the keys to my bike. I did not want to give them to him, but at last I did."

Hours later, on one of Nairobi's chaotic streets, David lost control of the motorbike and fell under a moving truck.

"I think of him every day, Mark. It gives me no peace," my eldest brother said, his head looming over me, bent as in prayer, or as though he was carrying a monstrously heavy ghost on his back.

"David, do you love me?" I once asked my brother in a dream.

"No, I hate you, because you hate me and what I represent!"

"And what do you represent, David?"

"I represent your other side, the part of Africa you never knew. *Haki ya mungu!*" Swear to God.

"And you, David, do you envy me?"

"I think I do, because everyone knows you are the success of the family ..."

This is the first time I have written about this tragedy. I have had a particular talent all my life—an ability to blank out memories. But memories do not vanish; they sleep until roused, like photos removed from a dusty box. In Washington I also met Rita, who now calls herself Auma.

"Everything has its time," she said, speaking of our reunion, though the words spoke just as truly of my long-suppressed feelings of bereavement about my brother.

David was bigger than me, in spirit and in his love of life, and there was something about him that scared me. I realize now that what frightened me most was his ability to open his mind and welcome the things that I could not, or did not, want to understand. His goals were broader, centered on sharing his life with his brothers, whether that meant those within his family or strangers on Nairobi's hectic streets. My demons were his angels—and my angels were his to cast aside.

My brother David Opiyo and me, around the time of Ruth's divorce from Barack Obama Sr. We were fiercely competitive for my mother's love, and our relationship was fraught with sibling rivalry. c. 1971

Another photo of David and me in 1983, with our younger brothers, Richard and Joseph. A few years later, David died in a motorcycle accident while I was study-ing at Brown University.

CHAPTER SIX

Sex, Beaches, and Mixed-Race Families

MUSICAL EVOCATION

South Pacific: *Rodgers & Hammerstein*

After we got our first piano, my mother started to make music with a passion. It was as though her inner diva found release in the popular American musicals of the 1940s. Just as her parents had sung with her, David and I would gather around the piano as she belted out tunes from the musical South Pacific. *Even now I remember the lyrics of "There Is Nothing Like a Dame," the beautiful nurse singing about washing that man out of her hair, the unforgettable "Bali Hai," and the classic "Some Enchanted Evening." The stories and songs are of young love, but I remember them more for the memory of the three of us gathered closely around the old grand piano as a cool breeze wafted in the scent of flowers from the garden.*

MANY OF MY MOTHER'S FRIENDS WERE ALSO THE MOTHERS OF MIXED-race families. Olive-skinned children played and squealed with their darker friends and neighbors, or they hermetically sealed themselves away from the disapproving scrutiny of society, as I did. In many of these homes, there was a sense of desperation and dissolution. Because the men who could have molded these families into stronger units often were not around, control lay in the hands of these remarkable women. I sometimes think of them as athletes: battle-scarred contestants in a tug-of-war, slowly pulling their families across the dividing line.

In Yiddish the word *bashert* means one's companion, the ideal and destined love or match of one's life. In these untraditional, unconventional, and often unsanctioned families, love and hope were uniting forces. Captivated by their *bashert* and the allure of mysterious places, these women had given up everything to relocate to Kenya. Finding themselves under tremendous social pressures for which they were ill prepared, they were sometimes forced to return to their homes and birthplaces. They could also sink into penury or, worse, lose their children under laws drawn up to perpetuate patriarchal rights. Those who remained and survived were both idealists and refugees of a sort, but above all they were survivors. I remember around the age of eight going to visit the Russian woman who had been deserted promptly by her Kenyan boyfriend when she refused to have an abortion.

"She is so beautiful, and so good," my mother would say. "She is struggling to make ends meet as a secretary and is determined not to go back to Russia."

Valentina was a tall, slender, auburn-haired woman. "Ruth, I hate it here. Yet I must not go back," she softly murmured when we visited her neat and simple little bungalow.

Valentina's Russian accent could not detract from the huskiness of her voice, the emotion in her rich brown eyes, or the flush on her high arched cheekbones. She was so pretty, I thought, even when she was in despair. I could imagine her dancing in *Swan Lake* or *Les Sylphides*. She would spin and pirouette under the silvery moon while flowers and swans gently swayed to the music. Then she would rise up from the stage floor and into the air, as light as gossamer, as brilliant as a rainbow.

The edge of a cot was faintly visible in the small, adjoining room. Valentina glanced toward it.

"I am doing fine here, and here is where I want to be," she murmured at last, eyes downcast. Her gaze shifted nervously about the room, and her hand reached up to touch her neck. I could see her fingers trembling gently, like those of a smoker in withdrawal or a pianist who has been away from his or her instrument too long. It seemed to me she didn't believe her own words. Indeed, not long after, she returned to Russia with her baby.

"She did the wrong thing," my mother complained. "Her son should be raised here. He needs to be among Africans, not among people back there who will reject him."

But I understood. Valentina was not cut out for Kenya. She was a butterfly lost in a wilderness of lions and cheetahs, vultures and hawks.

My mother, on the other hand, believed that "back there"—America, in her case—was a place totally unsuited to the raising of mixed-race children. It had too many racial conflicts, too much violence, she said. Kenya was a relatively quiet land where she could raise a family in peace and dignity.

"We are lucky with Simeon," she said. "He is a man who accepts responsibility and is well off. He can be a father. He will not drink or run away, and he can support us. He is a good man."

She lamented the loss of Valentina, as she did the departures of all her foreign friends who had fallen out with their African boyfriends or husbands.

My mother was in a constant state of love. First she had loved a man, then a son, then a family, and later she would add strangers in need to that generous-hearted list.

Although she would sometimes rail against "back there," she still loved it too. They say love is blind, but in Ruth Beatrice Baker that blindness was a form of strength. That steel core of love for her family was always apparent in her. She had an unabashed willingness to champion those she loved, despite any smirks or disapproval that this earned her.

On the only overseas trip our family ever took together, when I was around ten, right after Ruth and Simeon married, we arrived at the airport in Rome with a very sick one-year-old Richard in tow. Richard had an extremely high fever, and we were eager to get to the hotel and call a doctor. On the sleek modern bus, we found out we didn't have enough foreign currency to pay the fare. The bus was about to leave.

Desperate, my mother went to the front, holding her little boy in her arms.

"Please, has anybody here got some money for our fares? We must take this bus, my son is very sick. Please help us!"

No one on the bus paid any attention to her at first. They continued looking at their newspapers or chatting among themselves, mostly avoiding eye contact with the strange white lady yelling and holding the brown baby boy.

"Please help! We only need three hundred lira so we can go." Simeon, David, and I sat near the back of the bus, shrinking in our seats. I could feel Simeon's humiliation and my own as well. At that moment I wanted nothing to do with my mother.

For two or three minutes, which seemed an eternity, she stood there pleading for help. Eventually tears started pouring down her face. A hand reached out from the rows of passengers. I heard the clinking of coins.

"Thank you, *thank you!*" my mother cried. Eventually she had enough money and we could leave.

Mixed-race families always had to make their own way. It was as though the love of the women in these families was constantly being tested.

"When it comes to my children, I will do anything, anything!" my mother would say many times, her cheek pressed against one of ours, grasping our hands so tightly it hurt.

"But when you leave me," she would sometimes add, "don't forget me. When one day you go to live back there, don't forget me."

She loved America, but it was love that had brought her to live thousands of miles away from her home and family. *What type of love is this?* I wondered. I couldn't imagine how strong it was, for I had no experience in such matters. *What is love?* I often asked myself.

———

It was on the shores of the Indian Ocean that I first kissed a girl. It sometimes seems that I have always been happiest by the sea. With David I explored the waves off Diani Beach and Malindi, where the water was as blue as my grandmother's eyes and the beaches were as white as milk. Or under the palm trees where holiday friends and I would go foraging for shells and other flora, and even the occasional sting of a starfish or a sea urchin only seemed to intensify this kinship with the sea, like a dollop of chili sauce on a pretzel.

That summer in 1976 Simeon drove us to the coast. Malindi was to the Obama homestead at Kogelo as night was to day. Kogelo's harsh scrubland was forgotten in the wonder of white sands. The smell of dung gave way to the pungent odor of decaying seaweed, scrawny birds to white pelicans. Here we ate salads, fish, and macaroni instead of *ugali* and *sukuma wiki*. There were no loud sounds in the night, only the hum of an overhead fan lulling me to sleep. Loud radios were replaced by shells held up to my ear so I could hear the songs of the waves.

There was always this music, formed of beating hearts, crashing waves, forsaken shells, and wind that rattled windows and scattered palm leaves. In Africa the world is rhythm, and at the coast rhythm was an ineluctable, brutal, and unadorned force. Yet like yin and yang, these phenomena were not in opposition, but complemented each other.

"We'll be there by six!" Simeon declared, grasping the steering wheel as one greets an old friend by the shoulders. His Mercedes Benz 180 was his prized trophy. Not a dent marked its shining paint and chrome trim. Washed each morning, it stood in stately elegance upon the drive. Other than on occasional Sunday drives, David and I were used to traveling in Mother's old green Fiat. Simeon's car was a smoother drive, and we could fall asleep on the wide seats, dreaming of lush hotels and the pounding surf.

The journey of four hundred miles from Nairobi to the little coastal town of Malindi lasted approximately ten hours. The road to the coast was long and straight. For several hours we would see only endless carpets of tall, dry, yellow grass to either side of us. The occasional acacia trees seemed to sink like flattened umbrellas beneath the weight of the oppressive, sun-drenched sky. Wandering nomads grazed their cattle and goats at water hole after water hole, as their fathers and forefathers had before them. Wild animals, such as giraffes, wildebeest, and occasionally elephants, would cross the road now and again, heads turned in our direction, always warily watching us.

Once in a while a speeding *matatu* would overtake us, careening wildly from side to side. Once, as we drove along the edge of the Rift Valley, more than a mile above the valley floor, one rushed by us, human arms and legs dangling out of the doors and shining dark faces peering back at us through its dusty windows. As it sped away the most amazing thing happened. Whether it was a rock in the road or some other obstruction that caused it, I don't remember. Suddenly, the whole vehicle jumped into the air, flipped over, and landed back on its wheels, just like a cat falling from a height. It wobbled slowly to the side of the road, a few feet away from the edge of the cliff that dropped down for a mile into the silent valley. Dazed individuals poured out of the car. No one appeared to be hurt. We passed by slowly and peered out of the windows in astonishment. A few minutes later the same vehicle rushed by us, belching black smoke, racing as if pursued by invisible furies.

We had set off at dawn and arrived at Lawford's Hotel at 6:00 p.m., just as Simeon had predicted. While we were checking in, a voice rang out behind us.

"You rascal! Simeon, my love. . . . Where have you been? I've been waiting for you."

Marjorie Freeman, the hotel's owner, bestrode Lawford's like a colossus. A Kenyan of British descent, she was one of a small population of whites from the colonial era who had stayed on in Kenya. In this little dominion on the edge of the world, Marjorie still exercised total control. The African workers obeyed her without question and welcomed the Kenyan, German, and English families who thronged the popular hotel.

Marjorie swept up to us, her bangs of golden-streaked hair surrounding a red face lacquered with lipstick and blush that couldn't hide the toll of age. But her body seemed to defy gravity, swooshing across the lobby with irrepressible energy.

"My loves, where have you been? It is soooo good to see you. And Ruth, how wonderful!" Marjorie's voice was deep and harsh as a result of years of chain-smoking. She used an actor's emphasis, exaggerating the drawn-out vowels. She kissed both adults on the cheeks. She kissed us children, too, but somewhat more frostily.

"Now, children, you must behave. . . ." she cooed warningly.

My mother must have seen me shrink away from her, telling me later, "Marjorie was very beautiful when she was young."

During the day David and I played on the beach, plunging in and out of the warm, frothy surf. Around us, where the African sky met the sea in an unbroken crescent, the world seemed to reach its apogee.

At night, when we poked our heads out of the hotel window, it was as though a vast, kind, and powerful presence surrounded us. As the cool cotton pillows stroked our cheeks, the mantra of the crashing waves quickly shushed us to sleep.

Sometimes Maasai or Kamba villagers would come and dance for us, bringing their ceremonial bright red-and-blue garments. The women were draped in traditional jewelry, the men carrying drums and the fearsome wooden clubs called *kibokos*. Above the glow of the poolside lamps, the faces of the tribal dancers shone and dissolved into the blackness, silvery reflections on dark water. The drums would beat the rhythm of the earth itself, as if beguiled by the smoking wood, the sweating and contorting bodies, and the red-rimmed eyes of those watching from the audience.

Disco night was held in a large marquee that was elevated slightly above the ground. The roof was decorated with brightly colored banners and balloons. Large speakers were placed next to the bar and a rickety stage erected on which the musicians performed their gig. At around nine o'clock, they would launch in, very loudly, setting the boards of the stage shaking beneath them as they pounded out the beat.

I would walk on to the dance floor alone, showing off my latest moves to no one in particular. After a few minutes of whooping it up to a Tom Jones or a Bee Gees tune, I would rejoin my parents, repeating this cycle every ten minutes or so.

I first noticed her long black hair. It reached down to her chest, skimming over her thin, pale shoulders. Her dress's shimmering shades of blue, green, and yellow were reflected in the brilliant disco lights above us, giving her a regal aura. Like a princess she sat shyly in the middle of her family, facing me, her arms crossed.

My legs shifted uneasily. The music suddenly felt very loud. My heart was pounding. Her eyes were alluring, irresistible magnets. I wanted to ask her to dance, but I stayed put. I shifted uneasily in my seat and pretended to ignore her.

Although girls found me attractive, I was tongue-tied in their presence and tried to impress them by pushing forward my chest, giving high-fives, and repeating lines I had heard in the latest movies, like *Saturday*

Night Fever. I did not yet know who I was, and my facade, like my clothes, changed from day to day.

All of a sudden the big bearded man sitting next to her stood and came over to our table. He came over to me.

"My daughter wants to dance. She asks if you will dance with her?" He had a thick German accent, with a slow and measured delivery.

I stared blankly back. The girl behind him had faded into a blur. My heart seemed to be crashing in my chest. *Is it so obvious? Can everyone see what I am thinking?* I wondered.

Simeon leaned over and whispered, "Mark, go on. Dance with her. She likes you."

The girl's father nodded his encouragement.

"I-I'm not sure," I stuttered. Simeon just smiled as he took another sip of his beer.

"Go on," he encouraged me at last. The German man nodded at him knowingly.

"No problem. We wait if it's okay!"

He walked back to his own table. I stood and walked after him. Those few steps seemed very, very long to me.

She had brown eyes, I saw, clear and intense. "You want to dance?" I asked.

She just nodded and gave a little smile. The music was fast and easy. I would have no problem with this, I thought.

Just as we got on to the dance floor, it stopped and a slow tune started.

I panicked. *This tune is way too slow! I have to hold her! I have to hold her like the old people hold each other!* I half turned away. I saw my parents staring at me. I could not see their expressions in the semidarkness, but I knew they were looking at me.

The two of us stood together awkwardly for a few seconds. I was afraid. I felt my heart pounding. Summoning up my courage, I stepped forward and held her close. I cleared my throat.

"What's your name?"

Such thin arms, and her silk dress slippery against my skin. I didn't know how to dance this close, but somehow I managed.

"Maria," she murmured.

Her face was so close to mine I could feel her breath against my neck. The music was slow, but my fear was rapidly melting away.

"Bravo!" someone shouted from one of the tables. The music had stopped. A few people clapped. We had been the only ones on the dance floor. Feeling as embarrassed as if we had been caught naked, we rushed back to our parents. The adults had pulled their tables together and were drinking, chatting, and sharing stories among themselves.

The next day I found David playing table tennis with Maria's brothers. I hung back out of sight. A voice from beside me made me jump.

"You don't talk much, do you?" It was Maria.

"What do you care?" I said.

She laughed but did not say anything else. While the adults traveled around the old city or slept, ate, and drank, we kids played together, often at David's instigation. I saw Maria look at him and felt a touch of jealousy. Why was he always so good at making friends?

Maria was carefree and fun. She often joined us as we dashed about the compound. At times we would run down to the beach and watch with morbid curiosity as the jellyfish stranded by the tide slowly died in the unforgiving sun.

"Do you think they see us looking at them?" she asked. "They're dead," I told her.

"No, no, they're waiting for us to . . ." And she would scoop up seawater in her hands and splash it on to the drying, shivering jellyfish.

When the tide went out, we would carefully tiptoe around the exposed coral and seaweed, trawling the shallows for abandoned cowry shells.

When we played hide-and-seek, I lost sight of her many times, but after a few minutes of breathless searching, her smiling, beautiful face would appear as if by magic from behind a chair or a wall, as though we were in a special, inseparable compact.

"I will go back to Germany soon," she told me one morning. Her eyes looked suddenly sad. She stared down at the white beach. Not far away, some local boys of our age were pursuing a tourist couple, shouting:

"*Shell, mzuri sana! Shell shilingi kumi, baas!*" [Shells, very nice! Shells ten shillings, boss!]

Their voices reached us across the firm, packed sand, as clear as ship's bells. Their skin was black and oily with perspiration, and their feet kicked up a small white blizzard of dust behind them as they scrambled ahead of their European marks.

Maria turned her face toward mine. "I will miss Kenya."

She did not say anything more; she looked at the tumbling waves and smiled.

That afternoon, in our game of hide-and-seek, we found ourselves crouched under a huge speaker together, the same one that had belted out dance music the night we first met. My face was close to hers. I could smell the seawater on her salty skin, feel the heat of her body. All of a sudden she pressed her lips to mine. It was quick and fleeting. A shy glance from under her lowered lashes and then she skipped away, giggling. I could still taste the saltiness of her lips and feel the pressure of her chest against mine. Embarrassed, I ran after her, but she was too quick for me.

My first, our only kiss. Afterward, as though we had stepped beyond a red line, we instinctively became self-conscious and slightly wary of each other. It was as if our dance and that fleeting kiss had arrived too suddenly, overtaking our formless longings with a reality for which neither of us was ready.

In later years my family would often return to Lawford's, and each time we did I would remember that dance, those walks together on the beach, the salty taste of a girl's lips, an outpouring of young love carried away like a jellyfish on the foam, or a butterfly on the ocean breeze.

After the divorce, Simeon would take the family to Malindi, a day's drive. David and I loved to swim and meet new friends. Here I am holding a bow and arrow Simeon bought for me that day. c. 1974

94

CHAPTER SEVEN

Of Grandmothers, Music, and Wandering Jews

MUSICAL EVOCATION

Kitten on the Keys: Zez Confrey

The Copacabana nightclub in the 1930s. The wail of saxophones. Sharply dressed couples dancing the fox-trot. All these images were evoked for me when my grandmother used to play this piece. Thirty seconds later she would abruptly segue into Chopin's "Minute Waltz", and then in turn into other pieces, creating a wonderful, uninterrupted flow of music that caused even young children to sit up and take notice. "Kitten on the Keys" was always the first piece. A light salon composition that stressed virtuosity and a catchy melody, it symbolizes to me not only my grandmother, but also the erratic, wayward, bumpy path of all dreamers who follow their hearts.

MY FATHER BARACK OBAMA SR. COULDN'T CARE LESS ABOUT RELIGION. Our home never had a Christmas tree, let alone a Koran or a prayer mat. If he was Muslim he never showed it. As for me, I briefly embraced Judaism, mostly to disprove Christianity and, after being sent to a Roman Catholic school, discovered I was a Jew who did not believe in God.

In my childhood, religion did not factor into my life, and when I adopted Judaism it was like an ID card of sorts, a stamp of identification.

My mother and father had Muslim friends, but like most Kenyans (except for born-again Christians), they kept their spirituality private and refrained from proselytizing. So far as Islam went, I knew of the art of the great Spanish Renaissance and of the contributions made to science and mathematics by followers of the faith, but I remained completely ignorant of the Koran and its messages.

Early in my life, I tried to imagine what religious ecstasy felt like. I had read of Joan of Arc and the "revelations" and "mysteries" of prophets. I imagined these as being like an orgasm, only longer and perhaps more intense. Then, as I grew into my teens, my intellect took over and I became skeptical of institutionalized religion. (I was perhaps more like my father than I realized in this respect.) It was as though we both considered the practice of religion to be a form of weakness.

Only when I read in a newspaper many years later that my paternal grandfather was a Muslim, and news reports accused my Christian brother Barack of belonging to the faith, did I realize there were Muslims in our family.

"[Obama Sr.] never once talked of religion to me in the seven years we were together," Ruth told me, followed by a dry laugh. "His father may have been Muslim, but he was no Muslim. He was not Christian or anything else. Those things held no interest for him."

My grandfather reputedly converted to Islam after returning from a tour of duty in World War I.

"He was in many wars, always away and fighting," one of my relatives told me.

Historians say that of the 150,000 or so porters and soldiers conscripted by the British into the King's African Rifles, more than 50,000 perished during WWI. Onyango Obama was in his twenties, or maybe just a teenager, at that time. Mandated to serve in a horrifying conflict, he must have returned a changed man. Exposed to other religions, peoples, and cultures, he would have seen the world in all its magnificence and diversity, pride and shame, hope and despair.

Perhaps he was the Obama family's first Global Citizen. People used to say of him that he had ants up his anus, always edgy and irritable, wanting to be different.

I can imagine the day my grandfather returned to his homestead, clutching a khaki kit bag in which was stored a copy of the Koran. His wives and children may have been dumbfounded, suspicious, or merely curious, but they could not ignore his wishes. From then on the family was Muslim.

My father, Barack Obama Sr., couldn't care less about Islam. He married a Jewish woman. But even if religion did not factor into his life, the beliefs of his wife's family factored into mine.

Mixed-race children seem to grow up faster than most. A decision to choose one part of their heritage becomes an implicit rejection of the other, with all the resultant conflicts. They are like snakes that shed their skin too early. Parts refuse to peel away. Too soon, they start the prickly process of forming an identity.

I always identified closely with my mother and grandmother's culture and values. Their sensibilities, and in particular their aptitude for education and the arts, were rooted in Judaism. But it was my Grandmother Ida's attitude toward religion and life in general that gave my otherwise banal existence some sparkle and, eventually, helped define me.

As far back as I remember, Ida Baker would visit us in Kenya. At first my grandparents' visits were erratic, and then, after her husband, Joe, died, Ida's trips to Kenya resumed regularly, about once a year.

She would arrive from the airport in style, wearing an old but expensive dress and sometimes a huge hat ("to protect me from the sun"). Instantly, a whiff of perfume and an aura of energy would waft into the house.

"Honey, I'm here! Hello, honey! Oy, what a day! That taxicab driver, smoking behind the wheel . . . I told him what for!"

I loved to see Ida. I knew she brought presents for us, like chocolate, clothes, and books, but mostly she brought *America*. The world seemed so full of power to me, so sweet with possibilities.

We visited America after my parents' honeymoon and stayed with Grandma and Grandpa in their Newton, Massachusetts, home. The milk was rich and creamy, the cheese sandwiches delicious. The TV stations were chock-full of color cartoons like *The Flintstones* and *The Jetsons*. I wanted so much to escape from Kenya and be part of the rich, white world where she belonged.

So whenever she arrived, we would surround Grandma in the guest room, impatiently waiting for her to unpack luggage.

"What did you bring, Grandma? What did you bring?"

She would turn to her daughter, who let David and me do most of the shouting. "Ruthie, here's some food from the plane."

And she would fish out some oranges, tea bags, and the occasional hand towel with Delta emblazoned on it and hand them to my mother.

"I can't bear to see things go to waste!"

Finally, after endless dithering, she would open the suitcase and give us our gifts. I would get my chocolate, maybe a book or two. David would get a nice sweater, and perhaps a toy. It never felt like enough, and I would make the chocolate bar last for weeks, nibbling small pieces at a time. When everyone else slipped away to do their various errands, I would stay in Grandma's room and sit on the bed next to her while she asked me about school and told me about her life in America. Once I asked her about my grandfather.

"I miss Grandpa. I wish he was here too."

Ida just shrugged. "I remember the death rattle the night he died," she said. "A horrible sound. I had heard it before. Afterward I was relieved. Those last two years were so hard. At last I was free to do what I wanted."

I did not understand that. She sounded so heartless. I remember little about my grandfather, except that he was tall, kind, always smiling, and enjoyed smoking and drinking Chivas Regal with Obama Sr. and then Simeon. If he was sick and she had to care for him, shouldn't she have been happy to do so? How hard could it have been looking after someone with lung cancer? Wasn't she supposed to?

"Didn't you love him?" I said, shocked.

"Yes, of course, but those years when he was dying, I just wanted it to end! *Oy veh!* When I die, you can just cremate me, and that's that. We all die, and there's nothing afterward."

Ida constantly used words like *died, goy, terrified, oy veh, Shalom,* but drily, without emotion. It was as though her memories had been bled dry of all feeling and rattled round in the corners of her mind like old bones.

I would sit next to her as she leafed through a book written in Hebrew and tried to explain the meaning of the characters. "Teach me Hebrew, Grandma!" I blurted out.

Somewhat surprised, she assented. She read the words aloud, but when I asked her what they meant, she looked at me a little sheepishly.

"I don't know. Only a few of them. See, that's Yahweh, the word for God."

I was disappointed. I had hoped she could teach me more. Yet I loved to hear the sound of the language as she read it aloud. They seemed to be the words of a song, evoking a proud and irrepressible culture.

"I can speak Yiddish," she said, and quickly added, "but Hebrew is hard to read."

Like my mother, Ida's sense of religion had more to do with shared worldly experiences and history than it did with any notion of a deity. If God existed, He or She was like the soft earth beneath our feet: undeniably present but indifferent to our struggles.

As for me, I was proud to be Jewish. In my opinion, Jews were the bedrock of Western culture, from Christ through Einstein. In my teens, Sigmund Freud, Albert Einstein, and Friedrich Nietzsche were my three greatest intellectual influences. Nietzsche was my philosophical guide and he had nothing but praise for Jews, though his writings often have been appropriated and misinterpreted by anti-Semites, whom he loathed. During my teens, I was convinced that every great man of letters had a Jewish connection somewhere in the family tree.

"You're Jewish because I am Jewish," my mother had told me. "In our culture if the mother is Jewish, then so is the child."

"And if my father was Jewish and my mother wasn't?" I asked. "That wouldn't count?" She just smiled.

I was around eight or nine when I first visited the Nairobi Hebrew Congregation synagogue. The brick building always seemed hidden away, as though wary of attracting attention to itself. Large, leafy trees branched over the two-story brick building. Inside, a hushed atmosphere prevailed.

Like their place of religious observance, Nairobi's Jews were discreet and minded their own business. They had lived in Kenya for many years, even generations, and some of them were wealthy. They rarely professed their Judaism openly, perhaps fearing the sort of backlash they had suffered elsewhere in the world.

Once inside the synagogue, I remember someone placing a yarmulke on my head. The silk was cool and comfortable.

"This is my daughter Rachel," a woman introduced us. While the adults chatted, the girl looked at me. She had dark long hair and bright hazel eyes.

"What's your name?"

"Mark Okoth Ndesandjo."

"Strange name. It doesn't sound Jewish."

"What's yours?"

"Rachel. You want to see around?"

The girl led me around the small building. I sometimes wonder if people join religions and political parties because of the allure of the women they meet there. It seemed that my dark skin did not seem to matter here, the yarmulke on my fuzzy head was my badge of membership. In the religious instruction classes, I mingled freely with the other children and afterward played with them under the tall trees. I attended only for a few afternoons, but during those heady moments I felt I belonged.

For some reason my mother eventually stopped taking me to the synagogue. There was something intensely personal to her about her religious creed. I believe she had had an epiphany, and from that point forward traditional rituals, places, and customs had no bearing on her Jewish identity. I never once saw her observe the Passover or celebrate seder. As if by osmosis, her ineffable Jewish identity was translated to me in a heartful of light, and I welcomed it like a flower absorbs sunshine.

"All Jews are circumcised, why wasn't I?" I asked her one day.

"I think it's natural, that thingy you have. Why cut it away?" my mother said. Then, almost apologetically, as though I had blushed, she added, "When you were born they asked me, your father asked me, but I wouldn't let them do it, and he didn't force the issue."

Simeon persuaded my mother to talk to me about having the operation. Shocked, I told her I wouldn't discuss it. That was that, and I didn't hear about it again for several years. Then when I was about twelve or thirteen, Simeon came home with a frown on his face. He didn't say anything to me while we had dinner. Because we did not talk much anyway, I didn't pay much attention. However, after dinner he retired to his sofa to watch the news. Now and then he would glance at me fleetingly, as though he wanted to say something but did not know how. Soon my mother went to her bedroom and my younger brothers left us alone in the room, in front of the TV. Simeon looked at me seriously. He cleared his throat.

"I want to have a man-to-man conversation with you, Mark." I nodded.

"You know, Mark," he said matter-of-factly, "you should get circumcised."

"Really?" I said. I was a little taken aback but tried not to show it. I listened politely.

"It's dirty not to be circumcised. Later you'll get sick. And you're not a man until you're circumcised."

"I sort of like it this way," I replied, a queasy feeling in my stomach.

"If you do it later, there will be lots of blood. Now is a good time," Simeon continued. I realized he had been thinking about this on and off for years without telling me directly.

"Simeon, I really do not want to be circumcised," I said. "I'm quite happy the way I am."

Little did I know then but Obama Sr. probably would have agreed with me. The Luo is a tribe that traditionally frowns upon male circumcision. Simeon didn't push it. He respected my decision, but I know he was disappointed, just as he was disappointed when I wouldn't play golf, play chess, drink beer, or find a girlfriend. I was a weird boy in those days, and he knew enough to back off and give me a little space.

In my teens I went through periods where, in our unreligious home, I would try to be a devout Jew—as long as it did not involve pain or a lot of sacrifice.

For a time I stopped eating pork. I controlled myself for a few weeks and then reluctantly headed back to the bologna sandwiches I loved.

Ida answered my continuing interest in my family background. Although her ignorance of Hebrew disappointed me, she taught and influenced me in other ways, often without my knowledge.

Her thickly rouged face was enlivened by beautiful blue eyes that glowed with curiosity.

"Tell me about when you were a young girl and how you came to America," I would say.

"Oy, what do you want to know about that for? Those were hard years."

"I just want to know, Grandma."

"We fled the pogroms in Lithuania when I was a child," she told me. "It was about 1900 when we arrived in America. We took a big boat from Lithuania. There were many pogroms. I was about eight years old. I don't remember much about it. People didn't like Jews, but I was different. I had golden hair and blue eyes. So I was accepted more . . . like I was a goy," she said proudly.

I looked at her wizened face and imagined a younger Ida. My golden-haired and blue-eyed grandma. These were marks of superiority, and Ida was proud to say so. She still had the striking eyes, but at this point she wore an ill-fitting wig that I once saw her remove. I was shocked by the almost-bald dome beneath. Ida just ignored me, fussed around with the wig, and put it back on.

"What about Grandpa?" I asked.

"When I married I took my husband's surname, Baker. He was Jewish, too, but Baker was more accepted in society then. My family name was Indursky."

Years later, other relatives filled in the gaps for me. Around the turn of the twentieth century the Russian Imperial family and its bureaucrats often turned popular dissatisfaction with government policies and failed wars into reprisals against Jews. For example, in 1903 there was an extremely violent three-day pogrom in Moldova, resulting in the death of forty-five people.

I can only speculate, but perhaps this event prompted my great-grandfather, Abraham Indursky, to leave for America. As Onyango Obama had been impelled to change his life after serving abroad in the Great Wars, so my maternal grandfather was influenced by forces beyond his control to change his life and culture.

Abraham, along with his brothers and sisters, left Lithuania around 1905, and the family dispersed to different parts of the world, including France and Denmark. According to family members, my family had held respectable positions in society in their homeland; one of the Indurskys had been a photographer for Czar Nicholas II.

Leaving behind his wife and children, my great-grandfather arrived in Milton, Massachusetts, to live with a relative. He would travel up and down the streets with his horse and wagon, collecting bottles, scraps, and metal refuse, singing:

Any bottles, rags, any junk today?
The old rag picker is coming your way!

When he had enough money, he sent for his children, including Ida, and his wife to join him. Eventually he had enough saved to buy a small gas station in Allston, Massachusetts. When the family arrived, everyone chipped in to work. His wife would pump gas, and the children would sell brass candlesticks. Little by little, the scrap turned a good profit and they opened up Cambridge St. Metal Company, which eventually went worldwide.

"I wanted to go to college, but my father would not let me," Ida told me. "He wanted me to work instead. 'Woman should not go to college,' he said." It was one of my grandmother's greatest regrets. Like me, Ida was an exile from her family, and from her father, but she didn't care.

"We were the black sheep. They looked down on us," she said of her richer relatives across town. Then, lifting her head proudly, she added, "But I have my own house and I don't have to go to the rest home down the road. I live my own life!"

Most of her relatives in Boston looked on her as an oddball. Others looked on her as quaint. No one could ever accuse her of being boring.

Years before my conversations with her, Ida had developed breast cancer and had a mastectomy. She regularly placed padding under her clothes, and although it tended to sag, her chest seemed normal enough for an old person's whenever I looked at it. (A relative told me years later that during a family Passover dinner, Ida, in a huff, removed her false breast and placed it on the table.)

With my grandmother in the house, there was always music. "Kitten on the Keys," "The Minute Waltz," various salon pieces from the 1800s—all dashed off with blazing fingers and tidal waves of sound. Wherever there was a piano, she would gravitate toward it.

"When I was young," she once told me, "I won my high school music talent competition. I wanted to win the Victrola so much, but because I was Jewish, they gave me a book instead. The night of the prize-giving, I cried so hard. That was one of the saddest nights in my life."

For the rest of her life, she would always be seeking the Victrola. Music gave her an identity and a reason for being part of society. She was terrified by the thought of anonymity; her piano playing was her admission ticket to the world with all its marvelous gifts and prizes. Through music she could forget all the slights and criticisms, all the failings and setbacks. She found glorious meaning in the appreciation of others, with a tempo that rushed allegro con brio through her life.

"When I play piano, I forget everything. It even makes my arthritis go away," she said to me, her head bent slightly over the keyboard, almost as if she was praying.

Her piano playing was not very exact. According to connoisseurs of classical music, the tempos were inappropriate, the phrasing clumsy, and the dynamic contrast absent.

Later, when I studied the classics myself, I would complain to her, "How can you play Beethoven like jazz? That's a rest . . . and you can't change the tempo in the middle of Bach like that."

Ida would just ignore me and go on. She liked her own interpretation. The rhythms were pointed, the accents abrupt, but the notes were correct, and she believed in her performance.

We would sometimes visit the French Council in downtown Nairobi for an art event, or go to a movie at the 20th Century Cinema. Tightly holding her little green pocketbook on her lap, Ida would crouch in her seat, slightly hunched forward, her eagle eyes scanning the vicinity for any hapless child.

"Hello, dear, and what is your name?" she would say in the sweetest voice.

"Umm. . . Jimmy."

"Jimmy, do you play piano? Does your mother give you lessons? Huh, dear?"

"Umm, no." Sometimes the child would not speak at all, and he would stand and peer at Ida as though she was a strange species.

"Here, give me your hands, honey, let me show you something." And Ida would take the child's hands and start stretching exercises. Her wrinkled, pink fingers carefully held the small, trembling black hands.

"Do you know how to play a scale? Here, let me show you how it works."

Although there was no piano, she would drum out a scale or two on any flat surface nearby. Meanwhile the child's mother would look on, bemused and impatient.

"Say hello to the nice auntie, come on, come on!"

I would look away, embarrassed. Why did she have to be so intimate, so familiar with people we did not know? Why couldn't she just be quiet for once?

If there was no prospect of gaining a piano student, she would turn her efforts toward matchmaking.

"Honey, what a wonderful dancer's body you have," she would say to a pretty woman passing by the produce section in the supermarket. The young woman would inevitably be white, and often blonde.

"Have you met my grandson Mark? He's brilliant and will one day be the president of Africa!"

Tongue-tied, I would stutter a few words.

"But I want you to marry a beautiful blonde!" Ida would retort when I complained.

"Why does she have to be blonde? And anyway, I don't think I'll ever marry."

"Don't be silly!"

As I was growing up, I started to make sense of remarks I once found strange. For instance, Ida's refusal to live in the past. If we looked at old family photographs, she would say, gently but firmly, "Why keep those things? Everyone in them is dead. We should look to the future alone." Wasn't that what I had tried to do with my memories of the Obamas? Shut them away? Like Ida, I'd buried the bad memories deep inside me.

She had her own theory about miscegenation too.

"One day all of us will be brown, so why worry?" Somewhat flattered, I would nod. I wanted to believe her.

"There are three things that are important in life," she used to say to me. "Music, money, and men."

Unlike Ida I definitely did not need men, and money was never very important to me. But when it came to music, it was my oxygen, and Ida and I knew everything else was secondary.

Though Ida encouraged me to develop my musical abilities, my first teacher was my mother. I was about ten or eleven when I sat down and fingered the smooth yellow keys of the battered baby grand. It felt like it had always been there, waiting for me to play it.

My mother stood alongside me.

"You see the marks on the paper, Mark? Each represents a note." She bent down and played a simple piece.

"I will give each of your fingers a number. The thumb is one, the index finger is two, and so on." Underneath each note on the sheet music she wrote a number.

Placing my thumb on middle C, she instructed me, "Now just play the sequence of numbers I've written down." I did so. To my delight, although the rhythm was off, a tune emerged.

She taught me the differences between quavers and minims, crotchets and rests, and my tempos became more accurate. Because she was too busy to give me regular lessons, I painstakingly went through a Chopin nocturne note by note, line by line, assigning each finger to keys and phrases. After a few months I had learned the entire piece. People who heard me play encouraged me. I had at last discovered a way to satisfy an elemental hunger that had been buried inside me as long as I could remember. Playing piano gave me the strength to overcome adversity and the peace that comes with meditation.

My mother was happy to see me play, but for a long time she did not understand how deeply I loved music. When I talked of concert appearances and a music career, she brushed such thoughts aside. "It's a hard life, being a musician," she said. "Best to be a lawyer or a scientist. Have a job, but always keep your music."

She no doubt said this because she loved me, and I now know she only wanted me to be happy. How could she, or anyone else, understand the pull that music had on me? At that time even I did not know how much music would shape my life, or how many years it would be before I had the courage to seize this skill and use it to make a difference.

—◦—

My mother was always reading, and as with music she passed on to me her deep love of books and learning. I was always reading, and I was fortunate to have teachers who encouraged me to do so.

From the beginning my mother had made a point of placing me in good schools, even when she was living with Barack Obama Sr. and money was scarce. I had gone to Mrs. Taylor's nursery, one of the best kindergartens in Nairobi.

I still have a photo from those days. My head has been recently shaved and I look deeply embarrassed, standing in the middle of a group of about twenty African, Asian, and European students. Behind me is the cottage-like building in whose large bright rooms we would spend hours drawing with crayons and eating pudding. Outside, we played under leafy trees on swings and climbing frames. It was a happy place. But the day that photo was taken, before arriving in school I had been in tears.

The haircut was uneven. I looked like a black kiwi fruit. Always vain about my looks, I was miserable, though I would never show it.

I was never popular, and thus used to being alone. Picture books and the strange creatures within them, such as Dr. Seuss's the Drum-Tummied Snumm, the Four-Way Hunch, and Sam-I-Am helped me dream the hours away.

This isolation was partly my own fault. I loved showing off my precocious knowledge.

"Look at the genius," my mother's friends would declare. "What a talented boy!"

I loved to hear this praise, particularly from older women. Most of it was unmerited, as I knew only too well. Although I was viewed as a high-achieving child, I usually did not understand the facts and theories I parroted. I so wanted to be loved that for a long time I settled for praise. The admiration of others was like the ink that printed out my ticket to success.

My grandfather, Joe Maurice Baker, Ruth, and Ida. An immigrant Jewish family from Lithuania and Poland, they had attained the American dream, a home in the suburbs, a steady job, and a beautiful daughter. c. 1952

I like this photo of my grandmother Ida Baker taken in the States in the 1980s because it has something of that wanderlust, rebel quality that I associate her with.

My maternal great-grandparents, Abraham Indursky, Ida, and Sara Indursky in a photo taken around 1910, shortly after they arrived in Boston after fleeing the Lithuanian pogroms. Ida was terrified of her father. "I always used to hide under the table when he came home," she said. She was proud of her blonde hair and blue eyes. "People often did not know I was Jewish!" she once said to me. Shortly after they arrived, it is said, a relative of my great-grandfather found him sleeping on the couch. He was rudely awakened and chastised, "In America, you don't sleep, but you must work hard to succeed!" He eventually set up a successful international corporation in the metals industry.

Out of respect for my mother, and to find out more about my heritage, I traveled to Israel in 2011. In Jerusalem I had a memorable meeting with Chief Rabbi Yona Metzger. The following day his office announced I would ask Barack to free Jonathan Pollard, the jailed American spy—although we had never discussed politics. This photo was taken at Megiddo a few days later, where I was glad to turn my attention to Israel's long history and forget politics.

CHAPTER EIGHT

Saints and Sinners

MUSICAL EVOCATION

Goldberg Variations: J. S. Bach

This work consists of an opening melody (aria) and thirty-two variations, and it was composed by the great Baroque composer Johann Sebastian Bach (1685–1750). In my twenties, I wrote a series of poems to describe each of the variations in literary terms, but I gave up: There was no way words could capture the unique vitality and diversity of the music.

The greatest performance of this work was by the Canadian Glenn Gould, recorded in the 1980s. The music often employs a particular musical structure called a fugue, in which multiple melodies are simultaneously played and interact according to certain rules—rather like life itself.

I associate this work particularly with my adolescence, a time when I encountered many new people and experiences that altered and enriched my life. Some things, however, remained the same, such as my drive to excel and the importance of music and learning. Similarly, the aria that opens this piece goes through thirty-two changes but recurs at the end, apparently unchanged but spiritually richer.

DURING MY TEENS, I BOUGHT MY BOOKS MOSTLY AT TWO PLACES: THE Nairobi University bookstore, a grim building in the center of a campus that was often deserted due to student strikes, and Westlands, a relatively upscale suburb about ten miles from the city center. The university store had a huge variety of books, from annual government crop reports to the Larousse Encyclopedia, Wordsworth's *The Prelude* to Laurence Sterne's *Tristram Shandy*, Franz Kafka's *Amerika* to Jean-Paul Sartre's *La Nausée*, plus leading African authors such as Fanon, Soyinka, and many others, all at rock-bottom prices. Discovering cheap books was easy; choosing which ones to buy wasn't. I had limited pocket money and an insatiable appetite for reading. The bookstore was a vast, quiet room stuffed with countless shelves. I could rummage there undisturbed for hours, finally finding a bargain or two. The clerks hid away behind antiquated counters, nibbling their lunchtime sandwiches or chatting in quiet murmurs to pass the time.

The little bookstore in the Westlands Mall was owned by an Indian who, naturally meek and retiring, left most of the daily work to his wife—a short middle-aged woman with a perpetual frown, as if she had been wronged and could not shake off the injustice of it all.

If I had money and found something I liked, a comic or a book, I would pick it up and timidly walk to the cash register.

"Twelve shillings!" the woman would command as she pushed the plastic bag and receipt across the counter toward me. After tilting her nose as though she was about to sniff the ceiling lamp, she would then turn back to whatever she had been doing.

Down the road from our house, besides the jacarandas that were stained brown from the fumes of passing cars and buses, there was a little secondhand book and record store, also run by an Indian and managed daily by her African assistant. It may have been just my overactive imagination, but here too I felt myself to be under constant scrutiny. Eyes seemed to be trained on the back of my head whenever I browsed through the stock. Most of the time I would just be happy, even thrilled, to find a particular used recording, such as one by Maurizio Pollini, or a long-sought-after book, but other times I would get so angry I did not know what to do.

Once, I had no money and stole some comic books.

Another time I slipped one into a larger title, planning to pay only for a single item. I was overjoyed with the scheme until I reached the counter.

The assistant pulled out the hidden copy.

"Where did that come from?" I said in mock astonishment.

He didn't say anything, just looked at me, his eyes sad and disappointed. I expected him to be angry, even to call the police. Instead he shook his head as though I had broken the faith. He waved me out of the store, disgusted, and I walked home with my head down. Little did I know then that this tendency to act rashly and look for a quick result would come back to haunt me in the future.

Yet, at the time, I hadn't cared about the possible consequences. I felt I would do anything, even steal, to get something to read. Books and music were my raison d'être.

⁓

Saint Mary's, where I studied from the age of eight until graduation, began as a tea farm in the early 1900s. At some point, seduced by the cheap and beautiful highlands and the prospect of saving thousands of lost souls, a group of Irish Fathers of the Holy Ghost built a lofty church among the tea bushes. In 1939 they started a school. The students were white, and the mission of the Fathers was to proselytize their faith to all and sundry.

To this day the church is in remarkably good condition. The pews are made of solid oak, varnished and gleaming beneath the scratched or even carved initials and mottos left behind by generations of bored teenagers.

We students attended services there regularly, and during morning mass we sat dutifully under the lofty white walls and beautiful stained glass, which depicted the Stages of the Cross.

When I attended St. Mary's, it was one of the most respected schools in the nation. Its students went to the best universities in the world, and teachers and priests came from India, the UK, the United States, and many other countries to work there.

The twin pillars of an education at St. Mary's were religion and sport. The school occupied a huge site with dozens of acres of forest and lawns. The entrance was through two massive iron gates at the end of Ring Road in the suburbs, surrounded by the opulent houses of Indian merchants and expatriates. Once past the gates, the road wound past the rugby fields and golf course, swooping down the hill toward the main buildings and up to the magnificent church.

The ethos of achievement in sports hung heavy over the long, echoing corridors. Abandoned fourth-floor rooms held wooden chests bulging with rusting trophies. When I arrived around 1975, I was at once recruited onto the rugby team. I quickly discovered that thrashing around in endless mud and being pummeled by my fellow classmates, in frantic pursuit of a soggy ball, was not for me.

As for religion, I remember going to mass on Wednesdays. Though it was compulsory for the students, I felt distinctly uncomfortable praying to Jesus and complained to my parents.

"Jesus was a very, very wise man. He was a prophet, but he was no god," Ruth said in a determined voice. Afterward I was not required to go to prayers anymore, and the other students would troop off, leaving me behind, not knowing what to make of it.

Before the quadrangle across from the school banner was a huge statue of the Virgin Mary. Her white marble features looked out over the students every Friday morning as they gave a stirring rendition of the school anthem "When the Saints Go Marching In." There was something of the Jesuit tradition of salvation through pain at St. Mary's, so physical pain was an accepted part of school life. Fistfights between pupils were common; the Fathers tried to discourage them, but to us they were as natural as studying geography or playing soccer. Unless parents complained loudly, it was accepted that rule breakers were punished with "six of the best," the colorful description for being thrashed by the headmaster. We feared his leather belt or wooden ruler, but accepted them as necessary evils.

Every Friday, after assembly, we would gather in the huge school auditorium to publicly receive merits or demerits. We would line up in neat rows. The headmaster would open with the school song, say a short prayer, make some general remarks, and finally someone would read out the respective points awarded to each boy. Seven points was regarded as a good score. Eight could win you the number one position and an award of five shillings. Then the students who had scored five points would be named. After the assembly they would go to the headmaster's to receive six lashes of his cane. As they stood, one by one, heads bowed, surrounded by the deathly silence of five hundred or so fellow students, I felt their ignominy. Once I misheard my name and stood up in a daze, until someone tugged at my jacket and roughly pulled me down.

"They didn't call your name, man! Sit down!"

I still remember the feeling—a bolt of ice striking my belly. Failure was my bête noire.

As an A-student, I was never belted except for once—for starting a fight. I secretly slipped a rolled-up copy of *Captain Marvel* into my pants and bent over. The *whaaaackkkk*-ing noise sounded unnatural, but the headmaster didn't notice.

At "Saints" (our name for St. Mary's), there was a sense of belonging to a club of confident children who would one day grow up to form the backbone of Kenya's middle class: the doctors, lawyers, bureaucrats, and, above all, the politicians. In some ways, though, it was also about honor and atonement, the idea that one must confess one's sins, state the facts, and to hell with the consequences.

I was unpopular, but it was years before I realized how much. Then one day, in primary school, after an important exam, the marked-up papers were returned to us. Normally the kid with the highest grade, I was shocked to see my latest score: a dismal 85 percent. Looking closely, I started and raised my hand. "There is a mistake in my grade!"

Mrs. Parsons, an elderly Scot who had taught at Saints for decades, looked at me and shook her head, white locks bouncing energetically about her flushed cheeks.

"There can't be!"

"Yes, there is. I can show you," I persisted.

Up to this point the rest of the class had looked on with curiosity. Then I heard a shout from the back.

"Shut up, Ndesandjo! You're wrong as usual!" Then, as if on cue, the whole class chimed in.

"Yes, shut up, Banjo! You're wrong as usual!"

Goaded, I stood and walked down the aisle toward the teacher. The class murmured loudly. It was a bestial sound, deep and inarticulate, a wave of dislike so powerful that even the prim-and-proper Mrs. Parsons seemed disconcerted.

They glared as I passed. "Sit down, Banjo. Sit down!"

I handed my paper to Mrs. Parsons and showed her that I had the correct answer

She looked long and hard at my paper. My legs wavered but I stood my ground. I knew I was right.

Finally, Mrs. Parsons looked up at me, chastened.

"Yes, Ndesandjo. Your answer is correct. You get ten more points."

I walked back to my seat to utter silence in the classroom.

———

I visited the school library countless times, thumbing through the annual yearbooks, looking at photographs of bold, bemused, or angry faces, captured en masse, year after year. I saw the same poses repeated, the same expressions. But something was changing. First a lone African appeared, then another, and each year more and more, until the few white faces resembled scattered snowballs in a dark field.

Before Kenya's independence from Britain, the school was exclusively white. As the years passed, it became more mixed. Inevitably, African students would socialize with Africans, whites with whites, their lives rarely intersecting except on the rugby field or the concert stage. At the open-air swimming pool, these white Kenyans—Brits who had lived in the country for generations—would cluster together like a tribe. They would change clothes in full view of the other students, stripping down to their lily-white bottoms. They flaunted the virile bulges in their thin Speedo swimsuits like trophies, at one with the uniquely British and macho locker-room tradition. I for one would change into my togs with a towel tightly wrapped around my nether regions.

By the time I left St. Mary's in the mid-eighties, this small clique had disappeared, and almost all the students were either African or Asian. Most white families had moved their children to exclusive schools like Hillcrest, where Africans were still not welcome. The few who enrolled there were rarely on display. These strange weeds among flowers were probably too poor to go anywhere else, or maybe they were locked out of the social loop. For them, the only other alternative—public schools with barefoot students and chronic corruption—was out of the question.

Kenya was now an independent country, ruled by African politicians, yet the webs of economic and racial separation criss-crossed the dark corners of the republic, and not infrequently could be seen out in the open. St. Mary's was perhaps the most political school in Kenya. Government members sent their children there as a matter of course. Uhuru Kenyatta, the son of Mzee Jomo Kenyatta, and now the president of Kenya, was a few classes up from me. David Kibaki, the son of a former president, was my classmate. The Koinange family, itself a powerhouse during Kenyatta's time, sent their sons, with whom I played rugby, there. Saints was an institution in Kenya. And, like Kenya, it mirrored the racial divisions, battles, and contradictions inherent within Africa, now and probably for all time.

On a short return visit there in 2006, I remember walking under the entrance arch and seeing the school motto: *Bonitas, Disciplina, Scientia*. The blue letters were mottled and faded, but the buildings and other structures were mostly as I remembered them.

Several lawn chairs were scattered across the grounds in the aftermath of a gale. That weekend the students were away, and a few workers milled around, tending to the gardens, stonily viewing passersby as they exchanged small talk or smoked cigarettes with friends. Occasionally a priest would walk by in the distance, his face limned like a brass penny against the green and brown of the quadrangle. The bricks around the swimming pool were a gritty ochre, and the ridged steps around it painted light blue.

Right below me was the spot where powerful blond David Asquith, one of the last British Kenyans at St. Mary's, fought and lost to the equally large, pug-nosed Jeff, scion of a powerful political family. That savage fistfight symbolized, on a smaller scale, the movement of power from white to black that had started with the fight for independence, and which accelerated fast after 1963.

The fight was brief, a quick flurry of flying fists in a throng of mostly black, and some white, faces. David and Jeff had seemed almost reluctant combatants, pushed into contact by the two groups of screaming boys. Each side would claim victory although the whites' vehemence seemed to fade in the weeks following, as though they had lost their moxie. Part of me wanted to leave, another part looked on with a morbid curiosity. It seemed I had two hands—one white, one black—and at the moment they were in an uneasy alliance, almost clenched, not yet forced apart.

I was used to viewing these conflicts from the sidelines. Never participating, but instead walking my own path.

It hadn't always been this way.

About the time I arrived at Saints, boys would often play soccer or marbles in the quadrangle during the breaks. The moment the bell rang, they would run from the classroom and kick their footballs down the stairs or clutch their marbles in their pockets. For days I would loiter by the football players, too nervous to join in. I saw other students arrive and casually jump into the match, but still I struggled. One day I gathered up my courage. I took a step forward, and someone shouted out.

"Stay away, Banjo, we don't want four-eyes here."

I retreated. The next time I tried was no different.

"Go and join your white friends, half-caste," another boy called out.

I pretended not to hear him and just laughed nervously. On the verge of tears, I turned away.

Soccer was for teams, but marbles were for individuals, so I turned to the art of bombies, sparklers, and steelies. There was no greater pleasure than when I launched a fat marble across the pit, and it slammed into my opponents' marbles with a deep *craaaaacccckkkkk* that could be heard across the courtyard.

———

At St. Mary's there were two types of priests, or fathers, as we called them. Most noticeable were the pumped-up, adrenaline-soaked ones who helped run the school. The more scholarly types mostly kept to themselves and occasionally flitted across the limits of our vision, like pale wraiths fleeing the burning African sun.

Cormac O'Brolchain was a towering figure. He single-handedly developed rugby teams that dominated Kenyan amateur sport for years to come, guided St. Mary's to national championships in swimming and football, choreographed and conducted annual operettas, and still managed to supervise a school of several hundred students, teachers, and fellow priests. To a young boy, this silver-haired, handsome man with boundless energy was a colossus.

The first day I met him, he strode into my Standard 3 classroom, steely gray eyes focused on the teacher and some of the students. As if stung by hornets, the boys jumped to attention.

"Good morning, Father Cormac!" we yelled.

He stood at the front of the room, a faint smile on his thin lips. He locked his eyes onto some of us, as though we had some terrible lashing in store. I felt guilty under that piercing regard, a sinner unaware of my exact sin.

"What are you nincompoops up to?" he asked in a deep baritone. His voice was a beautiful thing. Smooth, resonant, and commanding, it was a deep Irish brogue. Its thrilling energy soared above our heads and out the windows like a banshee, driving away all distractions and focusing our minds on the task at hand. When he coached students for the school operetta and sang in a low mezzo-soprano, he morphed into something asexual, half-man, half-woman, evoking images of lakes of caramel and angels praising the Almighty. We were in awe.

Cormac did this or *Cormac did that*, we would whisper, in hushed voices. When he passed by, a tremor of both fear and exhilaration would run through our bodies.

I did not know what nincompoop meant, but it sounded like trouble.

Once he wagged his finger at a boy who often got into trouble and boomed, "What are you up to, Njoroge? Come here, boy!"

Njoroge slunk over, not sure what to expect, and stood next to the short, dapper priest. Cormac looked at us sternly.

"Now remember this . . ." Here he paused, slowly raising his hand as though he were about to bless us.

His knuckles sharply descended on Njoroge's curly scalp.

"*Njoroge* is a nincompoop."

Njoroge tried to duck, to no avail. *Knock*. Realizing it didn't hurt that much, he gave a shy, bashful smile.

"One *must* listen to the teacher." *Knock*.

"Or else . . ." *Knock. Knock*. The sounds rang out like a horse's hooves.

Gazing steadily at us throughout, he slowly expanded his Cheshire cat grin. Everyone, even Njoroge, laughed or smiled. Finally composed, eyes flashing with mirth, Cormac grabbed the boy's jacket lapel with one hand, but gently this time, and belted out his final words of wisdom.

"You are *all* nincompoops. Listen to your teacher and study hard!" Then he walked out while we shouted in thrilling, grand, and stentorian unison:

"Good-bye, Father Cormac!"

We feared him—but loved him.

Cormac was a human dynamo, packing his days with administrative work, inspecting and managing classes, and supervising season after season of memorable performances. The Gilbert and Sullivan operetta was an annual rite at St. Mary's. He conducted the orchestra like a fury, his body a blur of motion, while his gray hair flailed about his face and sweat rolled down his flushed cheeks. He would glare ferociously at the violins when they were off the beat.

"More, more! Nitwits!"

His passion was infectious. The orchestra played as one, the violinists inhaling, the woodwinds exhaling, all in glorious harmony, borne along by the energy of the silver-haired man astride the podium.

He once walked into the performance hall as I was playing Chopin. I had never seen that particular expression on his face before. He gestured to the other students in the hall.

"Boys, gather round. I want you to listen to this. Play that piece again," he told me.

I had never felt so proud.

Cormac eventually retreated from administration and took charge of sabbatical programs that required less contact with the students. I learned later he was working on his master's thesis for a college in Ireland. Sometimes I would spot him strolling on the third-floor corridor, his face slightly turned down and hands clasped behind his back. His broad aquiline nose seemed to cut through the air like a bird poised for flight. He looked so handsome and composed, I wondered how such a man could shut himself away from women, family, and worldly things. *What a waste,* I thought. But then I concluded, *what dedication.*

Once I told Cormac about my bitter argument with a teacher over grading. "Grades aren't everything," he replied. "Sometimes other things are more important."

"Like what?" I said.

"Friends," he said quietly.

Such deepness of character reached me better than any lashing or scolding could have done. Cormac, in his simple statement, was speaking to me as a human being, but beneath the words lay great wisdom and high expectations. The last thing I wanted in the world was to disappoint him. It might have been Confucius speaking to me in Gaelic-accented English:

学而不思则罔
Study without thought is deception.

I began to understand that I could study and win good grades, but if I did not know how to use my knowledge—if I failed to develop emotional intelligence—I would be deceiving myself, and others.

———

As Cormac was with people, Father Frank Soughley was with books. Soughley was a huge grizzly bear of a man, but gentle as a lamb. More than six feet tall, he wore a big, baggy, gray cassock that barely covered his huge paunch. He would meander slowly down the corridors, thick spectacles focused on his shuffling feet. He picked out each step with great care, and because his feet were unusually small, he always looked as though he was about to topple over.

He had taught for many years at various schools throughout Kenya, and some of his students had or would become prominent figures, including a former president, Mwai Kibaki. He lived as a scholar, in a small room behind the school quadrangle, among an island of apartments on a quiet corridor.

I often wondered what the non-teaching priests did with all their time. Some studied for degrees or were on sabbaticals from Irish institutions; the rest, like Soughley, were retired and puttered out their last days at Saints.

He loved history and taught it for one term. He would shuffle into the classroom almost reluctantly and then shyly proceed in a whispery Dublin brogue. He had an encyclopedic memory and knew his books inside out. His lectures had their own logic, beginning from subjects ostensibly unrelated to the topic but finally, ingeniously, transitioning to the main point. For example, a discussion of the French Revolution would begin with something unrelated.

"Well, do you know how the flushing toilet was invented?" He would peek at us from behind his glasses, then turn to the blackboard and draw a precise schematic of a toilet, detailing the flushing mechanism.

"The Irish were at their wits' end, and the economy was in the tank, you see . . ."

Most in the class didn't see, and dozed off. A few chatted loudly among themselves. Unperturbed, Soughley continued his monologue.

"The toilet was one example of how the Industrial Revolution enabled the growth of cities through sanitation . . . but only an actual bloody revolution made that possible."

Finally, after several highly detailed diversions, we would get to the point, which, unlike the preamble, I always forgot.

"I have a ton of books, Ndesandjo. You may come over and see them sometime," he suggested, after a fifteen-minute tour de force of a disquisition on his favorite book, Frederick Bodmer's *The Loom of Language*. "There is no finnnnneeeeeeer explanation of the English language." He drawled his vowels with all the sated languor of a gourmet.

I was his star student and began to visit him often. His studio apartment was piled to the ceiling with musty books. He sat on a little chair behind a wooden table, with a rusty typewriter and reams of papers scattered before him. The soft light from the window above his small pallet bed illuminated his smudged glasses and halo of yellow-white hair.

"The roots of language are quite amazing, Ndesandjo. Most English-speaking people don't realize that they are speaking Latin and Greek all the time, you see."

His large trembling fingers paged through a small book.

"Take the word *eudaemonism*, composed of Eudaimos and -ism, Greek for joy and French for thinking. French is a romance language, all based on Latin." He nodded his head vigorously, half grimacing, half smiling, peering at me intently over his wire-rimmed glasses. "As are Romanian, Spanish, and Italian. Combine the two fragments and there is a new word. Just understand the roots and you understand the word."

"So that's what the book is about. May I borrow it, Father?" Although he let me borrow it, I only read a few pages. I preferred to listen to him explain things to me; his love of words would pour over me like a rousing call to arms.

After one Friday morning assembly in the quadrangle, I looked up at the gleaming white marble statue of the Virgin Mary as she gazed down on us with her beatific smile, dazzling in the morning sun. Thoughts of Einstein and Freud flickered through my mind. Around me, uniformed students stood to attention in serried rows, all eyes fixed on the headmaster.

I shuffled my feet impatiently. Overhead, trees swayed gently in the breeze. The sky beyond them seemed impossibly vast, intensely blue. At once, like a sudden gust of icy air, an unreasonable fear took hold of me. Do we all just die? Did Einstein's beautiful, wise face just vanish into nothingness? Is this what is in store for all of us? To perish, never again to be conscious of our uniqueness, of this marvelous world and its kinship with each of us? In this moment of existential doubt, I saw Soughley standing to the side.

Afterward, I went up to him, distraught. "Father Soughley, may I ask you a question?"

"Of course."

"What happens to the genius of people like Einstein when they die? Does it all just vanish?"

He tilted his head slightly to the side and then looked at some spot in midair, as if he were a child examining the board in an ice-cream shop, searching for the perfect flavor. Finally he shook his head quickly, gave a little shiver, and faced me, eyeball to eyeball.

The clown had vanished. He looked at me, his expression serious.

"You see, Ndesandjo, such spirits do not die. Energy like that cannot disappear. They are still here!"

Soughley passed away a few years later. I took it hard. I couldn't remember the last time I'd cried. He was a shuffling, awkward man, but brilliant and caring. I felt the loss of him keenly, but faintly hoped that the life force he believed in would follow me to distant shores, for soon I would leave Kenya bound on a great adventure.

Richard, me, and our ayah (maid) Juliana shortly before I left for Brown University. The skin on her hands was so tough she could grasp pans of boiling water without any pain. Through her years of caring for me and my family, together with her amazing cooking, she was part of the family and we all loved her. c. 1984

Facing page, top: Here I am playing in a national musical competition. I won four trophies! c. 1981

Bottom: For a while I also played the clarinet in the school orchestra, before I gave it up for the piano. Music helped me connect with others, including my good friends Konstantin from Greece and Natsuhiko (pictured with flute) from Japan. c. 1982

CHAPTER NINE

Being Brown at Brown and Other University Stories

MUSICAL EVOCATION

Piano Concerto: Edvard Grieg

In many ways my peripatetic journey through Brown and Stanford was a sequence of collisions between inflexible rules and high expectations on the one hand, and an instinctive desire to break free of systems, complacency, and dead ends on the other. Music was my solace. In my junior year at Brown, I entered a university piano competition. The winner would play his or her concerto with the university orchestra. I selected the Grieg Piano Concerto. I did not win the competition, but I remember how one night, after the audition, in the piano bar of the Brown Graduate Center, a little drunk and lonely, at the stroke of midnight I played the cadenza of the first movement for my friends. Something that evening made me give a great performance, that connected with all the people in that smoky room. Perhaps because I could let myself go, through drink, I managed to achieve what I did not in the formal audition.

I REMEMBER CASUALLY WALKING INTO MY FRIEND JONATHAN'S ROOM AT Brown, thinking we would have a quiet chat about music. The door was half open. Day-old pizza slices were scattered on the floor next to CDs and under racks of music equipment. To the left of the door, Jonathan was lying on his slim pallet of a bed with nothing on except an unbuttoned shirt. A girl who I recognized and had flirted with just days before was sitting on top of him, half naked, panting and sweating.

"Hey, Mark, what's up?" Jonathan weakly waved me in, a smile on his handsome face.

He grasped a can of Budweiser, delicately balanced on his bare chest, and took a long sip, keeping the rest of his body perfectly still while the girl did all the work. He looked totally bored, as if he were doing the laundry. She looked impatiently at me, shook her blonde hair as though I was an annoying gnat, and continued bouncing up and down. Too embarrassed to say anything, I made an excuse and quickly backed out.

For one raised in a priestly establishment in Kenya, living in close quarters with other men and women was a radical shift. Brown University not only pricked my intellectual ego but also put a dent in my solitude. These people were all so free, so unbounded.

In the end, these social scenes weren't for me. Women at Brown were like beautiful trophies on a shelf—to be seen but not touched. The freedom that characterized America seemed unattainable to me. Would I retreat into my shell? Worse, would I eventually spin out of orbit like a top on a cracked table?

No matter that my decision to go to Brown was preceded by years of preparation.

When my father was growing up, he had used mango leaves for toilet tissue and herded cattle until his feet bled. But he had maintained his high aspirations and had gone to Harvard. Like my father, I felt I could go far. Barack Obama Sr. had sunk into oblivion afterward, but so what? He had reached the acme of academic life. So could I.

I was seventeen and confident of my talents. Going to Harvard or Stanford, I believed, was my due. Yet I always sensed a deep skepticism from others when I mentioned my goals.

"You think you're a genius, Ndesandjo. You think you're the greatest. You'll be disappointed," some said. I shrugged. I had a tough skin, and if comments occasionally penetrated I would retreat into my room. In my opinion, these people were like the small, dark flies that swarmed around my father's cows.

In high school I had been a multifunctional freak. I didn't know about rock and roll. Instead, I loved classical music (many called it dead music). I didn't know Swahili, but instead memorized Latin and Ancient Greek. I couldn't get laid, even when my brother had tried to treat me. I played marbles, because I had not been "black enough" for the school kids to let me join their soccer games. Most important, I didn't cultivate friendships because, in my limited experience, they led only to pain and rejection.

For years I had spent hours each day hunched over books. I got seven points in the all-important mock "O"-levels, a phenomenally high score nationwide and the top mark in my school. I would wake up at six in the morning every day during the three-month holiday break before the SAT and read books straight until eight in the evening. It was easy for me. I just needed a goal. I wanted to go to the best schools in the world. After that, who knew what I could become? Mediocrity was not an option. Kenya did not reward failures, of any stripe, color, or social class.

"Brain cells start to die at twenty-eight!" a high-school friend told me. "That's why most great men and women make their mark before then."

I was in a hurry. I was going to be eighteen. I would be old! I had to make my mark now.

—❦—

In 1983, St. Mary's was just starting to implement the International Baccalaureate Program. I applied to university before the year was out, disappointing my teachers.

"You should finish the program. You will have a better chance. More schools will accept you if you wait," they advised me.

I was headstrong and disagreed.

I was convinced that excellent recommendations were key and that people should be encouraged to see me as a well-rounded scholar with multiple talents. My national awards—many for music—also stood me in good stead.

I applied to Harvard, Princeton, Yale, and Brown, all East Coast universities close to my grandmother's home in Boston. In the end only

Brown accepted me. My teachers had been right. Disappointed, I relented and prepared to wait another year to apply. I was determined to go to Harvard. Then my mother stepped in.

"Brown is one of the best schools in the country. You should go. Everyone wants to go there."

I wasn't so sure but I pondered.

"Brown, what is that? Never heard of it, old fellow," classmates said.

I read up on the college. At that time it was the most popular undergraduate campus in the United States. The ratio of applicants to admitted students was the highest in the nation. Brown was also Ivy League. What I didn't understand was how I could have gotten into the most competitive university in the United States and still not have gotten into Princeton, Yale, or Harvard.

"These schools collaborate among themselves. They probably already discussed you and decided you would go to Brown," someone said to me.

After a few days of soul-searching, I went for Brown. While my parents would pay a portion of the tuition, the vast majority of the fees were covered by grants and loans. Later, I won a Ford Fellowship.

The morning I left Kenya, my mother came into my room to talk to me. She was pensive and had a sad smile on her face. She didn't say much. I probably said, "I will miss you, and I feel sad to leave," but it wasn't true. I was delighted to leave. I felt elated and guilty at the same time. Elated for adventure, guilty from appearing happy in front of my family. Ruth had persuaded Simeon to give me his beautiful leather bag, strong and expensive. I have it to this day.

My seven-year-old brother skipped into the room and jumped onto the bed.

"I am going to miss you, Mark," Richard said, looking sad for a moment.

"I'll miss you too, Richard," I answered. My mother stood silently next to the door, her hands folded, her eyes red and moist. Sunlight streamed through the window onto the green quilt she had knitted for me and onto the secondhand books and records I had collected throughout the years. Like the flowers of paradise in my garden, I was prepared to fly toward the sun. Unlike them, I would not let mere roots hold me back. I shut the suitcase with a bang.

I had been to America only twice before, first in 1966 for three weeks when I was one year old. At the time my mother had fled Barack Obama Sr. and returned to Boston. After Ruth married Simeon we again visited the United States for several days. During this second visit, my mother took me to the local Social Security office, where I registered with Selective Service.

"All Americans do this," she explained. I looked at the small silvery-green card with a slight frown. I read with dread that all recipients could, at will, be drafted into the army in times of war. I felt I was being press-ganged by a huge, amorphous bureaucracy.

"Now you can get an American passport. You're an American," my mother told me.

Eventually, I was won over by McDonald's milk shakes and hamburgers, fresh milk, and cheese toast.

"You must try the milk, Mark. It is the best in the world," my mother said when we first entered my grandparents' house.

She poured me a glass. Indeed, it was thick and frothy, sweet and rich, and that is how America itself appeared. From afar, it had an allure that appealed to billions, and I was one of them.

—

The first few months were probably the happiest part of my stay at Brown. We were still too naive to form cliques and as a result were relatively open to chatting and sharing. We were all new; my strangeness and reserve were viewed as normal.

I would soon discover that for all America's tasty food and pleasant surroundings, it hid a deeper, more complex, and troubling social structure than I had expected.

Surrounded by other high-achieving students, I encountered serious competition. I was a perfectionist. Bs were intolerable to me, but now common. A+s were a necessity, but few and far between. I was humbled and miserable. Furthermore, whenever I produced an essay I personally valued or music that I believed I performed well, there was always a professor who would pick at the typographical errors or wrong notes and judge it all as mediocre. I could have lived with this and even welcomed it as an opportunity to improve. However, there was a problem with me being a minority student who wanted frank discussions with white teachers: political correctness. It was about sensitizing every word, every gesture, until discussions about race were like walking on eggshells. There was an absence of frank dialogue, which muted the honest airing of anyone's opinion.

"That's a dumb idea," would have been a welcome comment sometimes.

But what they said was, "I see. I see. Yes, you get it."

From the moment I walked into their office, some professors clearly thought I was not bright enough to be in their class but seemed wary of saying so. How I yearned for a frank discussion! I kept silent, too, often too proud and sensitive to tell them I didn't get it even after they'd tried to explain.

I knew I wasn't stupid. I just had a different approach to learning. I had always been taught that asking questions was the way to do it. Here, hundreds of Brunonians burned the midnight oil and, out of inherent good sense or canny intuition, never sought help. The American student nurses a stubborn, proud silence—he or she fears that questions reveal weakness. As for me, during hour-long classes I would be the only one who raised his hand.

After awhile, I got the impression that there was an invisible majority that wanted me to remain part of the wallpaper. I could sit and listen but should never attract attention to myself. I felt like a stranger in a vast, alien world. I knew I would need to fight every step of the way.

It was my music that helped pull me out of this isolation.

—◦—

During my sophomore year at Brown, in the summer vacation of 1986, I won an internship at CBS Masterworks records in Manhattan. For several weeks I lived at New York University, splitting time between the Black Rock downtown, where I worked, and the rest of the city.

One week I heard through the grapevine that the great cellist Yo-Yo Ma and pianist Emanuel Ax would be recording the Brahms cello sonatas at Wellesley College in Massachusetts.

My supervisor found a way to get me to the recording session, which included the two great musicians, CBS producer Stephen Epstein, some engineers, and myself. Yo-Yo and Manny were good friends and had partnered professionally for many years. They were going to record in the Houghton Memorial Chapel, an 1899 Romanesque structure with many Byzantine and Gothic elements, dominated by a massive spire.

"The acoustics are superb," Stephen said to me, "and it has the perfect sound for Brahms."

I sat in one of the pews. There was a hushed silence in the great church. A complete change came over the musicians' faces when they started to make music, as though they were listening to an inner god. I was overwhelmed. The first take was flawless. Yo-Yo Ma always manages to produce a wonderful tone that is perfectly on pitch.

At the nearby cafeteria we chatted about music over a lunch of burgers and soft drinks.

"This is really a recording of Yo-Yo accompanying Manny," the famous cellist whispered to me. "Manny really loves burgers . . . he puts me to shame."

"I heard that!" Portly Manny smiled and shook his head. "We get along well together and enjoy making music. But a lot depends on the instruments. Yo-Yo is lucky because he can carry his cello around. I have to make do with whatever piano is available," he added, laughing. They were clearly both very humble, comfortable with each other, and very sure of their craft.

I had other memorable encounters at CBS. As I was listening to some Mozart in an office one day, a tall silver-haired man wearing a bow tie walked into the room. He saw some of the Glenn Gould recordings I had stacked on my desk, and his eyes lit up.

"Wow, you managed to get a copy of his Chopin and Scriabin recordings. That's hard to come by!"

It was the great record producer Samuel H. Carter, who shared a passion for the Canadian pianist. Carter had recorded a number of Gould's last discs, including his remarkable performances of Bach's *Goldberg Variations*. We got chatting about music and became friends. Together with the CBS PR Department, he later helped me set up a special film screening at Brown University devoted to the pianist.

Another afternoon, a short, stocky man with a wild head of brown hair and a puffy red face lumbered into the room. Like a conductor, he waved his hands in time to the music that was playing and looked hard at me.

"Who are you?"

"Mark Ndesandjo, the summer intern."

"Ah-ha! A man who appreciates classical music!" And he burst into a peal of high-pitched laughter. I stood up to introduce myself, but he waved me down and gestured to me to listen.

"You see, you see! The woodwinds are suddenly hushed there. Only Perahia can manage that while conducting and playing at the same time. He has balls!"

This was Peter Munves, the last great eclectic of the classical-music industry. Recognized as a marketing genius after his crossover hits *Jurassic Classics* and *Switched on Bach* opened up new markets and revenue, he knew more about the industry and its customers than most executives on the planet. Munves was known to treat life with a ribald sense of humor. He told *Time* magazine in 1971 to "call me the P. T. Barnum of the classics." We became fast friends after he invited me to visit his immensely untidy and disorganized home in Merrick, a tony suburb of Long Island. He had collected a vast number of LPs over the years, including thousands of rare and remarkable recordings.

"I conduct every morning and evening," he said, dressed in nothing but his underpants and waving his baton in front of his high-end stereo system. "It's better than sex!" We would listen to hours of music—Toscanini conducting Beethoven, or piano rolls of Josef Lhévinne and Alfred Cortot interpreting Chopin—as the sun streamed into the living room.

Peter was remarkably generous and bighearted, freely sharing his thoughts on music and life, introducing me to his friends in New York, giving me loads of records, and often treating me to meals and concerts. Our love of music bound us together.

"I knew that you were special from that day I heard you listening to Mozart. And of course, you had to be Jewish like me. I knew that too from the shape of your nose. Only Jews have such noses. Oy!"

I met Wynton Marsalis as he was chatting with a studio executive in her office. When I mentioned I had listened to all his recordings and greatly admired him, he was disarmingly modest.

"Thanks, man, I appreciate that." He invited me to a concert of his that week in the Village.

While working at CBS, I remember seeing cabinets stocked with LP recordings gathering dust.

"Oh, those are all from people who wanted to get contracts with us. Some have been here for years," a secretary told me.

I sorted through and listened to some of the music, astonished at the high quality. Even these accomplished people had had no luck. I was slowly accepting the complexities of the recording business and the difficulty of getting a contract.

How could I succeed if even these artists had no chance? I asked myself again and again. Music was like breathing to me, but to make a career of it—was that possible? With mixed feelings, I returned to Brown to resume my studies.

During these years Ida Baker was my enduring source of comfort.

Brown University was about an hour's drive from my grandmother's Boston home. Every weekend I would take the bus to see her. It was a respite from the pressure of studying and allowed me to avoid the ostracism I felt at Brown. On those weekends we would discuss food, make music, and visit Boston together. On Sunday evening I would take the hour-long bus ride back to Providence.

Above all, I remember how much she believed in me. "Mark, one day you will be the president of Africa!"

"Africa is a continent, Grandma, not a country," I said and laughed.

"It doesn't matter," she would curtly reply. Then, changing the subject, she would point to her Baldwin.

"Go and play me that Fats Waller, dear, or the Chopin ballade. I so love those pieces."

I would oblige while Ida opened the front door wide so all the neighbors would hear.

Without her, Boston would have been cold, bitter, and unwelcoming. Fresh from the plane at Logan, I would have been hard put to manage without her. Although I came to America with just $230 in Amex checks (which were quickly used up), Ida would always help. Even after I started work-study at the college and earned a little money, she would send me the occasional $25 check and house me on weekends and for the odd holiday.

One weekend in 1986, I returned to Boston to find her house strangely quiet. Rock and roll was playing somewhere in the back. Sandro, a crude South Bostonian who often missed his rent payments and boasted of his sexual conquests, was renting Ida's spare bedroom.

"Ida, where are you?" I called out.

No answer. For five minutes I wandered around the house and the backyard, calling for my grandmother. There was no sign of her. Finally, I entered the bathroom. The tub was half filled with filthy, brownish water. The walls were stained with fecal streaks. Towels were tossed about and the floor was soaked. Cold with fear, I rushed to Sandro's room and pounded on the closed door.

"Sandro, where's Grandmother!"

No answer. The loud music continued to play. I pounded the door again. "Where's Ida?"

He didn't even open the door.

"What? Oh, Mark, your grandmother . . . You want to know about your grandmother? She died yesterday."

He turned up the music. In shock, I wandered back to the living room, where the silent Baldwin stood. Ida had died just feet away from her beloved Victrola.

The cause of her death was unclear. My mother believed she fell asleep in the tub. A sudden brain aneurism, her doctors said.

Grandmother's death hit me hard. I had lost the person who had encouraged me, praised me, supported me, pushed me, and welcomed me to this strange new land.

I had the use of Ida's car while probate was being decided. On weekends I would drive long and late, roaming about Boston's red-light districts and porn shops, trying to forget the little old lady who had washed dishes deep into the night and played piano at the Museum of Fine Arts, and who was always there for kids.

After Ida's death I did not cry, perhaps because I considered it weak or overly sentimental. Instead a deep sense of gloom pervaded me. The death of people close to me would always feel like an injustice, perhaps because I was so completely powerless to reverse it.

David, Soughley, now Grandma. That I shed no tears should have been a cause for alarm, I see now, but mechanically I continued with my studies. Though I still didn't know where I was headed.

After Ida's death school became more of a challenge. I had intentionally made my syllabus difficult. I wanted a double degree in Physics and Math. I knew neither I nor my parents could afford two separate degrees, so I was determined to complete the double-degree syllabus.

"Why go for two?" someone asked me.

"Because I can," I retorted.

When backed into a corner, I could perform miracles. I once took an advanced algebra course, found it very difficult, and barely passed the midterm.

"It's a very tough subject. Perhaps you should consider dropping this for now," the professor said almost apologetically one day after a frustrating tutorial session in his office.

I knew he was sincere and well-meaning, but there also seemed to be that expectation of failure lurking behind his words. The weeks before the final exam, I applied myself with an energy I did not know I had. When I aced the final, the professor was astonished. Although I was pleased I was also a little disappointed. I had half hoped I would fail. It would have given me an excuse to give up mathematics, which I didn't like anyway. It was a case of my heart going in one direction while my overactive brain was moving in another. I seemed to be blessed and cursed with an ability to succeed in almost anything I applied myself to, and as a result could never decide what to follow. These conflicts between my heart and my head would cause me grief in the future.

It was through music that I found friends, such as John Duvar. We met during a music class one semester and hit it off, particularly after he heard I was a Glenn Gould fan.

"Fucking A, man, I love Gould. He's awesome!" John said.

Kindred spirits, we listened to Gould, Horowitz, Lipatti, Pollini, Michelangeli, and other musicians, ordered pizza and Coke, and talked late into the night of art and music. John studied the classics and read Latin and Greek fluently and with enthusiasm. I looked at him a little enviously. Physics could support me, I believed. Could Greek or music do the same?

As a senior I chose to live in the Graduate Center, a grim boxy building that tended to attract nerds, older students, social misfits, and those, like myself, who just wanted a little solitude. I spent much of my free time in the bar downstairs, a dark place filled with bleary-eyed older students, women squinting through the cigarette fumes, and men grabbing pool sticks and Budweisers in the red haze. Graduates and undergraduates would gather there in the dead of night and, amid howls of drunken laughter, discuss philosophy, poetry, football, sex, and even chess.

In a corner of the bar, amid this Dionysian frenzy, stood a small upright piano. Once, at the stroke of midnight, drunk and lonely, I staggered over to it and launched into the cadenza of Grieg's concerto. For a half hour I lost myself in the music, wrong notes and all. My companions and the beer-drenched bodies at the bar had ceased to exist. I was startled at the end by a burst of applause.

"That was bloody good, mate. You ought to do more of that!" Dennis, an Irish poet friend, opined. The faintest of smiles flashed across his wan face. My other graduate-student buddies and John nodded their heads.

At last I had found my milieu. My studies improved and I got straight As in the difficult final semester, although there was still my troubling lack of passion for physics. I completed the double-degree requirements. Because I could not afford the actual math diploma, it would instead be duly noted on my transcript that I had met the diploma requirements.

I had no clue what I wanted to do. I did not want to continue in physics, but wanted to start work even less. I was riding between places like a magnolia scattered to the wind. Like many other undecided students, I applied for graduate school. One day I got a telephone call from Stanford telling me they were looking forward to welcoming me.

My last days at Brown also heralded an unhappy reckoning with my mother. These past four years had been my first extended absence from Ruth Ndesandjo.

When she had flown over to attend my graduation, I was bitterly disappointed that I had not achieved cum laude. Some of the courses I had taken, such as advanced math and English classes, had been unnecessary for the diploma, and risky, shaving a few points off my GPA. What should have been a joyous day turned into a wholly depressing one. At the graduation events, professors, students, and family seemed so happy. I may have had a diploma from a celebrated university, but there was an empty feeling inside me.

Although I was graduating, I felt I had failed my mother. I really did not know what I wanted out of my life or what she wanted from me. All I knew was that I was no longer the boy who had left Kenya. My mother immediately noticed my low mood but didn't say anything—she'd just ask a question now and then about who this or that person was, or where we were.

"Why are you so unhappy, Mark?" she finally asked. We were having lunch after the awards ceremony at a small deli on Hope Street.

"I tried so hard to get cum laude, but they wouldn't give it to me. They said they required a three-point-five GPA and mine was three-point-four-eight or something. I don't know . . . I was so close. I hate them! All the time I was here they always tried to put me down!"

Mum continued eating. She ladled soup into her mouth with a slow careful motion, slurping and blowing on it noisily. I expected her to say something but she didn't.

"Don't you care?" I asked her. I looked around the deli. There had been a few stares from locals as we walked in. Always the outsider, I thought, always this feeling of being the other, of never belonging. I looked back at my mother's face. She was sipping her soup, avoiding my gaze.

"I do care. I want you to be happy," she said, her face reddening. I just looked at the window. It was drizzling outside and the sky above Providence was slate gray. This city was dull and boring. It had always been that way, I realized, filled with people struggling through their dreary lives, often under rain or snow. I would be glad to leave.

"I wish I had never come to Brown," I said. "I should have waited another year and gone to Harvard. You said it would be okay."

"I thought it was the right decision."

"Well, I hated this place!" I lashed out at her. Her eyes flashed in response.

"What happened, Mark?" she said after a pause.

"What do you mean?"

"You used to tell me everything that was going on in your life. Then you stopped. Your letters . . ."

"What?"

"You didn't say as much. We used to tell each other all our secrets. I loved hearing of what you had done . . ." Her voice trailed away.

"Mum, I don't want to discuss that."

She looked down. We finished the rest of the meal in silence. We left the restaurant and crossed the street. The traffic was heavy but I did not notice. I felt annoyed by my mother's slowness and caution and wanted to be away from her. I crossed the street rapidly. She could not keep up with me. I looked back.

"Mum, come on. Hurry up! What the hell is the problem?"

She panted over toward me. Cars were honking at her, and people on the street were staring at us. A car passed by very closely. For a moment I thought it would hit her. But I wasn't alarmed. I was shocked to realize I half wanted the car to hit her. I looked at her face. It was flushed from exertion, and I could see that she was crying. I realized that part of me wanted to be away from her for good, and another part did not ever want to leave her. I was deeply ashamed of myself. I wanted to take her hand, but I could not reach out. It was too much. She burst into tears.

"What do you want from me?" I said, exasperated.

"I just wanted you to be happy, Mark . . . I just want you to be happy."

I looked at her. There were new wrinkles around her eyes. I reached over to her but she brushed my hand away. Her hair was whiter than I remembered, and her bad back caused her to bend over more often.

Was that all she wanted? I was astounded. What about high grades and other achievements? Weren't those what she had really wanted? I realized that my mother's goals had not necessarily been the trophies and plaudits I'd won. She'd thought only that they made me happy. I had mis-understood her for so long.

I had grown up under my mother's close care and love, and, in case my memory was faded, she would sometimes remind me with a song:

> *For nine months*
> *I carried you*
> *No charge.*

"You see, it's like you owe me!" she would playfully conclude.

I indeed felt I owed my mother, but that day I learned what she always had wanted in return.

At that moment, seeing the tears on her cheeks, I loved her more than anyone else in the world, and, inexplicably, I hated her more than any-one else in the world. I vaguely sensed that we had reached a watershed moment. I was on my own path, and my mother was not, indeed had not been, part of it for four years. I wanted it to stay that way. I wanted her to leave me, to let me go. Without fully knowing it, I had violently broken from her. In doing so I hurt both of us, but, at that time I knew no other way.

While at Brown University, I would often visit Ida on weekends at her home in Newton, Massachusetts. She would open the door so neighbors would hear me play her piano. c. 1986

While studying at Brown University, I spent a summer as an intern at the CBS Masterworks record division in New York. This picture is from a write-up in the *Brown Daily Herald* at that time. Highlights were meeting pianist Glenn Gould's Grammy award–winning producer, Sam Carter, and musicians Wynton Marsalis and Yo-Yo Ma. c.1987

CHAPTER TEN

Sibling Atonement

MUSICAL EVOCATION

Ludus Tonalis Op. 24: Paul Hindemith

This beautiful set of piano pieces composed in 1943 begins with a praeludium and ends with a postludium. The first note of the praeludium was the same as the last of the postludium, the second the same as the second last, and so forth. It thus plays on two mirrored themes. This piece reminds me of Barack and me, in that the two of us, at different points in our lives, seemed to switch the racial ties that identified us, with profound consequences. Mixed-race, our bodies were like prisms, in which the light passing through us would emerge a different color, and those who saw it would identify with one or another. Sometimes when we met, as in 1988 or during the second term of Barack's presidency, identities fluctuated, or it appeared that way. Like these prisms, we could control how others saw us by showing one side or another. At such points we seemed to identify with, reject, or protect family. In reality, we did not know how complex the tune that runs through our lives is, as in Ludus Tonalis, and how inseparable is the darkness from the light. Put another way, we were often on the same page, but the melodic lines were moving in opposite directions, as in that first meeting more than twenty years ago.

"WHY, HE'S AN OBAMA—OF COURSE! WHAT DID YOU EXPECT?"

I could imagine my father's words had he learned of his son Barack's sudden ascent to glory. He would have slowly and deliberately barked them out in his deep voice. He might then have furrowed his brow, plucked the meerschaum pipe from his mouth, taken a sip of Johnnie Walker, and, with a tad of condescension, flashed a bright smile.

Dreams are funny things. Just when we think everything is humming along smoothly, they lurch out of the darkness and cause upheaval in our lives. In some ways dreams are about guilt and unfinished business. Barack Obama Jr. may have had a dream from his father, which impelled him to come to his family in Kenya and then write a book about them.

Many years later I had a dream that would urge me to meet my brother again after a long separation. Dreams are the stuff of atonement. Those who dream are blessed, as the name Barack suggests. Barack Obama Sr. had his own dreams; it was his sons and daughter who ended up trying to achieve or atone for him. His son Barack Jr. was among the first to do so. I sometimes think that had the stars aligned differently, I could have been in my brother Barack's place and vice versa. Our lives were in some ways so different and yet so similar.

As I write these words, I feel a great sense of pride. It took me many years to reach this place. Ten or even five years ago "He's an Obama" would have signified nothing to me; in fact, it would have repelled me. It would take Barack's meteoric ascent to persuade me to look anew at my birthright and embrace it in its new light.

——◦——

In 1988, after graduating from Brown, I had returned to Kenya for a brief summer break before heading back to the United States to enroll at Stanford in the fall on a fully paid scholarship. I had the vigor and confidence of youth, caught in those halycon years when death is still an abstraction and patience is unknown.

But before I headed back to the States, I had an unexpected visitor.

That first time Barack arrived at our house in Westlands, I was reading a book in my room. I heard the crunch of gravel outside as a car entered the gate. I thought it was just a friend of my mother's or perhaps some business to do with her kindergarten. I heard voices talking and then silence, as though the guests had gone into the living room to chat. A few minutes later my mother knocked on my door.

She wore a worried look on her face, as though she did not know how to broach a subject. Her stocky figure trembled slightly in the doorway; part of her wanted to move forward while the other wanted to step back.

"Mark, it's your brother Barack . . . here to see you."

"Who?"

"Your brother from the United States. Barack Junior. He came here to see you."

My brother from the United States. What did she mean? There had been whispers about a son of my father who lived there, but I had banished these to the back of my mind. There had been just too much pain associated with Barack Obama Sr. to even consider this. I hadn't even known this other brother's name until my mother told me at that moment.

"Where? Where is he?" I said.

"In the living room. He's waiting for you."

I looked at my mother in disbelief. I likely shrugged and turned back to reading *The Devil Drives*, Fawn M. Brodie's biography of the explorer Richard Burton. It was a good read, and in any case, a suitable reason not to meet this so-called brother of mine. The feelings coursing through me were confused to say the least. Burton's experiences of cheating, betrayal, and mutilation seemed preferable to facing my own troubled family relationships. The shadows of forbidden marriages, of the bigamy I had always suspected, rose inside me; it demanded release. Who was this person? What should I call him: Brother or Barack? Why did he want to see me? What could I possibly do for him? What did he want? There was a cold, empty feeling in the pit of my stomach. For some reason I felt like a fraud, imperfect, even impure.

"Tell him I'm not here," I said curtly.

"But he's in the living room!" My mother had seen the troubled expression on my face. Quickly, her tone turned softer. "He is your brother. You could at least say hi," she pleaded. "He came all the way from the United States."

If I have to see him, I consoled myself, at least I can let him know I'm going to Stanford. It was all that shored up my precarious self-confidence.

"And he is going to Harvard," she added, a touch of astonishment in her voice.

The last sentence deflated me. I had failed getting into Harvard.

If I staunchly refused to meet guests—which I frequently did—she would often half tease, half coax me, bringing her face so close to mine our noses almost touched. "Now, now," she would say, "they just want to say a quick hello to my handsome son!" Vanquished but flattered, I would burst into laughter.

This time the mood was different. She just stood in the doorway expectantly. I sighed, put down the book, and stood.

I walked into the living room. Rita and a lanky brown-skinned man were sitting on the sofa, talking to Simeon. My younger brother Joseph, whom we called Joey, was sitting on Simeon's lap. The man had a similar complexion to me, much lighter than Rita's, and he was nodding carefully as he listened to Simeon speak. They both stood when I entered.

"Barack," he said to me, reaching out his hand.

We shook hands. I behaved matter-of-factly, able to hide my anxiety very well. Rita smiled at me, but I knew she felt too uncomfortable to say much in front of my mother. They had loved the same man, and where one had seen too many faults and convinced herself she did not love him anymore, the other had fought to remain oblivious to his flaws. (Even now, years after our family breakup, Rita dislikes my mother.)

"How interesting. Your brother from America is here!" Mum interjected.

Barack looked at me and then at Rita. Seeing our sister's unease, his smile quickly vanished. For the rest of the meeting, he was deadly serious. There was an embarrassing silence as we all stood there in the living room.

"So, I hear you are going to go to Stanford soon?" Barack said to me casually, without any real interest, as if to break the silence.

I nodded. I did not want to talk to him or Rita.

"Do you want to see some albums?" my mother suggested. Without much else to do, I picked up some photo albums and we all sat down. I sat next to Barack, while Rita and Mum sat on two other chairs, as though unwilling to be too close to us. Barack placed the book on his long lanky legs. I noticed how plain his clothes were and that his hands were huge and spatulate.

Simeon silently observed us. "Regarding those people, I want nothing to do with them," he had always said. "Always fighting among themselves . . . just big mouths. I want a quiet life."

This time, however, Simeon was interested. I could see it in his eyes, particularly when he looked at Barack. They had talked before I came into the room, and I could see that he was impressed with the young man.

Barack flipped carefully through the pages with those bony, big hands that closely resembled mine. He paused over some pictures of David.

"Your brother . . . ?" he said. I noticed he did not say *our* brother. My mother's eyes met mine for an instant. I saw her hands grip the chair, her knuckles white as chalk.

He casually flipped through the pages. From this point on, other than small talk between me and Barack, Rita and my mother hardly said a word. There were many awkward silences, broken only by Richard, who came into the room to play with Simeon.

We did not have lunch together. Overall, it was a very awkward, cold meeting. As though the skeleton that no one ever talked about had strayed into the middle of a family party.

"Maybe Mark and I can meet again," Barack said finally, his eyes focused on a spot somewhere between Ruth and me.

Suddenly animated, without waiting for my reply, my mother assured him, "Yes, I am sure you and Mark have many things to talk about!"

Actually I did not want to talk to Barack any more. I wanted to go back to my own room, to Fawn Brodie and Richard Burton. I nodded slightly, avoiding their eyes.

"I have some things I need to do." My feelings in turmoil, I left the room.

⚊ ⚊

Barack and I met again, a few days later. He had driven to my home, this time without Rita.

Now that I think of it, I wonder why he was waiting for me outside, as though he wouldn't enter the house. All our other guests had always come straight in, sometimes surprising us. Did he refuse to enter? It was as though there was an invisible barrier between his part of the family and my own. They were the Obama clan, living in scattered places across Nairobi and Kisumu, centered around the "Old Man," as many family members later called Barack Obama Sr. But my mother and I, with the help of Simeon, had escaped the squabbling, poverty, bigamy, and domestic violence that had tainted my early life. It was a sign of how insecure I was that I faced this second meeting with trepidation. My mind wanted to shut out my past but it had grown into a menacing presence, a hungry lion hidden in elephant grass.

Barack stood in front of a car, I believe a Volkswagen. In the sunlight I could see him better than I had the last time. He was taller and thinner than me, with a huge mass of unkempt hair framing an angular face. His nose was large and broad, his eyes piercing and direct. His clothes again were very plain: a simple cotton shirt and green or pale blue trousers.

"Hello, Mark, how are you?"

He spoke very loudly and clearly, almost paternally. He didn't smile. It was as though he had recently been upset. I reached out my hand.

"Hello, Barack. How are you, man?"

We shook hands somewhat awkwardly. At the time I said *Ba*rack, as everyone called our father. Many years later I learned that my brother preferred Ba*rack*. He didn't correct me, and I probably repeated this a number of times during our conversation.

I looked more closely at this tall brown apparition that had suddenly appeared in my life. *Why so serious?* I thought. Had he been dispatched on an unwelcome but necessary mission? His was the face of a person with secret plans and goals. It was discreet, earnest, but very wary of me and my immediate family, particularly my mother, perhaps on account of what others had told him.

From the way he stood in the driveway that bright afternoon, rigid, his head tilted a little to the side as though listening to an inner voice, I saw a person who was searching for something. It was the look of someone who has already decided on the verdict but is still struggling with unformed questions and imprecise doubts. As we talked later (and we discussed a good deal), I sensed he was looking for something in me, something deep but simple, like a melody among the noise. "I wanted to meet you," he had said during that first meeting.

"Let's take a drive. I want to talk to you," he suggested.

I obliged. His tone was gentle but commanding, that of an older brother. It also was so deep that it seemed to belie his age. I associated that type of voice with sages and elders, not with young men in their twenties. *Who is he?* I was thinking. I looked at him sidelong as we drove into town. His face was swarthy and his hair was shorter than mine but more frazzled, as though he hadn't bothered to comb it. His large hands firmly gripped the steering wheel.

From our conversation, I gathered that Barack had come to Kenya to find out about the African side of his family and, in particular, our father. We made small talk as he drove, about Harvard and Stanford, although I sensed he did not want to talk about university. He spoke casually, his eyes on the road as he steered through the pandemonium of honking cars and bicycles of downtown Nairobi. I watched him as he effortlessly changed gears. "Do you have a license?" I said half seriously. He laughed, "I don't need one!" We had driven to an Indian restaurant in a commercial strip adjoining the industrial area, a smoky godforsaken place that belched dark factory fumes into the pristine blue sky. Inside, it was simple and clean. As we ordered the food, I could feel Barack's eyes boring into me.

Whereas our first meeting had been superficial, strained, and skirted about the edges of what Barack really wanted to talk about, this second encounter had a brutal directness to it. It was just the two of us, and there was no one else around to change the topic.

I still remember my brother Barack's words to me then:

"What do you think of our father? What do you remember about him?" He peered at me earnestly.

All these years I had kept my memories of my father far from me. Yet, sometimes I remembered my estranged siblings Rita and Bobby, my mother's cries of pain, and the bitterness of the family breakup. I would recall the drunken rants of Barack Obama Sr., and the sounds of whisky bottles clinking and sometimes breaking on the floor.

Some strangers walked by to be seated. Barack looked at them calmly. I felt hemmed in, but grateful for the interruption. In the few seconds of silence, my eyes wandered around the mostly empty room. The glossy red and white walls seemed to shout out, and greasy plates still lay on some of the checkered plastic tablecloths.

I remembered that Barack had selected the restaurant, and thought it ironic that he, not I, had located it. The food arrived almost immediately: spicy masala and rice. Not hungry, I nibbled at a *mendazi*, a fried donut. I remembered how David and I had used to make *mendazis* together. We would drop spoonfuls of the syrupy batter into boiling oil. Our mouths would water as we looked at the golden crispy donuts expand and fill the kitchen with their sweet smell. As though reading my mind, Barack stopped eating and turned his calm brown eyes to me.

"I'm sorry about David," he said.

"I think you would have liked him," I replied, glad to change the subject.

"Everyone I know here speaks well of him," Barack said, his brown eyes suddenly warm.

We lapsed into silence.

What I wanted to say was: *He would have been more interested in meeting you than I was, and you would have liked him more than you like me.*

The exact words of this conversation more than twenty-six years ago have faded from my mind, but the overall meaning and import of what was said is clear to me still—as clear as the bright sun and cloudless sky of Kenya.

"Why don't you call yourself Obama?" Barack asked.

Obama. I had tried to forget that name. Now here it was again. It was as though I was on a revolving treadmill, and no matter how hard I ran, I was always coming back to where I had started. Again and again people and events would cross my path uninvited, bringing in their wake a flood of unresolved questions.

Several years before I met my brother Barack, I had met some American tourist friends of Lois, my mother's cousin, during a visit to Kenya. My mother drove me to a downtown hotel to meet them.

"They just want to ask you some questions about life here," she explained before she dropped me off at the gate of the hotel. Two people, a man and a woman in their fifties, were waiting in a grassy, deserted, and largely untended garden behind the main building.

Expecting them to ask me questions about Kenya, I looked forward to telling them about our national parks, the different tribes, maybe even teaching them a word or two of Swahili. Instead they had asked me how I felt about being mixed-race, whether I felt ostracized by Africans, whether it was hard for me, and the like. I don't remember exactly how I answered. At the time I was too polite to refuse to talk to them, but during the next hour or so before they wound up the interview I felt that my psyche had been forcibly invaded. My skin had crawled with reluctance and embarrassment.

Now, with Barack, it was happening all over again.

"Do you consider yourself African?" he asked suddenly.

"What do you mean?"

"Your father was black, a Kenyan. Do you just want—?"

My mind completed the thought . . . *to be white?* "I don't think about those things," I said, interrupting him.

"When you leave for Stanford, what do you want to do afterward?"

"Probably get a research post in physics."

"Will you come back to Kenya?"

"Probably not. I'll be studying theoretical physics. But the university here is closed most of the time because of student strikes. What would I do there?"

I looked at Barack. His skin was paler than mine, and yet he seemed so *African.* I knew he thought I was black on the outside but white on the inside. The way he walked (with a slight *Shaft* bounce), the way he talked (as though trying to purge the middle-Americanisms in his accent), the clothes he wore (like those of ordinary *wananchi* on the street)—this was a person trying very hard to be African.

"Maybe you can return to Kenya after Harvard and help out here?" I joked.

Barack didn't laugh, but he looked at me as though I were a little crazy. I realized that in some ways my brother was ashamed of the whiteness that was part of him, whereas I was ashamed of my blackness.

"Do you think you will get what you want in just a few weeks of visiting here?" I asked.

He shrugged.

"Do you even know what your father did to us?" I asked him suddenly.

"I don't know. I don't really care." Barack shrugged. "What do you want to do with your life?"

He did not want to address this either, so he had changed the subject. There were so many places both of us did not want to go, so many topics that were just too close, too raw, too sensitive to be alluded to, let alone actually confronted.

"How do *you* feel about your family?" he asked.

As he asked his questions, I grew increasingly tense. It was as though I was back on that hotel lawn, answering those tourists from America.

Then again, that move into dangerous waters:

"What do you think of our father?" he asked. "What do you know about him?"

This man sitting across the table from me was my brother, granted. But we had barely met and now he was exploring my darkest past, asking me these intensely personal questions. These were things I would not have discussed lightly, even with a wife or a mother. Barack was relentless in his questioning, like a barracuda in a bloody sea. And he had absolutely no sense of humor. His voice was dry and lawyerly, clearly a man in control of his emotions. That day he had shunted those emotions to one side.

What Barack might really have been saying was: *"Mark, are you happy?"*

I prefer to think that that was his real meaning. Because what more fundamental yardstick could there be than happiness itself? Back then I was a desiccated being, my heart and my head constantly at war. On the surface I was happy, but there were many factors clouding my emotions. To my brother's questions, the ones he asked and the ones he implied, I had no real answer.

Twenty-six years is a long time. Events recede from one's memory like the view from inside a speeding train or the flutter of a waving hand from a cab. I do not remember his exact words but there was a special mood about our conversation, and the gist was clear. To Barack I was 40 percent a brother and 60 percent a sidebar, an index card, a data DVD that might answer some questions about our father. Some conversations have a pattern to them, a certain kaleidoscopic quality. In these conversations questions coruscate like a strobe light on a dance floor. Such questions remain in one's mind. Although the words shift, blur, and evolve, the core meaning remains.

With Barack there was a uniform monotony to the questions, as though he wanted to shut out any emotional involvement with me or my immediate family. Long after that first meeting, I would speculate that perhaps he had been upset by something I or my mother had said when he arrived. Years later I finally read his book *Dreams from My Father* in its entirety, after having skimmed through it over the years. My mother and some friends had talked about it and mentioned accounts of this and that. One section I had read when it first came out claimed that she had been astonished enough to say to Barack Jr., "You were lucky not to grow up with Obama. Why did you keep his name?"

Or something like that. I asked her if any of this was true. "Mark, you know me," she said. "Do you really think I would have said something like that?"

Perhaps Barack had been angry with her for another reason. Then again, it simply might have been that I was too sensitive to accept his emotional distance: the plodding, persistent objectivity of a lawyer. I tried to change the subject but to no avail.

In time I would begin my own search, and ask the same questions he had asked of me. Life would repeat itself, though haltingly, years at a time, in an odyssey encompassing family, discovery, and redemption.

Yet Barack started his odyssey much earlier than I, and being on the receiving end of his blunt inquiries jarred me. At times during our conversation I saw someone else behind those words and carefully played-down looks. I recognized a darker, more insidious presence that was as much a part of him as his DNA or the color of his skin.

I probably knew my father had died by then, though I do not remember for sure. I knew that Barack's return to Kenya had some connection with our father from the way he talked about him. I do not remember Barack mentioning his death, and though he referred to our father in the past tense, it seemed natural to me, like old history. To me my father had always been dead. I would read my brother's first book many years later and wonder why it had come to pass that no one, not even my mother, had told me of my father's fatal car accident somewhere in the dusty hinter-lands of Nairobi. Or perhaps someone had told me, and in a reflex action I had refused to remember. Regardless, someone had made the effort to call my father's son in America, but no one had called me in Kenya.

Now it was as though my father refused to let go—that no matter where I went there would always be some relative to reappear uninvited in my life, bringing along the memories I had tried so hard to obliterate. I was ashamed of myself for my pettiness, and for letting history overcome what should have been the joy of the moment. Despite the tone of our conversation, I truly felt Barack was trying to be honest with himself and with me, focused on reaching a higher level of self-understanding. In the presence of such honesty, it is imperative to respond in kind, but the shock of it was like being dipped into a lake of ice-cold water.

This off-kilter image of myself sitting across from me was my brother Barack. I felt I could hide nothing from him, that there was nothing in my life that I had experienced that he had not, though for him the results might have been different. He looked so like me in some ways: his gait, his face, his hair, even his voice, though his was deeper than mine. I should have been happy to see him, but I was not.

Like me, he was mixed-race and must have been rejected as I had.

Like me he'd been educated in an Ivy League university.

Like me he came from a broken family.

Unlike me, he had wholly embraced his African side.

Unlike me, he was attempting some sort of reconciliation with some-thing or somebody, even if not with me and my mother.

Thoughts tumbled through my mind as I looked at his half-familiar face.

If this big brother who is going to Harvard has accepted the Obamas, then why can't I? I thought. *He is probably smarter than me, and can discern lies from the truth, including mine.*

I felt afraid and exposed, like there was something dirty about our kinship, that it was founded on a lie, that we had been dealt a grubby, fragile deck of cards on which to base our brotherhood. Yet the quest that Barack, and later I, would embark upon required honesty, however brutal it was to ourselves or others close to us.

So with all this in the back of my mind, I lashed out at him. "Why bring up all that garbage about my father? He was a drunk, he beat my mother and us kids. I've learned to move on. Life is hard enough without dwelling on all the problems of race and bad dads."

Barack seemed to flinch, an almost imperceptible movement; I saw his eyes turned hard as he stared at me. It was as though he did not understand. After a moment of silence, he continued with his questions.

Had he not heard my outburst? I was astonished. A part of him seemed to have shut out my words, as though Barack was pretending I had not said them. In this way, we were both blind. Whereas at the time I could not see any of my father's virtues, Barack might have formed high opinions of our father, even idealized him. Likely no one had told him the truth, the shameful details of episodes of anger, drink, and violence within the family. It was as though he had been conditioned not to explore these matters, having already formed an opinion, clinically and without passion. His demeanor was cold. I felt he was an arrogant bastard but was too polite to say so to his face. I did not enjoy being treated as a research subject.

I was tired of carefully parsed, politically correct sentences, while visitors to Kenya tiptoed through or barged over my personal history.

I did not want to discuss my father and my early childhood with someone who had never lived with the man.

I did not want to be pitied or ignored by members of my own family.

What I really needed was someone to tell me when I was being a jerk and needed to straighten up. That would have been okay, too, and we could still have shared a beer. How I would have loved for him to have thrown his arms around me and said: *"Brother, your big bro is here. I'm looking out for you, man."*

I probably would have cast his arms aside, but I would have broken up inside.

Instead he said: "I see."

I was succeeding academically, but I'd already started sowing the seeds of my own failure. A big brother's advice might really have helped me then! I wanted him to hit the ball back at me, like a tennis ball off the practice wall. That would have woken me up. But it was not to be. Barack was not made that way. He absorbed my answers and digested them, like an amoeba in a vat of sugar.

I talked about music and physics. He rolled his eyes.

"I see. That's good. But do you see any meaning in it?"

"I love music and philosophy. Physics is cool, but Chopin, Beethoven, Nietzsche, and Freud are my idols."

"But don't you want more?" he said. Nonplussed, I stared at him.

"What more is there? Thousands of years of Western culture. There is so much one can learn from them."

"And will you come back to Kenya?" he asked.

"Of course, my family is here. But my home is where my family is. If they lived in America, that would be my home. However, it would be difficult to get a job as a physicist in Kenya. It is hard enough getting a telephone service here. Who knows?"

Barack seemed to sigh. I tried to change the topic of conversation again. "How do you like Kenya so far?"

"I like it. I'm having a good time here," he said casually, his eyes on the place mat, his hands casually resting on the table like a poker player's.

There was much that we discussed that day, but I particularly remember how similar Barack was in some ways to my brother Bobby. I remembered how, during his teens and early twenties, Bobby had railed against the colonialists and the imperialists. Even after my mother left him with Rita and my father, he had come to our house a few times, always reluctantly, always ill-at-ease, as though picking his way through a minefield. I was about thirteen or fourteen, naturally arrogant, and, like Bobby, had a head filled with half-digested quotes from books I did not understand.

"The whites have tried to take over Africa," Bobby told me. "All this development is at the expense of the black man." We were sitting together under the leafy tree in Simeon's backyard. My parents were hosting a goat party for friends at the time. As was customary, a live goat had been slaughtered and barbecued in the garden, to celebrate some achievement or to welcome someone back.

"Come on, man, why are you so angry?" I said.

"You just don't understand."

Bobby laughed at me. His eyes glowed with contempt. He did not suffer fools gladly—a marked trait among many members of our family. In front of him, I often felt like a fool and would imagine him thinking, *And you, Mark, you're just another tool of theirs. Brown on the outside, white on the inside.* Bobby was angry at many things: his life, his father, his sister, his responsibilities as the eldest in a traditional Luo family. Like me, he was instinctively intellectual and yet highly emotional, which probably didn't help him in dealing with the many people who were in positions of influence in Kenya. My father had the same problem.

Even my stepfather, Simeon Ndesandjo, harbored an instinctive distrust of people with "fancy" degrees, who didn't understand "how hard it was out there" in the world. Bobby then was a natural intellectual who, without the certification of a degree, was doomed to remain an outsider. At my mother's urging, Simeon had provided him with some job opportunities, which Bobby had derided as beneath him.

Simeon was a hands-on man, simple and direct, without a prestigious university degree. He had built his business from scratch and, because he loved my mother, had made an effort to help my brother. Bobby had rubbed him the wrong way and probably would go through his life unaware of it, in the way of those whose high intelligence is bookish and innate, rather than inculcated by a nurturing mother or a wise father.

As I talked to Barack, I sensed a fusion of two distinct attitudes in him.

One was a harsh rejection of, or at least a powerful skepticism toward, Western culture, a milder version of Bobby's anti-Westernism. This intellectual and emotional reaction against the last vestiges of colonialism and imperialism, on reflection, was common among bright young Kenyans. In time it would often disappear, like water spots on white paper. I talked about Chopin, Beethoven, Nietzsche, and Freud, saying nothing about Frantz Fanon, Wole Soyinka, Ali Mazrui, Kwame Nkrumah, Malcolm X, or Ngugi wa Thiong'o. Barack was too polite to interrupt me but he was disinterested, as though he had heard all this before.

Another aspect of his character had to do with something I had noticed in my teens. When I was very young, I remember how white, black, brown, and Asian students played together in activities such as marbles or football. Later, as I grew into adolescence, I noticed how mixed-race boys I had known from childhood started adopting mannerisms that seemed to consciously reject Western culture. They would form cliques with their African brothers. Even their speech patterns would change. The American or European tones and colloquialisms bequeathed them by their white mothers would turn into something less fluent, rough around the edges, like the speech of Kenyans recently arrived from the villages around Nairobi. These teenagers, which included my brother David, started to surround themselves only with their African friends, and they slowly distanced themselves from Asians and Caucasians. It sometimes seemed as though they wanted to prove themselves more African than the Africans. I felt strongly that Barack was on the same path.

He doesn't like white people, I thought at first. Then, as I talked with him more and more, I realized that the white parts of me, like my love of classical music and Western books, were irrelevant or simply not attractive to him. I felt guilty because he made me feel like an Uncle Tom. If he felt bitter about his own whiteness I could not tell. Yet the indisputable fact was that we were both white and yet we were black too. We were both on paths toward an accommodation with that, even if we did it in different ways.

—⁓—

Years later Simeon recalled that first meeting with Barack Jr. "He sat right there and talked about the community work he was doing. He wanted to help the lower-class people."

"Did he talk about Harvard?" I asked.

Simeon shook his head. "Nothing. He just wanted to learn about Kenya and his family. Charity work. I was so impressed by that young man."

During the second meeting, what struck me was that, to Barack, going to Harvard seemed unimportant. There was a moment when I had complimented him on his achievements. I had asked him when he would be enrolling.

"Oh, sometime in the fall," he said.

He said it so casually, so modestly, that for a moment I sensed a unique greatness and humility in him—everything a boy would have wanted in an older brother. For a moment the fog of suspicion cleared and I wanted to hug this stranger. He asked for the check.

Years later I would realize, after getting to meet Barack and my extended family again, that his humility was grounded in an instinctive sense of duty, as well as a refusal to be overwhelmed. At the time of our meeting, Barack was already aware that his duty was to give back to society in some way, which he would achieve through law school, and later community service, and much later, through the presidency. In a sense when he had asked me whether I would return to Kenya, he may have been wondering if there was a similar feeling in me. How were we to know that one day I would experience an epiphany that would lead me to China, not Kenya?

His coldness, in a sense, was part of an instinctual refusal to be overwhelmed. In turn, I refused to be overwhelmed by him. Perhaps Barack had expected me to warmly welcome and accept him, but I didn't. Instead my words and questions were critical, and my attitude toward the West contradicted his. The result was that we each refused to be overwhelmed by the other. It felt as though we were polar opposites.

Little did I know then that this trait of refusing to be overwhelmed is a common one in our family. It can be seen as arrogance, but it stems from what I call a high emotional threshold. Just as a high pain threshold can enable a boxer to tolerate pain and accept what someone else would find excruciating, Obama family members are often underwhelmed by things many people would give an arm or a leg to experience.

It took a lot to impress me. Even sex would fall short of my expectations. When I lost my virginity, I remember thinking, "My God. Did I wait so many years just for this?"

This high emotional threshold drove me, and probably others in my family, to constantly exceed expectations, to pursue the absolute or perfect simply because it was never there.

I wanted that hug of reassurance from him, but my older brother was intent on his own quest. In Kenya, we were two ships passing in the night. Our lives had yet to intersect.

What a stuck-up asshole, I thought. Barack may have felt the same. He had to have realized that we had made each other very uncomfortable, had disrupted each other's equilibrium, and that he had jarred me out of my (white) middle-class complacency. When he dropped me off back home hours later, I was exhausted. As we parted he gazed at me as earnestly as he had a few hours earlier.

"Maybe we will link up in the States," he said.

"Perhaps we shall. Let's stay in touch."

To me that sort of farewell was normal: a shake of the hand, an exchange of glances, a vague but implicit dissonance. To him, as he later recounted in his book, it sounded insincere. Yet our conversation had been painful. To me it was as though, with the skill of a true lawyer, he had pried open the lid of our family's box of secrets, and left me to close it while he flew back home. Barack was like a radioactive isotope: get too close and it travels through your system, illuminating the cancers within. It was a painful experience and, like a true porcupine, I wrapped my quills about me. Before long we had gone our separate ways. I had wished him luck and didn't think I would see him again.

That evening my mother came into my room. "Well?"

She stood in the door expectantly, reading glasses still perched on her nose, her eyes bright. She spoke carefully. Like a spider extends its skein of silk, or a technician draws wire from a detonator. I was lying on the bed, on the woolen quilt she had made for me so painstakingly. I avoided her inquiring gaze. I knew she wanted to talk about Barack.

"Well what?" I said, offhandedly.

"Barack, of course! How did your meeting go?"

"It was okay. We'll stay in touch," I lied to her.

In fact, over the years we would meet again. On a number of other occasions I tried to reach Barack, but it was always a spur-of-the-moment effort. There was one such time I happened to be in Chicago for a job interview, right after I left Stanford in 1991. I could have planned more carefully, found out more exact contact information by reconnecting with Rita and Bobby, but I didn't. Then, for some reason, I desperately wanted to see him and talk to him. All I knew of him by that point, from the news, was that he was in state politics. I left my hotel, headed for the State Office building, and promptly got lost in a ghetto downtown.

After meandering around for hours, I gave up and ended up having dinner alone in an Ethiopian restaurant. From that point onward, our relationship lapsed into a silence that lasted more than a decade. Our interactions always seemed destined to alternate beyond warmth and coldness, like the sun's drowsy rays abruptly being replaced by the cold blast of winter.

President Barack Obama with my wife, Xue Hua, and me at the Regis in Beijing in 2010. This was the first time he had met my wife. "She's lovely!" he said in an e-mail to me. I agree.

CHAPTER ELEVEN

Harvard of the West

MUSICAL EVOCATION

"Les Adieux," Piano Sonata No. 26 in E flat major: Ludwig van Beethoven
My Stanford University experience was about love and fear, recklessness and
new beginnings. I performed this piece at a concert I gave there. My tutor,
George Barth, one of the most perceptive and purist teachers I had the privilege
of studying with, would sometimes playfully criticize me when I complained a
piece was too hard. "You're always saying this or that is too hard. Just do it!" he
would scold. This work from Beethoven's middle period seems easy but is decep-
tive, as I discovered in concert. Beethoven wrote these farewells in response to
the enforced absence of a dear friend in time of war. During the period of my
life when this piece was important to me, I left behind my study of physics and
a woman's love.

IN THE LATE SUMMER OF 1988, RONALD REAGAN WAS FINISHING HIS
last term as president, while Democratic presidential nominee Michael
Dukakis was bumping around in tanks. Attorney General Edwin Meese
had outed 7-Eleven for selling *Penthouse* in the latest of America's incessant culture wars. Tiananmen Square was in the future and Japan-bashing
was still in vogue. I had three hundred dollars in my pocket and my newly
trimmed hair looked like a brown Nazi helmet.

In late September I drove through the dry terrain of central California into what seemed like an oasis, Stanford University. My dreams were

coming true. I was about to enter one of the most prestigious universities in America. Some said Stanford was the Harvard of the West, while others retorted that Harvard was the Stanford of the East. Little did I know that Stanford would reorient my life. I was twenty-three when I first saw The Farm, as the University is also called. How could I know then that I would fall in love here, lose my way, and leave two years later, humbled and newly enlightened?

On either side of the road stood huge palm trees. Adobe roofs glimmered in the distance like the faint vestiges of ancient Nubian palaces. The sky was very blue that day, and in the steamy haze the distant roofs of bloody brick looked to be straight out of a fairy tale. As I drove along roads that stretched like streams of spaghetti across the five-thousand-acre campus, through endless stop signs and speed bumps, I breathed in an atmosphere of great confidence, wealth, and self-sufficiency.

Brown had been small and concentrated, insular and incestuous. Stanford by contrast was like the earth mother, wide and embracing. New England had been socially closeted, driving people into cold little rooms and houses, shut within their windowless spaces with PDAs and televisions galore. California, on the other hand, seduced people into the open, and cured them of their agoraphobic mindlessness. It seemed to be calling out to me:

"Behold me, behold my warmth, have fun, be true and welcome nature!"

I savored my arrival. I had completed a three-week road trip across America from Providence to Palo Alto. My old Ford Escort had limped over three thousand miles and was still chugging along. Shortly after driving through the university gates, I was pulled over for ignoring a stop sign. The campus police officer saw my Rhode Island plates and asked me a few questions. Finally she said, "I'll just give you a warning this time . . . welcome to California." With a stern look at me and my dilapidated car, she drove off. Little did I know this would not be my last brush with authority at Stanford.

In the center of campus, I stopped beside a square marble building that was surrounded by bronze sculptures. There were a few other people wandering around and some students playing Frisbee on the lawn.

Walking closer, I recognized the distinctive outline of a Rodin sculpture: massive carpenter's hands bigger than a head; a wiry muscular torso that seemed to rip the air apart with suppressed energy. I looked around me with delight. *Rodins were everywhere.*

Stanford University had more than a dozen Nobel Laureates, had students from more than ninety countries, and was more than one hundred years old—but at that moment I couldn't care less. Since I was a teenager growing up in Kenya, I had always admired Rodin. Now I actually stood before some of his works. They were powerful and sensual, filled with a remarkable awareness of texture, line, and rhythm; almost voluptuous, it seemed to me. I forgot the time and lost myself in their bronze beauty. The discomfort of the police stop completely vanished at the sight of those huge welcoming bronze hands.

I got back in the car and continued driving. After about ten minutes I arrived at the Physics Department. It was quiet and deserted. I met a student in one of the corridors and asked him where the central office was located. He looked at me with open curiosity. He was a short and muscular African American.

"Here, I'll show you," he said, and led the way. "Are you the new student?"

He said "student" as if I were the only one in the incoming graduate class. In fact I was the only African American admitted to the graduate school that year.

I told him who I was.

"No kidding!" he exclaimed.

We talked for a bit and I told him I was bunking in the back seat of my Escort until the dorms opened in a few days. His eyes were bright with vivacity and he spoke rapidly.

"Hell, you can stay at my pad. You can't sleep in a car," he said. I couldn't say no to such a generous offer.

Al was a second-year graduate student who would be my unofficial guide to my new environment. If I wanted to know where the best supermarket was, he would take me to the local Safeway. If I wanted to know where the best library in which to study was (Stanford had many libraries), he gave me his opinion. All the while he would flash his welcoming smile, trying to make my first few weeks as easy as possible. Al embodied

Stanford's relaxed air and sense of self-confidence that was worlds apart from Brown's brittle facade.

He quickly introduced me to the staff at Varian (where the Physics Department was situated), who were hidden like hobbits in rooms deep within the dark building. Then he invited me back to his apartment in Escondido village, a small group of single-level graduate houses close to the center of campus.

There were twenty or so students in my class at Stanford that year, all low-key, stable, decent individuals. They talked in level tones, critically, as though things had to be proved, always with a sense of intellectual gravitas. Even when they laughed they seemed, in a nonoffensive way, to be thinking of other things.

We all socialized and even shared homework discussions, but I kept largely to myself. I saw them as competitors that I had to keep at bay—at least until I figured out what to do with my life.

I liked California. There was something about going west that made me feel blissfully free. It was not just the sunny weather that reminded me of Kenya, but the way the students and faculty acted. Everyone was serious, but also focused and determined to learn for the sake of learning. The professors did not look like professors. They were older, of course, but almost universally white men who wore polyester shirts and needed good tailors. There was little or no eccentricity among them, though once in a while a Nobel Laureate wearing a bow tie would cross my path.

I was surprised to learn that one of the students was living with a professor. She was gorgeous. *Please God,* I thought, *let me, too, become a Stanford professor and be free to cohabit with lovely students.*

I took advantage of this freedom. In some ways it was as though I was finally liberated from a windowless box where I had been imprisoned for ages. When I was not studying, I was exploring California. Allergies that I had suffered from back east magically vanished. I had a car, and San Francisco, a bastion of various cultures and immigrant communities, of multitudes forever linked by art and asymmetry, was close by!

On the one hand, the Italian cafes, the Chinese market, the inscrutable Nob Hill district, the dysfunctional Haight-Ashbury, were a coruscating dazzle of the unknown and alluring.

On the other, hidden beneath the bright post-psychedelic sheen, unlighted alleys were slick with urine and poisoned dreams. Beside the sleek limousines parked outside the Hyatt Embarcadero or the Marco Polo, not far from the expensive incense and sparkling necklaces of beautiful people on Haight Street, little old bag ladies thrust their cartfuls of worldly possessions past lines of honking cars.

On the Embarcadero filthy men whose white faces were burned to blackness by living perpetually on the streets wrapped themselves around at night with newspapers and old rags and huddled down in large cardboard boxes. *Why are they here? Why do they have to tarnish this lovely city? Don't they have anyplace else to go?* I angrily asked myself, and was immediately ashamed.

I knew that I might have been one of them were it not for life's turn of the roulette wheel. In San Francisco I first started to understand the plight of the American homeless. Extreme poverty and despair was not just a problem in Nairobi. It was here, too, in the Land of the Free. San Francisco's bums, urchins, winos, and castaways were an eye-opener and a reminder of life's vicissitudes at a time when I needed it.

<hr />

My first year went by in a rush. The classes were difficult but I managed to be a good, if not exceptional, student: mostly Bs, a few As, and the occasional C. Previously I would have been deeply ashamed to get anything less than a B, but all of a sudden it didn't seem important anymore. I'd fallen in love.

Caitlin was a music student studying singing at Stanford. I first saw her on a sunny Saturday at Stanford's Bechtel International House, where I often hung out. That afternoon I was the host on duty, an easy way to work part-time and make some money.

Outside the faded house, in the walled garden, the sun shone down on an Indian wedding. Brown faces, resplendent saris, and hats looking like burnt sunflowers surrounded tables laden with sweet *basundi* (a sweetened milk dessert) and *jalebi* (a melt-in-the-mouth snack item), *biryani* (a spiced rice dish) and sweetmeats arranged on fresh banana leaves, dried *paan* (chewy betel leaves), fresh juice, creamy *aloo kofta* (a delicious vegetable side dish), and other delicacies.

I discovered her upstairs in the otherwise empty administrative offices, doodling on a computer.

"You can't stay here. This is for faculty only," I said

"Oh, Greta's my friend," she said, turning to look at me.

I stared blankly. I had no clue who Greta was or what that had to do with her playing on the computers.

"She said it's no problem," she added.

Later, bored, she meandered over to my desk downstairs, and while I read a book she stood beside me, not saying anything. Uncomfortable at the prolonged silence, I looked up at her, a little exasperated at the interruption.

"What are you doing here? Do you like weddings?" she asked cheekily.

"I'm the monitor for the afternoon," I answered curtly.

"I'm hungry," she said, and with that she walked off into the crowd of wedding guests and came back with a plate of food.

"Here, have some." She pushed it in front of me.

Why is this gorgeous girl talking to me? I wondered. I sensed she was detached and lonely, and lonely people tend to gravitate toward each other. We started chatting about music and hit it off.

"There's a block party with barbecue in Palo Alto next week, followed by jazz in the park. Want to go?" I asked.

One thing led to another, and soon we were going steady. One day I heard her sing and was overwhelmed. She had a light bel canto style that could master fifteenth-century Schulz through eighteenth-century Mozart through nineteenth-century Franck. When she sang she glowed as though in a state of perpetual rapture.

Seeing Caitlin sing was enough to seduce me. Her lips, and the sound they produced, became erogenous zones. When she sang, her long, delicate throat and full, rosy lips seemed like romantic appendages. They became places where art, sensibility, the earth's rhythm, and the pounding of my heart mysteriously converged. I imagined kissing those firm, fleshy lips, that they were jewels from a diadem or tiara, adorned with stanzas from Bach and melodies from Schubert, parts of a kingdom that could be mine alone. Later, when we kissed, it was a long, sensuous embrace that was like a duet.

But she wouldn't let me sleep with her. Once, while listening to jazz in my apartment, she suddenly turned to me.

"Let's dance!" And she stood up and twirled her body like a ballerina. I danced, too, somewhat stiffly. We had been drinking a little wine, and I crashed onto the floor, barely missing the TV.

It was late and the music was turned up full blast. I jumped up on the table and kicked my feet around.

"Me too!" she cried, and jumped up to join me.

With that, we pounced on the sofa and then I followed her onto the dining table, all to the rhythm of Miles Davis.

Exhausted, we fell on the floor. I snuggled up to her. She was suddenly quiet, her lips close to mine. They were full and soft. She didn't pull away but rubbed her groin against mine. We removed our clothes and pressed against each other. She rubbed against me ever more violently, and we came again and again. The next morning I could barely walk, I was so sore. But I was happy.

"I wanted to save it for when I get married," she later said, a little guiltily. But we would pet and make love with increasing freedom: on picnic tables, in airplanes, on hikes. Everywhere.

I was falling in love with Caitlin, and she with me.

And little by little, I was discovering I did not care about grades, or classes, or studying. I just wanted to be with her. Finally, I wanted to be happy. It was what my mother had wanted for me, and now I understood what she'd meant. But from time to time, Caitlin and I had fierce arguments.

"You don't want to marry me," she once said, after a long phone call with her mother.

"What did your mum tell you?" There was a telling silence.

"You think we can always be like this? It's about responsibility," she said, suddenly animated.

"You're wrong. I don't want to be rushed. It's too quick. I don't care what your mum said!"

"It's not her. It's me. You don't really love me. We're too different. You even like California."

Dumbstruck, I looked at her accusingly. "Yes, I do, so what? It's better than Wisconsin!" Caitlin was from there. "Is it something I said about California?"

"You like these people," she went on. "I don't. Everyone here says this is interesting or that is interesting. I hate the word interesting!"

"I like California; it's true."

"And you don't like my friends."

"What do you mean? I thought Carol and her boyfriend were lots of fun," I protested. We had had two friends of hers over for dinner a week ago.

"Well, she didn't like you. She told me she thinks you're a chauvinist!"

I was shocked. "I'm a democrat and reasonably liberal!" I spluttered. "I'm no chauvinist!"

"Well, she thinks you are."

"She's a stuck-up bitch if she said so. And you said you would iron my clothes today."

"Well, I won't."

And before I could say anything more, she slapped me hard across the cheek. Speechless, I just looked at her.

"What did you do that for?" I gasped.

She smiled triumphantly. "I've always wanted to do that. It feels good!" Without another word, she walked back to her room, her back very straight.

The rest of that morning she was very nice to me, as if we had never had an argument.

We talked very little about each other's families, except once. We were sitting in the living room of my apartment on a quiet afternoon. For some reason Caitlin asked me how my mother met my father. Whenever I talked about him, I tended to emphasize the romantic aspects of the marriage, as though it would excuse my father's later actions.

"She eloped with him back to Africa. A long time ago." I recounted it as though I was proud.

"That's really romantic."

"That's right. She fell in love with him, and the next thing she knew she was in some hut in Africa," I said dismissively.

"Must have taken courage. Being with the zebras and the lions and all that."

I felt a slight sense of discomfort at her remark and went on defensively, "Her own mother wouldn't see her off at the airport. One of those crazy things."

"Why not? What type of mother is that?"

"She couldn't stand the fact that her darling daughter, the tennis pro, the belle of the neighborhood, was about to marry an African. Why else?"

"Perhaps she missed the bus." Caitlin turned a magazine page mechanically, as though she didn't want to miss a word I was saying without making it obvious.

"No bus was missed. She was probably tearing her hair out at the time."

"Well, that's over and done with. Hell, twenty years ago. No loss."

"She made up with her mum eventually. But I still remember my grandfather saying to her years later, when they visited us in Africa, 'Ruthie, Ruthie, what have you done with your life?' He was always the quietest of them all. If anyone understood his daughter's love, it was probably Grandpa."

"Yet . . ."

"Yet it was he who said she had wasted her life. Now I think, does that mean my brother and I were a waste? Is that what he meant too? I'll never know."

Caitlin nodded her head sympathetically.

I went on. "Grandpa was nice to me. He had a big tummy. I loved to run up and hug it. Then one day my grandma said, 'Don't do that anymore. It hurts your grandfather.' He died a few months later. Lung cancer from smoking."

She asked for me to tell her more.

"That's enough," I said roughly, wanting to change the subject. She put down the magazine.

"Something really frightens you, doesn't it? Why won't you tell me more?"

I stood and turned on the TV.

"What's with all this sound!" Caitlin shouted, a touch of exasperation in her voice.

"What about it?"

"Silence is beautiful. I love just lying in the tub and listening to the silence. Or the gurgle of the water slowly draining. You always want sounds around you!"

"Yes, silence is beautiful. But I prefer it in small doses," I said, glad we had stopped talking about my parents.

Near the Rains apartments, where I lived, there was a private club with a small swimming pool. It was surrounded by a wooden wall and always locked in the evening. However, when my roommates were out, Caitlin and I would sometimes slip over the wall, sneak in to the pool area, and have a swim.

Caitlin would be anxious, peering behind us when we were at the wall, as if looking out for the omnipresent police cars. We would clamber over the fence like escaping convicts.

One night we were in the pool making love when the lights suddenly switched on. Shocked, we retreated to the deep end, hoping no one would see us. A group of middle-aged people walked through the entrance.

"My God, my clothes are on the bench," Caitlin whispered in alarm. The two of us clutched each other tightly.

"Mine too," I said softly.

We remained for a few minutes at the far end of the pool. The group of people, a few women and a couple of guys, continued chatting. They didn't take any notice of us although we must have been quite conspicuous, a black man and a white woman, naked in a pool at an ungodly hour of the night.

"I've got to get out of here," Caitlin said suddenly. I also felt a little silly, and nodded.

"I can't move," she said under her breath. "Maybe you can go and get the towels."

"You do it," I said.

"You should go. You're the guy!"

"Right! I should go!" I said sarcastically. "If they see a naked black guy coming out of the pool, they'll panic and call the police!"

After a minute she said firmly, "That's it, I've got to get out of here." With a swish of cold water, she leapt out of the pool and dashed madly to the nearby bench. Before I knew it she had a towel wrapped around herself.

Suddenly confident, she waved at the group. "Hi there!" she said with a cheery smile.

I blanched but they waved back at her, not seeming to look at me, as though they did not want to.

"See, that's that!" Caitlin said, and threw me a towel. She wasn't nervous anymore. We broke into laughter and dashed back to the apartment, soaking wet.

The times I spent with Caitlin were wonderful. It was as though I was waking up in a new world. I had resigned myself to being alone in cold, passionless laboratories and libraries. Through this woman I was connected with the great river of life that surged around me. I was filled with a sometimes overwhelming love for not just her but for *everyone*, as though love for humanity was real, not just an abstract principle. My heart had grown a hard shell around it. Caitlin calmed me and slowly peeled it away.

In general, professors at Stanford felt research was more important than teaching graduate students. To them, graduate students should be independent and not count on faculty for advice. As at Brown, they tended to frown on my questions.

"I don't really see the point of going through this again," was a frequent reply, or else they would give a brief textbook answer and then go back to the board. Often, they simply wouldn't notice my raised hand.

There were exceptions. The student ombudsman, Walter Meyerhof, was a large, lanky, brooding man, careful in everything he did. Behind a wrinkled faded face masked by thick horn-rimmed eyeglasses, his huge brown eyes absorbed everything around him with integrity and compassion.

Meyerhof was a German Jew who had fled the Nazis. He talked in a deep, gravelly voice, using his adopted tongue in careful, monosyllabic responses and terse sentences—the analytical, emotionless manner of a born physicist. He spoke very slowly. At first I thought he was impaired. Then I realized that, unlike me, he actually thought through his sentences before speaking them aloud. He would just sit and look at me until I had run out of things to say. Then, while I felt more and more uncomfortable, he would wait several seconds more.

"As I was saying . . ." he would finally start, and follow up with a perfectly succinct answer.

Other than dutifully studying physics, I had to choose a graduate adviser for my PhD. This adviser would help steer me through the research and compilation phase of my doctorate. Of the approximately twenty professors in the department, none had research subjects or temperaments that appealed to me, except for one.

William Fairbank had made his name long ago with seminal research in the then-young field of low-temperature physics. He was, to me, a source of light in the depths of Varian.

"Fairbank is brilliant, but he's a bit of a dud," a fellow student told me, pointing out to me the grand old professor emeritus one day as he shyly passed us by, his head bent down as though in thought, moving quickly to avoid attention. Although he was respected in the department, it was more on account of his past work. His current ideas were greeted with polite skepticism by the faculty.

I did not care. With some trepidation I walked into his office one day. He was sitting behind an old steel desk, sheets of paper scattered about. He stood, and we shook hands before sitting down. After some small talk I got to the point.

"Professor, I would love to work with you, for example on the fifth force. It sounds fascinating."

"What do you know about it?"

"Not much, but I've heard that you have done research to prove that it exists. People in the department talk about it with great respect."

The last sentence was an exaggeration, but I would do anything to work with this man.

Fairbank laughed. "I'm not sure about that, but I know that we are getting closer each day. These anomalies in our experiments point to a constant . . ."

"There's gravitation, the weak force, the strong force, and electromagnetism. My God, if we can find another force . . ." I enthused, interrupting him. Sensing my eagerness, Fairbank took no offense, and he launched into a long explanation of the subject.

His work revolved around proving the existence of a natural force that had hitherto been hinted at in some of his earlier, groundbreaking experiments. Isaac Newton had "discovered" gravity in the seventeenth century. James Clerk Maxwell had discovered electromagnetism in the 1860s. In the twentieth century physicists had proven the existence of "weak" and "strong" forces. Now Fairbank claimed there was another, very weak but omnipresent force that slightly repelled gravity and was bound up with the existence of particles called quarks. He called it the fifth force.

Although I didn't understand most of what he was saying about the fifth force, I was confident I would eventually get it. He was like one of those salesmen who unknowingly sell themselves rather than their product. I wanted to buy the old man, from his silvery hair down to his neat brown shoes.

Fairbank also had something of the artist in him. He had reached for boundaries in physics that approached the spiritual and philosophical. What a lofty achievement it would be to discover the fifth force! It would be something akin to discovering gravity or electromagnetism. Even if it were to come to nothing, what a grand challenge! It seemed so far from all the dry, bureaucratic, and lifeless PhD topics then floating around.

Yet Fairbank's reputation at the department was decidedly tarnished. The prevailing attitude at Stanford toward him was a polite but deep-seated skepticism toward his ingenious, though controversial experiments.

Physics is a science that is colored by mostly bland personalities that fall into one of two camps: theoretical and experimental. The theorists see the experimentalists as intellectually lightweight, and the experimentalists see the theorists as impractical dreamers. A century after Einstein's Relativity Theory and Bose's Quantum Theory shattered the tidy explanations of Isaac Newton, theories grew more abstruse, experiments became more complex, expensive, and time-consuming; theorists and experimentalists were in a heightened state of complementary creative tension. A confusing spectrum of theories based on probabilities and the existence of small and elusive particles had proliferated as a result.

One of these elusive particles was the quark, smaller than an electron and with a fraction of its electric charge, proposed by Murray Gell-Mann in 1963. In 1977, Fairbank, in collaboration with George Larue, claimed to have experimental evidence for the existence of a quark.

He suspended a small niobium sphere between two metal plates at a temperature close to absolute zero and discovered that by measuring the electric charge between the plates, a quark was present. However, because the measurements were so sensitive and could be influenced by a number of factors, he spent years improving the experimental apparatus. Just like a hunter locates a bear by tracking footprints in the snow, ignoring leaves and debris that hide the trail, Fairbanks was on the hunt for his quark. The presence of electric charges was like the bear's footprints, and random particles, for example, were like tracks of other creatures that could smudge the prints. Finally, he announced in 1979 that, using modified apparatus, he had detected a second particle with a fractional charge.

However, no one managed to reproduce Fairbank's experiments. Although there was still a lot of skepticism about his work, he was sufficiently respected enough for his work to be taken seriously.

When some professors heard about my choice, they were apoplectic. They cautioned me that he was not considered the right type of adviser for students.

Usually, physicists are emotionally reserved types, focusing their joy and ire on observing the interactions of particles too small to be seen. But when they get angry, they tend to wave their arms for no reason, furl their eyebrows, frown slightly, and sometimes even jump about. There were suddenly lots of frowns, curled eyebrows, and a few agitated waves in my direction. I was even summoned into the dean's office, who warned me about studying with Fairbank.

"Fairbank is a little too imaginative. You know, he will retire soon. His work is unverified . . . You should consider another adviser."

"Why should I change?" I responded. "It's my choice and I like him. I think he is a great scientist and one day he may prove the existence of the fifth force."

The dean just looked at me, the corners of his mouth turned down. There was an awkward silence, punctuated only by the drumbeat of his fingers on the table.

"Is there anything else, Ndesandjo?" I politely shook my head. He turned his head away and I walked out.

Other professors raised their eyebrows and joined the chorus of disapproval. A few complained that I was too loud and assertive, according to friends of mine who overheard the meetings.

Meyerhof defended me. "It's time an African American came to Stanford who stands up for himself. Ndesandjo doesn't wear false humility as a badge of admission to white society," he scolded other faculty, or so said a staffer in the know.

I was surprised that what seemed unimportant to me in the vast scheme of things was causing such a ruckus. At Stanford, it wasn't someone choosing Fairbank as adviser that caused chagrin; it was that a *black* student insisted on it. It was as though I had created—with Fairbank as the catalyst—not a fifth, but a sixth explosive force, that resulted from the collision of two unstable particles, Stanford's Physics Department and myself.

Why can't they just see things without me being black or white? I thought. It was such a pain in the ass.

I did not really know or care about Stanford's politics. It was all very much behind the scenes and I could ignore it, even if it was to my own detriment. At the end of the day, although I very much wanted to study with Fairbank, I relented.

My eventual adviser would be John Lipa. Lipa's team did good research and we developed a low-temperature thermometer that was capable of measuring very close to -460 degrees Fahrenheit (otherwise called absolute zero or the lambda point); it was probably the only instrument of its kind at that time. The techniques would be used in the Gravity Probe B experiment, a multiyear space project headed by the US government and the seminal project that confirmed Einstein's theory of general relativity.

After much dull but rigorous experimenting, I was the proud coauthor of a paper published in the prestigious *Physics Review.* I often wondered what would have happened had I remained with Fairbank. Would I have been happier? Would I have discovered a passion for physics? Would my life have turned out differently? Such questions, perhaps, were as unanswerable as the quark speculations that once fascinated the kindly, white-haired professor.

While at Stanford University, I often visited San Francisco. On my first visit I was shocked at the disparity between the rich and the poor. c. 1989

CHAPTER TWELVE

Youthful Indiscretions: The Second Time I Realized I Was Ugly

MUSICAL EVOCATION

Bolero: Maurice Ravel

While Maurice Ravel's orchestral poem Bolero is seen by some connoisseurs of music as playful or melancholy, I don't like the work. To me the technique of repeated melody ad infinitum is like Nietzsche's eternal recurrence realized. "Why keep banging your head against the wall? You should just move on!" someone once said about me. My attempt to leave race behind, to become a neutral player in the racial ether of America, was frustrated by my own willful blindness. Perhaps even more than stumbling at the race fence, I had long been stubbornly persistent in finishing what I started, even if it had ceased to have any meaning. Refusing to correct this self-inflicted blindness and unreasoning persistence led me to make the same mistakes again and again. It was like being locked in a movie theater, viewing every moment of my life, looped without end.

Until I came to terms with things I refused to see, such as race, I would be in a hell of sorts, listening to an endless tune, played back again and again, as in Bolero.

FAILURE IS NOT EASY TO WRITE ABOUT, PARTICULARLY FAILURE THAT reflects on my character. Like intellect, character is bone-deep and almost impossible to alter. But while a person may clearly have intellect (or lack it), character is more ambiguous, its development rooted in a person's choices and their consequences. The truest failures are ones of character, because they incorporate choices made based on hopes, fears, and desires—the stuff of being human.

Whereas many memories of my early childhood have long since faded, my more recent history, particularly at Stanford University, stayed vivid in my mind for many years, like images from a Balinese shadow play, elongated silhouettes strutting behind white silk screens. These memories were full of passion and fear, delivering few clear questions or answers.

I had just turned twenty-three. Caitlin and I had moved a few miles off campus to a quiet three-room bungalow in Mountain View, situated on a dead-end street off El Camino Real. All the houses were small and plain, like little white boxes neatly placed on square patches of green lawn. The landlord and his wife left us alone. A fellow graduate student and friend rented one of the rooms, Caitlin had her own—as she insisted—-and I slept in the living room.

Our public and private lives were different. Alone together, we were free and happy. Outside, particularly when we met her friends, our interactions were reserved. She would introduce me with a big smile.

"Here's Mark. He's my friend."

Months of being introduced as a "friend" took on a dark, insidious meaning. It seemed to push me away. Whenever I heard it I flinched inside. One day we had quite an argument about it—she told me it shouldn't matter what she called me; she knew what I was.

What was she afraid of? I thought. Her lips professed commitment, but her eyes had the glazed, confused look of one looking for—but failing to find—a stable place, an anchor for the soul. This public distancing gnawed at me. Then one day, for no apparent reason, during a casual introduction to some new friends of hers, she gestured to me.

"This is my boyfriend, Mark!"

From then on, as if she had been doing it for ages, she started speaking of me like this. I had finally gotten through.

However, I couldn't tell her that I loved her. If I did, surely it would be a sign of weakness, I thought, an indication that I was ready to fall down on my knees before her. I didn't know that I could completely love anybody, for what was love but prostrating oneself and revealing inner flaws? It hurt. If anything, I wanted still more assurances from her. I didn't know how to trust her. I had long believed that trust was like ash—the moment I touched it, it crumbled in my hand.

"I love you, but I don't think I like you," she told me once. I was both perplexed and flattered by this.

"I'm glad to hear you at least love me!" I responded. She sighed and said nothing. I knew she wanted me to say I loved her too.

Caitlin was twenty-eight and thinking deeply about marriage. But mapping out my own life was the challenge before me; marriage seemed like an afterthought, an idealized impossibility, a bloodless ritual that dissected passion into a thousand sterile pieces of paper. Caitlin, on the other hand, wanted something more stable. Although I secretly loved her, I preferred the status quo.

I had seen the worst of marriage and what it did to people who were not ready for it, and I was spectacularly unconvinced it was the right thing for us. Scientists are by nature skeptics. Thus I willfully sought proof that she did not in fact care about me, doubting I was worth the attention of this beautiful woman. After all, she was a knockout. Tan and lithe, rich, glowing brown hair that tumbled around her face seductively. Even without makeup, her full lips and eyes turned heads. She was oblivious to her beauty, but I wasn't.

Finally, one day I asked her the question whose answer I feared the most.

"Why do you stay with me?"

She tossed back her hair and considered me calmly.

"Mark, I stay with you because I am lonely, and I want companionship."

Her words crushed me, and I constantly asked myself what they meant. It was like she was saying she didn't really love me, but I was as good a way as any to pass the time.

Other than our shared passion for music, she and I had vastly different characters and personalities. I had the outlook of an intellectual. Caitlin, on the other hand, was so intuitive she seemed almost psychic at times. I responded to the visual arts and always noticed the way other people looked, while she cared little about appearances and concentrated more on listening. She didn't talk much, while I was almost garrulous. Finally, as far as America was concerned, she was white and I was black.

I could not imagine being in a mixed marriage in America. I remembered the stares when my family had gone out for dinner together in Kenya. I sensed the hidden disapproval when Caitlin and I walked the streets of Palo Alto. It was like having a merciless spotlight constantly trained on us, one that we didn't talk about nor confront. What do they think about us? How do we look? I thought and acted like a self-conscious teenager, as though we were just high-school kids dating and not adults about to enter a serious long-term relationship. Caitlin deserved more, and when I realized I could not give it to her, a slow corruption stole over me, overwhelming what had been kindness, trust, and love. That chilly autumn we began to move apart, leaves on the same branch shriveling and ready to disintegrate in the cold blast of reality.

One weekend we were reading side by side on my bed, which also functioned as a makeshift couch, when Caitlin suddenly turned to me. "You know, Mark, maybe you should try to find someone else."

"What do you mean?" I said, not raising my eyes.

"We're not meant for each other. I notice you're interested in other girls . . . maybe you should go after them. Then you might develop a real lasting relationship," she said without a hint of sarcasm.

Her tone was casual, almost flippant. She gave me a half smile, as if she only half meant what she'd just said. But I felt like I had been stung.

"Sure, sounds like fun!" I replied, playing her game. I tried to laugh but couldn't.

"As far as I'm concerned, you can fuck whoever you want," I added spitefully, for want of anything else to say.

She didn't answer, but her smile vanished. I knew then I had lost her.

She doesn't care if I flirt with other people! I realized with a sense of shock. There was a time when it would have made her furious and I found myself missing those days—even while we still lived together.

Cracks were appearing elsewhere in my life. Caught up with Caitlin, I had neglected my studies and prepared little for the important doctoral qualifying exam. One day I picked up a copy of Landau, Akhiezer, and Lifshitz's *Mechanics and Molecular Physics*, the textbook bible of graduate physicists. Flipping through the pages, I was shocked to realize I understood practically none of it! I had missed many classes and had no notes. I had been out of the loop so long that I had even forgotten much of what I had understood a year before. I saw myself speeding toward a brick wall. Cold fear took over.

Where was I to go if I failed? I could never go back to Kenya in defeat. Repeating the exam was out of the question. There was no one I knew in the United States who could support me. My family's expectations for me were so high. I had never failed an examination in my life. I had gained a solid B average at Stanford—without studying really hard. But the second-year exam was just weeks away. To fail at this stage in my academic career would be unimaginable ignominy for me.

I had forced myself to succeed beyond expectations, to be perfect, even in things I did not love. I had driven myself on and on, studied for hours, and never asked myself why. Academic success had been fundamental to my sense of self-worth. Without it, what was I? Who was I? What value did I have?

Even music was no solace. Around this time I had tried to convince myself I could have a concert career playing piano. I had convinced myself that if I gave a good concert then and there, I could succeed professionally. George Barth, my tutor, a professor of music at Stanford, helped me plan the concert. George was a wiry, bearded workaholic whose passion for detail was exceeded only by his love of music. Our lessons were musical séances, in which we could argue over the proper phrasing of four bars for thirty minutes and produce glorious music for the remaining fifteen.

The program was difficult—Beethoven's Les Adieux together with the Brahms Opus 21 Variations, and some Chopin, but my technique was up to it, or at least seemed to be in my practice sessions.

In the end it was Les Adieux's damned double notes that did me in. The audience that afternoon was not large, just a handful of people scattered throughout the auditorium. Stricken with nerves, I could not concentrate and found myself playing too fast. In the first movement, I stopped midphrase and looked down in consternation at my hands. The white keys looked dazzling, and a sinking feeling took over. Then those double notes came up again and I couldn't remember the sequence. There was silence in the auditorium. After a few failed attempts, I looked at the audience and said, "I should have brought my book." Someone tittered. Several seconds later I found my way back and finished the piece, but my memory had failed me, a no-no in classical concert recitals. My dreams in that moment were dashed.

At Stanford I lost faith in my music. It was like the slow passing away of a friend, accentuated by them being public performances. It would take me years before I could really enjoy making music onstage and realize not everybody cared if the notes were not perfect.

I tried to hide my failures by not talking about them. The only person I was willing to confide in, Caitlin, had already drifted away. Grandmother was no longer around. There were support groups at Stanford, but I evaded them—seeking help would be admitting weakness. What worse failure could there be than recognizing my emotional weakness?

Big mistakes and great successes often hinge on snap decisions.

I discovered, in a matter of moments, that I was ready to lie, cheat, and steal to pass a damned exam.

The professors never locked their office doors. Late at night anyone could walk through the corridors. I knew that it would be easy to take a look at the exam questions and answers. One night as I was working on a laboratory project in the deserted building, I decided that I would do so. What does it matter if I see a few answers? No one will ever know—and in any case, doesn't everyone cheat?

I furtively grasped the door handle of a professor's office. It was unlocked. *Why do they make it so easy?* I quickly shut the thoughts out of my mind, almost recoiling from the door. Then about an hour later, as I was heading back from the laboratory, I passed by the same office. As if to counter what I already knew was wrong, anger entered my mind. *Why should I suffer?* I thought. *I have worked so hard to get here, and now I could lose everything!* This irrational feeling of being unjustly persecuted took a hold of me. I grasped the door handle again. Just a quick look, I thought, and I was in. A heady feeling washed over me.

I felt almost giddy with power, as if I had just skydived out of a plane. I had the keys to the kingdom in my hands, and neither heaven nor hell would prohibit me from opening the gates. A quick look was all it would take. I had never done anything like this before and I was terrified. The exam papers were on the desk . . .

As expected, the exam was easy. The next day I opened my mailbox and found a short note: *Please see Meyerhof in his office.* I knew the game was up.

I walked into Meyerhof's office. Never one for small talk, he got to the point.

"Some professors say your answers are very close to their own. They think it is a little suspicious."

"What? That's ridiculous," I said. "How could they say that?" Meyerhof didn't say anything more for several seconds. Then, as though he had made up his mind about something, he suddenly turned toward the window. Outside it was getting dark. An indigo sky settled over Stanford's red roofs.

"If you defend this I am sure that things will swing your way." His voice seemed to float in the ether, his back turned to me so I could not see his expression. "There can be a student trial for you to defend yourself against accusers. Students and professors would make the final judgment."

Meyerhof was probably right and I could have prevailed. I told him I would think about it before deciding what to do next. That night I returned to my apartment. It was very quiet. I heard a voice inside me ask: *Is this really how you want to end up at Stanford, defending yourself with lies, fighting to stay in a career you no longer care for?* I realized I had to tell the truth even if it meant my life there was over. I felt very alone, almost suicidal, but I had to face the music. The next day I confronted Meyerhof in his office.

"I did it," I confessed. "I panicked about the exam. I am really sorry, Professor."

He flinched as though I had just struck him in the face. I realized that I had broken his trust, and that hurt me most of all. Why did I have to be one to shame myself in this way? If only I had resisted temptation.

Blackness consumed me for days afterward. I tried to continue my life as though everything was normal. Then, one afternoon, I found myself at the International House, where I had met Caitlin. I locked myself in a small room on the first floor, behind the reception counter. At that time of the day there were few people in the building. How different it felt now from that day I had met her. Back then the world had been bright and full of love, rich with possibilities. How I'd loved everything: the sunshine, the trees, the people around me, even the threadbare carpets and rusting, creaky furniture. Now the sunlight seemed to burn me, and people's voices seemed to accuse me. How quickly everything had changed.

Someone knocked on the door. "Mark, are you in there?"

"I'm fine, just relaxing," I shouted out.

"Are you okay?"

"I'm just great!" I said. I seemed to be outside my body. My voice sounded shrill.

I looked around the shabby room, saw the olive green wall and the broken TV that no one had ever gotten around to fixing. I sat behind the metal desk and thought of how I had finally become that *half-caste failure* that I had feared becoming since my early days. I didn't want to live any more. If I had had a bottle of sleeping pills, I would have swallowed them in an instant.

I was in a strange state, in a cocoon almost. I wanted to remain rooted in my chair. Time had stopped for me. I could hear my heart beating even as the sounds of people outside faintly reached me. I had an overwhelming desire to sleep and forget everything.

Cllaaaaaaanggg.

The old rotary AT&T phone's tinny sound jerked me out of my stupor. It rang noisily on the table, amplified by the small room. Reflexively, I picked it up.

"Mark . . . Mark, is that you? It's Dean Swinehart."

At that time I did not know who she was, but her voice sounded gentle and anxious. I mumbled something in reply.

"Mark, can you please open the door?" she insisted.

"Who . . . who is this?"

"I'm Dean Swinehart, the Student Affairs Dean. Can you open the door?"

Perhaps I was too polite to say no. Perhaps I was ashamed of my weakness and wanted to do something decisive. Perhaps it was just that she sounded genuinely concerned.

"Okay," I said as I stood and opened the door.

The dean was a stocky blonde lady in a business suit. Her bronzed complexion made me think of someone who had enjoyed her younger days hiking and surfing, and who would have continued to do so had she not been lured into a job in the university's bureaucracy.

"I know what's going on, I'm here to help," she said gently.

We walked back to her office. That afternoon Swinehart was the shrink or kindred spirit I had always feared talking to but so obviously needed. While I unloaded she calmly sat back, nodding her head sympathetically.

"I'm sorry I had to tell you all this," I would say again and again, feeling I was burdening her.

"It's okay," Swinehart urged me on.

It was a relief to tell somebody about my problems for maybe the first time in my life, a revelation even. She seemed to just absorb all my offloading without criticizing.

I remembered when I was a child, at Lawford's, when David and I had discovered an envelope filled with money hidden behind some books in a small guest library.

"Keep it," David had joked.

"No. Let's give it back."

He had looked surprised for a moment and then nodded his head. We handed the stuffed envelope to the surprised clerk at the reception desk.

In my mind's eye, David's pudgy face looked happy, his eyes a little red from the surf, his ringlets of long hair curled at his neck, dripping with water. I also saw Ida, leaning over her piano as her spry fingers tripped through "Kitten on the Keys," then images of my mother and Simeon.

Something inside me seemed to snap. Thinking of Grandmother and David, particularly of David, tears started to flow down my face.

"Don't worry," Swinehart said, handing me a tissue. "Think of this as a new start."

My graduate adviser, John Lipa, looked at me with compassion "I am sorry because of what this means for your future," he said.

Lipa would continue to hire me as a research assistant, giving me much-needed financial support while I figured out what I wanted to do next. He and his research team also eventually published the paper I had spent months working on, giving me credit for my work.

His words were perhaps the most prescient of all the comments I would hear in the immediate aftermath of my transgression.

More than twenty years later, I can analyze and ponder all sorts of reasons for that moment of ugliness: Ida's death and my loneliness, the breakup with Caitlin, the lack of interest shown in me by faculty, and my own fear of failure. In the end it was stupidity and weakness for which I had only myself to blame.

I had always secretly feared that I was a fraud, a cheat. For a long time I had not known where this feeling came from, but it had been with me most of my life. Whenever I received gifts or won prizes, I would feel that they were never truly mine. I felt that one day they would be snatched away, and that it was perhaps just as well, because I did not deserve them. So when others loved me or tried to love me, I could not appreciate their love. *It must be for someone else*, I reasoned. *It could not really be for me.* I had even distrusted my mother's love.

"Mark, Mark, I just want you to be happy!" she had cried that day at Brown.

Even those tears on her cheeks had failed to fully wash away the fog before my eyes. It was the trophies and awards that mattered most to me. Throughout my life I'd felt the ground shifting uncertainly beneath me, like jelly, or an ice floe with deep and dangerous crevasses waiting to suck me in. Yes, I was smart and gifted, but in the end, at Stanford, I finally realized how hollow and empty I was. It was the place where my longest-cherished dreams collapsed and died.

My actions threw the department into turmoil.

"Steven Chu wants you out of the school immediately," an African-American staffer who had befriended me told me later. "So do some others. They cannot forgive you."

Knowing the department chair wanted me expelled plunged me deeper into gloom.*

"What can I do? Maybe I can go to another school?"

---

* In an ironic twist, Chu would later work for my brother as Secretary of Energy in the Obama administration.

Even then, I flirted with the idea of hanging on in physics. I confided in Letisha, a staffer who had been instrumental in boosting black enrollment at Stanford.

"You don't get it, Mark." Letisha shook her head wearily. "You want to keep banging your head against the wall when it does no good. They want to make an example of you. That's what they do to you and others like us."

"What do you mean?" I said, a little perplexed.

"You were dating a white girl, openly. You struck some as arrogant with the adviser thing. If this had been handled right perhaps you would have gotten a slap on the wrist and could take the exam again. But this is all about big egos at the school. You will never be able to get into another Ivy League again, at least not in physics. Maybe someplace down South. But in the North, no way!"

I felt a tremendous bond with Letisha. "Others like us" was a statement of solidarity. I had mostly kept away from the African-American community who were in some ways like a separate species from me: the way they talked, the way they moved, the clothes they wore. We were all black, and we mutually recognized it, but I had always felt they had this victim mentality. Yet, in the end, it was the minorities at Stanford who best seemed to understand my situation and at least tried to help me.

I remembered how some of the faculty members had looked at me and Caitlin when the two of us walked by. I had asked many questions during classes, irritating professors, and making them snap at me in public. I realized they may have thought I was teasing them, perhaps questioning their authority and knowledge. My decision to study with Fairbank must have helped poison the water too. Years later I would read *The Other Barack*, a book on my father by the American reporter Sally Jacobs. I learned that Harvard had kicked my father out because of his relationships with white women, not on account of a poor academic record. I also read how he had been expelled from high school because of attitude and disciplinary problems. I wasn't an alleged bigamist. Neither did I have children by different women. However, I was arrogant and in your face, and I had attracted attention by dating a white woman.

There was perhaps some truth in Letisha's perspective. People had not looked at me only as Mark Ndesandjo, the errant student, they had looked at me as Mark Ndesandjo, the errant *black* student. That was Letisha's view. That was Stanford's view. Perhaps that would later prove to be America's view, a destiny I had tried so hard to avoid. It was selfish and easy to play the part of the victim, but another part of me wanted to take responsibility for what I had done and resisted being categorized as just another black failure. And why would Letisha and other minority staffers advise and look out for me? Because I was black or because I was Mark? It was all so confusing, and yet, for the first time, in my gut I felt that Letisha understood me and my situation better than anyone else at the school, or in my whole American experience.

"There is a lot of racism at Stanford," an Asian research assistant told me. "When I wrote a paper here, they would not publish it. I was not part of the establishment, not a tenured professor, and I am Asian."

"Meyerhof defended you," Letisha told me later. "He said, 'Ndesandjo came here and did his own thing, selecting his own adviser against your recommendations, and generally stood up to you. You didn't like that and now you want to make an example of him for this one mistake. His career is already in ruins but now you want to destroy him.'"

Tears came to my eyes when I heard this. The gruff old man who had been so supportive of me, and whom I had let down so deeply, still defended me.

"Steven Chu is going to be the next chairman of the department, and he can't stand you. He will do everything to have you kicked out."

"What have I done, Letisha? What have I done?" I cried.

Her voice softened, "Again, if you had let us know earlier, perhaps we could have done something. But it has gone too far now, too many people know. It isn't just about you now. Many professors hate the minority outreach programs we have here and will do anything to kill them. The knives are out and scores are being settled. They are using you."

So two camps were at war at Stanford, all because of my recklessness and weakness.

In the end, I was not expelled—but was suspended from the university. I could not attend coursework but was allowed to continue my research.

A few months later, on a quiet Sunday, Professor Fairbank passed away. I remember attending his memorial service. At the time I was in a sort of academic purgatory, still doing some research for Lipa while officially on suspension.

I sat in the back of the cavernous Memorial Hall while the service was being conducted. It was a beautiful occasion. Several hundred people quietly gathered beneath the famous stained-glass windows and the cupola of one of northern California's most famous churches. I sat in a pew at the very back, trying to be as inconspicuous as possible. No one seemed to notice me or care. A tear rolled down my cheek as I remembered the grand old man. Fairbank had been among the few to uncritically welcome and support me in my first independent steps at Stanford.

A few days later Meyerhof called me into his office. "Ndesandjo, some people saw you at Fairbank's service," he said. "You know you should not have attended, especially at this time."

"I respected and liked him. He was my friend," I gently protested.

Meyerhof shook his head. "You do not want to attract attention at this time!"

I nodded my head and left it at that.

I remembered old Fairbank, and his handsome, kind face. I recalled how he had eagerly shared his ideas and walked me around his lab, jabbing his finger at various rusty pieces of equipment, excitedly telling me about this and that idea or project.

He hadn't seen black or white or arrogance or subservience in me. He had just seen an eager student trying to find his way. Now, I could not even attend his memorial service without causing trouble. Stanford saw me as a rotten apple. Even Meyerhof viewed my presence as something infectious and debilitating. I bowed my head and walked away.

From that day on I stayed quiet and inconspicuous. I saw no point in doing anything much anymore.

I remember when I was about six and Barack Obama Sr. shaved my head. "You need a good haircut!" he growled and dragged me outside the house. Seating me on an upturned pail, he took out a razor and scissors and snipped and shaved off the soft, curly brown locks I loved. Then, my childhood vanity convinced me I was ugly, and I did not want to go to the kindergarten the next day. Now, at Stanford, I was ugly again. No one would want to look at me, ever. I had clothes, but no dignity.

Inside I was dead, without honor.

A few months later I requested and received my master's degree in Physics. I wondered why Stanford had approved it. It could have been for my two years of completed coursework as well as my final experimental research in low-temperature conductivity. The work had been ground-breaking and a paper would soon be published. I reasoned that it was just luck, or perhaps the administration had had second thoughts about the severity of my punishment.

In any case, I had lost all my passion for study. I saw no future ahead of me in physics and decided to leave Stanford for good.

I had hurt too many people, including myself. The shame would be long-lasting and deep.

For a long time I did not have the courage to tell Caitlin about what had happened. Information on the matter would be sealed forever. It would take a court order to make them reveal details to the public. When I finally told her, she was silent for a long time.

"I never liked those Stanford people anyway. They were all stuck up," she concluded.

Soon after that, Caitlin and I broke up for good. It had been a long time coming. For years afterward, I would shut her out of my life. The pain was so great, I couldn't bear thinking about her. It had been almost two years since we first met. It would take almost as long for me to recover from our breakup.

On the face of it, I had achieved a great deal in college, including three degrees in math and physics, a prestigious internship at Bell Labs, and even a published paper. And despite my ugly moment, I had still walked away with a master's.

I had also been through hell, and though my lonely road would be that much harder, I made a promise then to follow my heart. An inner voice, growing stronger with each passing day, was telling me not to give up. Call it stubbornness, call it steely persistence, but in the very core of me, I was cautiously optimistic about the future.

And for now, the future lay in San Francisco.

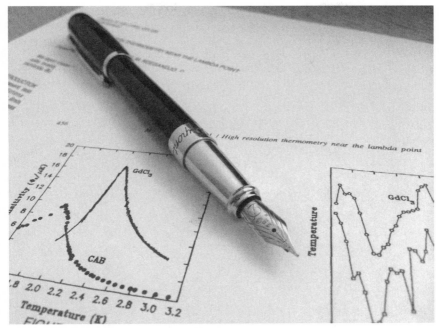

Our research team at Stanford University eventually published a paper on the low-temperature thermometer I helped develop. The results were used for the space shuttle's Gravity Probe B project, a test that confirmed Einstein's theory of general relativity.

CHAPTER THIRTEEN

Culture Shocks and Untimely Nuns

MUSICAL EVOCATION

The Untimely Ones: *Mark Obama Ndesandjo*

The Untimely Ones was my first CD, which included my own piano compositions, recorded in New Jersey in the mid-1990s, and inspired by the great nineteenth-century mystic Friedrich Nietzsche. Like the characters in his books, I was untimely. My shattered identity was late to develop, and it took years to understand the deeper significance of my American experience.

I was a cube of ice in a sea of salt, slowly dissolving into anonymity. Life's lessons would appear too early or too late. The road that had started in Kenya had reached a cliff edge. I had arrived in the wrong place at the wrong time.

OCTOBER 17, 1989, STARTED AS AN IMPOSSIBLY BRIGHT, CLEAR, SUNNY day. I was working in a laboratory in the basement of Varian until I could find a job. In nearby San Francisco, thousands of baseball fans awaited the Battle of the Bay at Candlestick Park—Oakland and San Francisco playing in Game 3 of the World Series. Then, at around five o'clock, the pen on my desk decided to move. Perhaps it had decided it was tired of its anonymity and wanted to startle me. Almost immediately afterward, my body began to shake. At first I thought I had eaten something bad and was just a little dizzy. Then I realized that my chair, not I, was moving.

My God, it's an earthquake, I realized.

I ducked under the solid metal table while the room shook around me. A few feet away a huge helium canister teetered precariously for about ten seconds.

It's going to fall and crack—I'll be suffocated by frozen helium, I thought as I watched it totter. When the shaking subsided, I scrambled out of the building. A few students were clustered outside.

"Man, you should have seen the cars. Like, they were on jelly. It was amazing," someone said.

In about fifteen terrifying seconds, California had suffered its worst earthquake since the Great Quake of 1906. Sixty-three people died, almost four thousand were injured, parts of the Bay Bridge collapsed, and Mother Nature inflicted billions of dollars' worth of damage.

California for me was about forces of every shape and direction, magnitude and intensity: forces of love, self-destruction, fifth forces, and earthquakes.

Soon afterward, I left Stanford for good. I had a few hundred dollars in my bank account. I wouldn't ask anyone for help. Instead I wanted to lose myself in the vast hinterland of America, to leave behind memories of shame and failure.

I destroyed myself in America and it was a good thing—because that way I could start afresh.

How do I start to explain those wandering years? How do I make sense of a confused life in one chapter? My world now resembled a Rubik's Cube, a block of jarring colors, multiple dimensions, random-yet-linked experiences: a telecommunications manager, a woman who loved me more than I deserved, forays into music, my first great encounter with the East. And a fateful encounter with a nun.

—◆—

Sometimes life changes direction completely thanks to a minor chance event. Like the leaflet someone wedged on to my windshield while I sipped a cappuccino one day in downtown San Francisco.

The Embarcadero Club is having a potluck in beautiful Marin Park this Saturday. Only $10 or bring your own!

In the park that weekend, about twenty strangers meandered and chatted before a long wooden picnic table loaded with food. An Asian woman was hovering somewhere between the grapes and the macaroni salad. She did not talk to the people around her, and perhaps that impression of solitude was what drew me to her.

We began talking. I noticed she ate her food carefully, as though every bite was precious, even a crumb must not be wasted. She had shoulder-length black hair and very beautiful marble-white skin. Somewhat stocky, she moved jerkily, as though unsure where to go next. Her face was round like a small moon. I thought her very pretty.

She told me she had taken the bus from town, so I offered to give her a ride back. She feigned a protest but accepted.

"I'm from Japan," she told me. "I will get my accounting degree and then get a good job here." Her English was quite good, but she had a strong accent.

"What were you doing in Japan?"

"I was a stockbroker." She didn't smile, but moved on down the table.

"What was wrong with your trading job?" I asked, following her.

"It was hard. I hated selling," she replied brusquely. I changed the subject.

Later, I dropped her off in the Mission District. As she exited, somewhat nervously I asked her out to a movie and was surprised when she accepted.

Ayumi and I started dating the following week. The night I made love to her for the first time, she turned toward me, her eyes a little dreamy. Without looking at me, she ran her finger over my body, lingering over my crotch, then held it up to her nose.

"Now I have your smell," she said in a low voice, "we are together."

I shrugged. I was interested in sex, not love. I thought her comment was a little strange, but maybe this was a Japanese thing, like ramen, peach blossom, or Kabuki.

At thirty-five, Ayumi was starting a new life in a new country when I happened to cross her path. Perhaps she saw in me something of the American Dream.

"I want a house in New Jersey with a nice white fence and a pretty garden," she once said. I didn't know whether or not she was joking. *Do people actually believe that?* I asked myself, imagining a scene from a Norman Rockwell painting.

One day I walked into her apartment, expecting us to go out to dinner and come back and cuddle.

"What's up?" I exclaimed.

She didn't answer. She was sitting on the side of her bed and did not get up. I immediately knew something was wrong.

"I'm pregnant," she said, her voice low and so hoarse I almost didn't recognize it.

I gasped. I did not know what to say.

Ignoring me, she quickly went on, "I should have a job soon, once I'm graduated. We can support the child."

It could have started from my toes, or perhaps my belly. Something powerful and formless was snaking through me.

The word was out before I could stop it. "No." I refused to look at her, and a pall settled over the room. "No," I repeated, softly but firmly. "I think you should get an abortion."

I was young and selfish, and I didn't care what she felt like. It was what *I* wanted that mattered. I was not going to have a child. I would never have children, if I could help it. I had told myself again and again, over the years, that there were too many marriages, too many children, and it would be better if fewer people married and had kids.

For me, the most important things about our relationship were sex and ramen noodles, which she was fabulous at making. We made love everywhere: on the beach, in the parks, on planes, in spas, and in offices. I was in my mid-twenties; sex was all I wanted and needed.

I was a part of Ayumi's dream, although in the end, for her, too, it was also mostly about sex. Some say that the less one knows of one's partner, the better the lovemaking. We did not know much about each other, and we had preferred to leave it that way.

Ayumi didn't try to change my mind about the abortion, but afterward things changed between us. She seemed older, her face more lined. I began to notice the difference in our ages.

Two years passed. Once we had a huge argument in my apartment. Reduced to tears, she had crumpled to the floor, into a small heap of long black hair and prim accountant's clothes.

"You never tell me anything!" she cried.

My apartment's kitchen opened on to the living room, and there were knives lying on the countertop, almost beckoning.

"You can kill me, I don't care!" Ayumi cried.

You can kill me. Perhaps it was something about those words, juxtaposed with the sight of knives, which caused a tremendous flow of guilt to wash over me. Suddenly I wasn't angry at her anymore. I tried to pull her up off the floor, but she wouldn't let me.

"You don't love me." She brushed away my hands. "You just want to use me."

"What do you want me to do?" I asked.

"You made me get an abortion. He would have been two years old . . . we should be married now," she sobbed.

"No. I'll never marry," I said. I sank on to the sofa. Quiet now, she looked at me.

"Why?"

I hesitated. "My father. My father used to beat my mother, and I couldn't help her. I remember so many bad things. I think . . ."

"Yes?" She had stopped crying. Her tone was curious rather than distressed.

"I think that's why I am so hard to be with," I said, tears coming again to my eyes. I wiped them away and looked at her apologetically.

"I can never be married. I don't believe in it. I can't be like him."

Ayumi let me lift her up then. The expression in her eyes was very tender, and she hugged me for a long time. At that moment she was more than just my sexual partner.

Much more.

When we made love later that night, it was different from the other times. I was fully connected with her on a spiritual level. This exposing of myself was also unsettling to me, as though I had flayed myself and rubbed salt in the wound. There was a part of me that wanted to be hard, to be spiritually alone, even when my partner was a woman with dreams, who had suffered too. And, most of all, a woman who understood me.

That precious day was not to be repeated. A few months later, when she had gotten her accounting degree and been hired at one of the Big Five Firms, she moved to New York. At once I missed her.

At the time I had been working at AT&T Sales, a job I got after getting my master's at Stanford in 1991.

During my first week at AT&T, I remember my manager giving me five minutes of coaching on how to make a cold call.

"Always push the customer to say 'yes.' Even if it is only a little yes, have them keep saying it. That's the key," he instructed me.

When we did a role play with him as customer and me as salesman, he was not convinced. "You just don't seem to drive to a close," he told me. "You don't have that killer instinct."

Somehow I kept my job. My manager lost his a year later. Layoffs.

I remember an older associate who'd been at the company for more than twenty years. Her eyes looked tired, but her suit was wrinkle-free and she moved with the alacrity of a person decades younger. The day she was laid off, her eyes were hard and resigned, flitting between the cardboard boxes in her cubicle and somewhere over my left shoulder, as though there was an invisible ether where the jobless go, like a graveyard for the whales.

"Twenty years and they let you go just like that," she told me. "You're young, fresh. I don't give a rat's ass. It was all for the money anyway." Her expression lacked conviction, but I nodded sympathetically. Then she vanished into the ether.

"They never fire you at AT&T," a friend once told me. "People spend their lives there." Although I hated sales, I looked at my pay stubs, bought a new car, and decided to believe my friend.

Four years later I was still there. "You're smart, and everybody says that you have talent, but you just can't sell," someone told me. I was given three months to get another job in the company, otherwise I would have to leave. My first manager had been right after all, and I only realized it four years later.

It was my turn to enter the ether.

A few weeks later, I got a call from the AT&T branch in Morristown, New Jersey. A thick throaty female voice boomed over the line. This was Esther Walson; from her accent I knew she was black.

"Mark, what is a person with your background doing stuck out there in San Francisco? Shuffled from one lateral sales position to another? We need someone like you."

I leapt at the opportunity. It had been several months since Ayumi had left. I missed her deeply and had often thought of joining her in New York. The next week I loaded my things into my car and drove across the country. Ayumi had missed me, too, and we were happy to be together again.

We moved into a rented house in New Jersey, not far from Morristown. I remember the gas station at the corner, and the quiet residential neighborhood. The house had a pool and several rooms. The owner, a Chinese businessman who spent most of his time in Shanghai, had only one request.

"My son who is studying needs someplace to stay in the summer."

We didn't like the idea of sharing the house, but the rent was very low and we took the deal.

Esther greeted me my first day at the office. She wore dangling earrings and a perpetual wide-eyed stare, as though life was always surprising her. Her lips were thick and fleshy. Some would say she was fat, but I saw her as voluptuous.

"You? You're Mark?"

"Yes, that's me."

"Mark Ndesandjo?"

I nodded energetically. I assumed she was surprised I'd arrived a few days early. I immediately started work as a promotions manager in her department.

Esther was a manager in the network equipment division of AT&T (what later became Lucent) and had worked there for more than ten years. Every company has a formal power structure defined by an organization chart. However, there is always the informal organization, where the real power lies. Esther taught me about this, the industry, and our customers.

She was always open to new ideas, and we would develop a good relationship based on trust and professionalism.

"When you walked into the office I took a double take," she later told me. "I didn't know you were black! You sounded white over the phone."

"Why? Was that a problem?" I felt a little offended.

"It sure was. I had hired another black person at the same time. When my manager, who is white and bless her soul, found out I had hired two blacks, I thought she was going to have a hissy fit! It took some explaining!" Esther chortled loudly, her hand over her mouth.

It was that race thing again, blundering into the picture unwanted, like a sudden flash of blinding light.

After she got to see my work, she confessed to me she had been puzzled why I had stayed so long in sales.

"You were dying out there, Mark. A person of your accomplishments being shuttled from place to place. I knew there was something wrong, but I saw your background, Brown, Stanford, and thought there might be something there, so I hired you."

Esther knew things were harder for minorities, but she was particularly demanding of me. When I first arrived she taught me to put forward my ideas in a less confrontational manner. "Watch your style, Mark, you have to temper down those hard edges."

And God forbid I ignore or criticize her. Then she would clutch the sides of her desk, roll her eyes balefully, and rail at me. I felt like a vassal cringing before a Nubian empress.

"Damn, sometimes you are soooo arrogant! I know you. But others—you really can rub them the wrong way." I braced myself as she continued. "You have this way of repeating what other people say, as if it were your own idea. And sometimes you forget to give other people credit for the work they have contributed. It's a simple matter of courtesy."

Others would have been upset, even angry, but her comments were welcome water in an oasis to me. I desperately wanted to improve, and I hadn't realized that attitude was the key in getting ahead. Esther's advice helped me gain my first pay raise. The things she told me might seem trivial, but I should have learned them years earlier.

Esther also taught me the importance of developing credibility with one's managers and associates. "You have to think carefully before you say something. The moment it comes out of your mouth, it becomes part of what people think of you."

She could be brutal in her yearly appraisals of my work, always ending the conversation with her signature phrase: "Wake up, Mark, and smell the coffee!" And I did. But I was smelling the coffee in other ways too.

—◆—

When I finally broke up with Ayumi, it was over another woman. On a trip to Paris, I had met a young Slovak girl. It was a beautiful afternoon in the Parc Monceau. I was listening to an open-air concert when I noticed someone sit down next to me. She had long auburn hair and was wearing a bright red-and-white dress like from a 1950s Technicolor movie.

"Great music!" I remarked, glancing at her. She smiled but said nothing.

"Are you from here?" I persisted. "Everything is so new to me. I don't know French . . . or much about Paris."

"Oh, I know a little," she said casually.

"What do you do?"

"I'm a nanny for some bullshit rich French family." We talked about music and America.

"I'd love to go to America!" she said, brightening up.

"I'm only here for a few days. Maybe you can show me around?" I suggested.

One thing led to another. I had left Ayumi in tears in New Jersey after another huge argument. We had grown apart. Now, alone in Paris, I felt as though I'd been reborn.

Dana was less interested in me than I was in her. In any case, on the third day I had to return to the States. We promised to stay in touch.

Back in New Jersey, Ayumi and I were living in the same house but it was like we were strangers. We barely talked. We slept in the same bed but barely touched. Constantly thinking of Dana, I called her one day.

"I miss you. Come to America. I'll pay for everything."

It was another of those things I did without thinking, and it would cause much unnecessary pain to the three of us. In retrospect I wonder how I could have been so cruel to Ayumi, where this indifference to her feelings came from. It was as though I sought energy and life, no matter what the consequences.

Dana arrived in New Jersey and I put her up in our house. I had told Ayumi a few days before that I would be inviting my girlfriend to stay. Although we were more like roommates than partners by then, we still occasionally slept together. It was as though I could not bring myself to break away first, yet that was exactly what I was doing, in the cruelest way imaginable.

Ayumi exploded: "She will NEVER sleep in our bed!"

Dana was dumbfounded. There were arguments and tears every day. Ayumi even wrote to my mother, who sent me a short e-mail. It was with shock that I read the last line:

"What sort of person have you become, Mark?"

It was as though my sense of right and wrong, good and evil, was in abeyance. I wanted to have my way, and to hell with the consequences. In desperation, I took Dana on an expensive road trip around Maine and Massachusetts. It was a failure. She flinched when I touched her, as though I had become a different person. I realized she had lost respect for me. Even then, I did not know why. After she returned to Slovakia, Ayumi and I had a final huge blowup.

"I never loved you. I only kept you around for the sex," she screamed.

I grabbed her throat and forced her against the wall. I felt her soft skin yielding to the pressure of my fingers. The frailty and lightness of her frame surprised me.

She looked at me. I saw the fear in her eyes and at that moment my anger evaporated, replaced by a sinking feeling. I was ashamed of myself. I lowered my eyes and looked at my hands. I had never physically attacked a woman before. What had happened to me? What had I become?

"What a fool I was, to waste so many years on you," she said.

Shortly after that we moved out of the house. I never saw her again.

Had I been a drinker, the problems would have been magnified. I might have killed her, as my father almost killed my mother more than a decade before. I wanted all these women around me, and thought I could control them, and keep them. I wanted to control everything, and just as at Stanford, I had impulsively and thoughtlessly ruined everything.

In the end, I lost them all.

I did not know how to love, or how to trust. I had lost my way.

I had a job, but money could not save me from myself. How was I to know that meeting a nun a few months later would do just that?

The Brown Club of New Jersey organized a group visit to the Central Ward one weekend. Volunteers would paint houses and help clean up neighborhoods. That week, things had been particularly difficult at work. I had more bills than I could pay, and I looked at the hair I'd shed in the sink and felt I was growing old.

"Just meet at the church at ten a.m.!" my contact gaily said, giving me the address in central Newark.

That Saturday morning the sky was a slate gray, and it seemed to look down on me with a grim intensity. I drove through neighborhoods I had never visited before.

"America has the best roads," I remembered a friend from Brown once telling me. An adventurous German, he had rented a car and driven across three western states on his summer vacation.

"So long, so straight, so well kept up."

Indeed, the roads before me in Newark were long, straight, and well maintained. That is, until that bend at the end of a long boulevard where high-rises blocked out what's around the corner. When I rounded the bend, it was like I had entered another world. Before me was a long stretch that sloped downhill. On either side were simple, unpainted, red-brick homes. I found myself in a vast concrete depression, a bowl scooped out of the earth. Gaps on the roads and pavements were covered with a lattice of white strips, like bars on a horizontal jail cell, forming a vast checkerboard.

Normally, even in poor districts, otherwise humdrum houses looked a little different from their neighbors: a potted plant or two, a lily blooming in the yard, an American flag furling outside the kitchen window. Here the houses were of a deathly sameness, as though all hope had been stripped away from them, and where life's games always had the same grim outcome—tedium, poverty, dashed dreams. I looked ahead and in the quarter-mile of road there was not a living soul to be seen.

Was this still America? I asked myself. How could people live here?

I eventually found my way to the church, a whitewashed wooden building that was the tallest structure in sight. I dutifully signed up and spent that morning painting houses with other alumni.

"Here, we need some people to paint!" An older woman in a nun's habit flitted between the youthful volunteers.

"Bless you, child, help me bring those tools over here."

I didn't talk much, yet the people around me chatted loudly. Everyone seemed to feel compelled to sound joyful, as if to counter the malaise of the place. I looked around. I had the only dark face in a group of twenty or thirty people. It was as though my darker brothers had retreated back into those grim Newark houses, ashamed.

"Hey, you!" I heard the voice but went on painting. It seemed that a stubborn patch refused to be covered, no matter how much whitewash I slathered over it.

"You, young man!" The voice was insistent. I looked behind me. It was the nun, her wizened face inches from mine. I saw the lines under her bright blue eyes. Her teeth, slightly yellowed, in a wide guileless smile.

"Gotcha! Please come with me," she said in a strong Irish brogue, a curved index finger beckoning me to follow her. We entered the dilapidated church.

Her office was large and dark. A huge wooden desk stood in the center of the room; a window behind it overlooked the broken streets and buildings behind, a threadbare carpet lay in front. It was a room steeped in the visual language of thriftiness: a window without shades, some scattered pencils, the smell of old, damp wood, and a paucity of light, as if even the sunbeams were rationed.

"Sit down," she said and gestured to a small chair. I did so, hesitantly.

"Why did you come here, Mark?" she asked. Traces of a Midwest accent broke through the Irish tones. Hers was a firm, purposeful voice.

"I wanted to help these people," I said, a little perplexed at the question, as I'd thought the answer would be obvious.

"I see . . . I see." She paused and resumed, "And what do you want to do with your life?"

"I work at AT&T and am interested in telecommunications," I blustered.

"You're different from the others," she said, almost apologetically. "You have so many gifts," she quickly went on, "and have achieved so much."

I nodded. There was a faint undertone of flattery in her voice, which both pleased and repulsed me. I sensed her words were the prelude to a request.

"Maybe you can come back and work here?" I looked away, avoiding her gaze.

"You could help us, you know."

Different. That word she'd used was still roiling in my mind. *How was I different?* I wondered.

"The children here, they need someone to look up to."

In a flash I realized what she meant. After all, we were in a black neighborhood. On the surface it seemed her comment was blatantly rude, but wasn't she right? Didn't kids need role models that looked just like them?

"These people need help!" she said, as though reading my mind

But her voice was changed. It didn't seem so confident anymore. It had that pleading, flattering quality, as though she had told her story to indifferent ears many times before. I looked around again. Everything here was so depressing: the crumbling plaster walls, the cold, dull gray sky, the roads that were so old they were cracked in a thousand places. Above all, the almost empty streets. No one wanted to be in this concrete wasteland.

"I really can't. I have other things I must do," I quickly replied.

"Surely you can spend some time here," she persisted.

I did not want to be surrounded by things that depressed me. I wanted my world to be light and airy, positive and cheerful. This place reminded me too much of those early years, when my mother struggled to make ends meet, when we dealt with my father's rages, when we were poor and desperate. I wanted help to be an option, not a trap that would suck me in year after year.

The old nun spent almost thirty minutes trying to persuade me to stay, offering me various assignments there, until conceding. I was glad to get back to the other volunteers. She watched my retreating back and called out, her brogue just clear enough for me to hear, "Don't forget us, Mark!"

Forget her? How could I forget her? Although I dismissed the slight sense of guilt, the memory of it lay dormant in my mind.

Little did I know then that the nun from the snaking streets of Newark had offered me a way out of the darkness.

It had just been too soon.

⸺ ⸺

Esther was my mentor and teacher for the four years I was at Lucent, the spinoff from AT&T's equipment division. When I was passed over for a promotion she felt I deserved, she encouraged me to move on. I had been working at the same job for two years and, in her opinion, had taken on the most challenging assignments and succeeded each time.

"Mark, there's a real resistance in this organization to treating you fairly. I've tried to argue your case, but I think you should finally tell them to shove it. I suggest you force them to give you that promotion or tell them you'll leave. I can find another place for you if you do."

I walked into the director's office that afternoon and laid down my ultimatum.

"I am the best manager you have," I said. "I am not going to wait. If you want to keep me, give me what I deserve or I leave this afternoon."

I had never taken control of my life like this before. My push back sent the department into a tizzy. Flustered associates hurried in and out of offices; a few people I had worked closely with tried to reason with me.

"You're pushing too hard. Just wait for a bit. You shouldn't worry so much," a colleague said.

Soon after my encounter with the nun, and emboldened by Esther's show of faith in me, I felt fearful but giddy, and immensely free. I remembered something Esther had told me months before.

"You're too trusting, Mark. You let people walk all over you and you don't even know it."

I had coasted along, assuming that people would give credit where credit was due. This time they hadn't done so. I stuck to my guns. The director wouldn't budge.

"Wait until next year. I am sure we can do something then," she told me.

I left, quickly finding another job at Lucent, with better pay and a promotion to boot.

From that time onward I decided that my career path in professional America would no longer be left to chance. I would take control, as Esther had taught me.

Taking control, however, also meant accepting certain facts about American life.

"Every day we have to prove ourselves," Esther had told me. "And we can't just be better. We have to be a lot better. If we are not, we will never get anywhere."

However, I would not frame it as us against them, like many people did. When faced with what my fellow African Americans would call a racist experience, I told myself: "He just doesn't like me, and that's life."

I had long seen *black*, *white*, and *racism* as nonwords. Depending on who was doing the talking, they could represent a source of power or a malady. To me they were words that represented permanent or incurable states, and to pay undue attention to them would only lend them more power.

I felt it would be weakness in me to ascribe any and every failure to racism.

But wasn't it foolish not to acknowledge that racism still had a part to play in the American way of life, with its dizzying vortex of etiquette, habits, attitudes, gestures, and speech?

What Esther and other African Americans taught me was that I needed to open my eyes and be aware of the racial distinctions that run like welts across the back of American society. Remaining blind and willfully refusing to see what was around me, as I had done for so long, was stupid and self-destructive.

I was learning to take responsibility for my choices, and racism was a fact of life in America, like stop signs or Starbucks. It was there in denied promotions, in a university's culture, even in a nun's attitude. It was here in New Jersey, just as it had been in Nairobi. It was not just an idea; it was a pothole on the road that could divert, maim, or even kill if you were not paying attention.

Now, with the help of Esther and other black mentors I'd met through the years, I was slowly equipping myself for survival. In short, I had to know what to say, how to say it, and then perform better than everyone else.

Or better than them, as my African-American brothers and sisters would say.

But "they" were also part of me. My mother belonged to them, as had Grandma Ida and Grandpa Joe Baker, whose big tummy I had hugged with joy and love. I could not deny them, just as America and Kenya didn't let me deny my father's heritage either.

I was unique. I did not see myself as black or white. I was black *and* white. If people claimed me as one or the other, that was their problem. No race or culture had ownership or exclusive rights to Mark Okoth Ndesandjo. In America, as in Kenya, or perhaps any country, people would always see me through blinders—as a black Stanford graduate, a mixed-race AT&T employee with a funny accent—and treat me accordingly. It was hard to acknowledge that even people I thought I knew well still primarily saw me as black. I had discovered that in America, unlike anyplace else I had ever been, race was the subtext of almost any social interaction, and articulating its language was a required art, but fraught with peril.

My younger brother Joseph (bottom) and me out for dinner. He studied and worked in the United States too.

CHAPTER FOURTEEN

Digital Revolutions, Sowing the Seeds of Rebellion

MUSICAL EVOCATION

__Piano Piece Op. 11 No. 1: Arnold Schoenberg__
When Schoenberg wrote this piece in 1909, the first in a set of three, its signifi-
cance could hardly be overstated. Historically, it helped usher in the twelve-tone
theory that dominated classical music for the next fifty years. To me, it sounded
like Wagner or even Brahms played out of tune, and its dissonances coaxed
new sounds and passions from the piano, while still linking it with tradition.
Schoenberg purposefully emphasized theory over subjective passion. Just as his
rigorous musical rules were bent in my own subjective performances of this piece,
passions always lurked underneath and threatened to disrupt my placid life.

IT WAS 1998 AND CHANGE WAS IN THE OFFING. BILL CLINTON WAS BEING impeached. Wars were fought in the Balkans, Viagra was resuscitating marital sex, and the prospect of technological chaos loomed over the coming millennium with Y2K. Yet the biggest battles were now being fought over bits and bytes of data. Much of this fight was over possession of the Holy Grail: the information superhighway.

The nineties were heady years. Chips and storage devices with ever-higher processing speeds and capacity were outpacing the ability to transmit information. Copper wire, for so long the medium linking telephones and computers, was now being replaced by wireless and optical technology with boundless capacity. The prospect of data and conversations being transmitted through the air was being realized, as the Internet was seizing the popular imagination. The information superhighway was becoming a fascinating and revolutionary reality.

Billions of dollars were to be made by the captains of this new industry. Wall Street was greedy for money and consumers were greedy for information. Whoever could manage and control the flow of information was on the road to fabulous riches. The consumer would also reap rewards: greater access to information and more lifestyle choices than people had ever known. Superstars Bill Gates and Steve Jobs seized the popular imagination, but the most substantial players lurked behind this dizzying and colorful curtain of electrons and photons. They were megacorporations such as AT&T, Pacific Bell, and Verizon. Though regulated, they accounted for a huge sector of the American economy. Upstart communications ventures such as Google and Amazon were already making inroads. Lucent, Nortel, Alcatel, and other equipment and software vendors were scrambling to sell products and services to these clients.

Soon my life would be at the center of one of these products: light.

A million simultaneous conversations taking place through a piece of glass the thickness of a human hair. This was optical technology, and it was going to be the future. A beam of light could carry these conversations faster—and with greater accuracy—than cumbersome copper wires. When combined with wireless technology, the possibilities were mind-blowing: telemedicine linking doctors on video screens halfway across the world, pay-on-demand movies connecting hundreds of thousands of multimedia libraries, video games networking hundreds of users over the Internet.

The information superhighway would be made up of light beams divided into numerous channels, or highways, each carrying a customer's unique information, such as video, voice, or data. Some highways have different speed limits and have levels of police enforcement to regulate the traffic. Customers can pay depending upon the level of speed, security, and privacy they choose. This was known as managed wavelengths, and it was exciting new territory.

Little did I know that this was to be my future as well.

One day I was working in my office at home when the phone rang.

"Is this Mark D . . . Deesha . . ."

"It's pronounced *Deh san jo*, how can I help you?"

Ever since I can remember, people have mispronounced and misspelled my last name. I was used to it. What often threw people for a loop was the silent *N* at the beginning, let alone the *d* or the *j* at the end. School wits had called me Banjo, in a mangled juxtaposition of music and bad poetry.

The caller made a pitch for me to work for Nortel in Atlanta, telling me that "some folks" had recommended me. I told him I'd think about it but expected that to be the end of it.

However, soon after that more headhunters were calling me about positions opening up across the United States. With my experience and increased skills, particularly in strategic marketing, I had unknowingly become a hot commodity.

The timing was perfect; I was ready for change. My manager at Lucent and I were at odds over the direction of our marketing department and now had a strained relationship. I accepted the Atlanta interview.

There, at Nortel USA's headquarters, a man fidgeted in his chair like a live wire. Every so often his thin hand would brush back his thick head of hair or nervously adjust his rimless glasses. He was telling me about the position.

"Why me?" I asked.

"You know about our industry and can help us lead the way, become an evangelist of sorts."

Evangelist! That religious theme again. First nuns, and now evangelists. It was as though there were prophets and messiahs hovering about me, all waiting for the moment they could finally plug the holes in my soul.

Rob was a Canadian and had invested much of his adult life in Nortel. One of the youngest directors ever at the Canadian communications behemoth, he had a deep knowledge of technology and the best way to market it. Rob was both a priest and a diplomat. He had a low-key intensity, and, rare for an engineer, he could move with ease between laboratories and boardrooms. I would learn later he was also unfailingly loyal to those he hired. I figured that if Nortel wanted me so much, I was worth the price of an MBA.

Rob agreed to make it happen, promising he wanted to "invest" in me.

With that he went to bat for me, convincing Nortel to fund my Executive MBA at Emory University, and promptly hired me with a six-figure compensation package. Nortel bought my house and relocated me to Atlanta.

It was perhaps the happiest and most rewarding decision I ever made in corporate America. I still treasure my connection to Nortel and its people for their warmth and openness, which continues to this day.

Most important, and critical to my success, Rob and others believed in me.

"You are doing great. Now we just need ten others like you," he often would say.

How I had longed for such words since arriving in America!

Many large companies and quite a number of smaller ones, despite their sophistication, tended to be seduced by their technologies, forgetting that for the customer (or the customer's customer) there were only three cardinal principles: price, speed, and quality. If a company could provide a lower price, faster delivery, or higher quality, it likely would capture that market. But the engineers in charge of such companies often lacked the ability or experience to see things from the point of view of the single user alone in his or her office or home. In communications, innovators such as Cisco dominated the market because they understood this intuitively. Many companies focused on their immediate customer or distributor instead, to their detriment. I would later find this problem endemic in emerging economies, such as China, which tend to be behind the curve in branding strategies and dominated by senior managers with applied engineering backgrounds. The key was in understanding not just the wires in the lab but also the politics in the boardroom and the passion on the streets.

The ability to develop and steer a clear message to a particular target market was also fiendishly difficult to manage. Large companies are like island societies, dominated by consensual, meeting-driven interaction. It is a challenge to bring people to agree on a key message. However, once developed, the brand develops a single unifying image in the marketplace that can be electrifying and very rewarding. In my business career, I was to use these core principles again and again.

This was the peak of the nineties technology bubble. Before I left Nortel two years later as a senior manager, I had helped steer the optical group to three billion dollars' worth of business. I had published papers and given talks at conferences. I was at the height of my game.

My Emory MBA only helped.

Emory University's Executive MBA (EMBA) program was ranked number eight in the country by *Business Week* magazine. Once every other week I would spend two full days in classes with other students. Unlike typical MBA programs, these students already had several years' work experience, which kept the quality of discourse very high. Whether analyzing the role of foreign currency conversion in the Asian financial crisis, or illuminating the psychology of leaders and followers, or explaining the necessity of creative destruction in business cycles, the faculty was amazing. Unlike at Stanford, where the emphasis had been on what I could not do, here the mind was opened to a wealth of possibilities, ideas, and open discussion. I was no longer a horse with blinders, but a fly with 360-degree vision.

Emory also introduced me to Asia.

The EMBAs traveled to Indonesia, Malaysia, Singapore, and Thailand to research Asian business. Those two weeks were among the most rewarding and fateful trips I have ever taken.

The economies of these countries, and China, were growing at an astonishing rate. Western companies saw the Asian market as a key area of growth and investment. From the least-developed (Thailand) to the most advanced countries (Singapore), there were lessons to be learned. These ranged from the importance of networks based on families, friends, and other personal contacts (called *guanxi* networks) in such places as China, South Korea, and Japan, to the overall importance in the East of savings and thrift.

Life's major moments are about finding the places you love. When I stepped off the plane in Singapore and the hot sun beat down on my brow, I felt as though I had been born again. The business allure was tangential. What struck me most was the energy that surrounded me, the youth and bustle of the dirty streets, the lovely women, and the language that throbbed in a uniform staccato wherever I went. I fell in love with Asia almost immediately.

On our last night in one of the cities, I visited a popular nightclub down the street from our hotel. The music inside was thumping fast and furious. Twenty-somethings were milling about, drinking and dancing, their blurry outlines fading in and out of the blue strobe lights. I moved to the bar and pretended to be cool, though I felt a little out of place. I caught the eye of a young woman standing a few feet away.

She introduced herself as Sasha and brought her work friends over. "How did you find this place?" they asked. Indeed, I was the only black guy in a room full of Asians.

I was thrilled to be making friends on my first night there. I was an exotic of sorts, something out of the ordinary for them. They also seemed to sense I was single and a little lonely. It didn't seem like they were flirting, just being friendly.

Sasha and her friends were white-collar professionals working in marketing and sales for clubs and businesses in the city. After chatting a bit, they wrote down an address on a napkin and handed it to me. I promised I would join the party later that evening.

Sasha and her friends were at an apartment complex on the city outskirts. The high-rises loomed over the city like black totems studded with pinpoints of light that barely illuminated the quiet streets below. The moon hung high and luminous, drenching the sky above the city with a faint milky whiteness.

I eventually found the apartment. Most of the furniture of the two-roomer had been moved out and it was filled with people, none of whom I recognized, sitting on the floor or standing. There was a sweet, grassy odor in the air.

"How're you doing?" I said to some guys on the balcony. They shrugged and looked at me as though I were a dinosaur. I didn't care. Looking over the balcony rail, I saw the lights of the city stretch away far into the distance. Each light, I imagined, had a soul, a life, associated with it. There was a hunger in me that seemed to grow out of the people and this city, like a musical river of energy and sound that would welcome me—if I were courageous enough to jump inside. For a brief moment I felt that time had gone by so very fast, and life had left me behind.

"Want to try some grass?" I heard a voice say behind me. It was one of the young women I had met at the club. I had tried pot only once before, at Brown. Perhaps because I had only smoked a small quantity, I had wondered what the fuss was all about and decided the experience was overrated. However, I wanted friendship then, as I did now. I glanced at the men who had ignored me, turned to her and bravely said, "Sure."

She handed me what seemed like a cigarette and I took a few puffs. *Nothing special,* I thought.

"What's your name? I forgot!" she said.

I looked closely at her in the dim light of the room. She was much shorter than me. Her long black hair was clasped behind her neck. Her skin was too light to be indigenous, and I guessed she had Chinese ancestry. Her eyes were almond-shaped, deep and black. She tended to talk jerkily, like a hummingbird flaps its wings, with a nervous, febrile energy.

"Mark, and yours?"

"Amyris."

Smoke in hand, I wandered around the room, taking a puff or two. A warm feeling stole over me and I felt blissfully light-headed. I looked around; Amyris had disappeared.

I tried to engage the crowd but no one seemed too interested in chatting with a stranger.

All of a sudden I felt terribly lonely and walked out of the apartment into the cool night air of the gardens below. I heard a sound behind me.

"What's wrong?" It was Amyris. She had followed me out. Her face looked anxious.

"I don't know," I said. "I just feel really, really sad."

"I guess it's the weed," she answered. We sat down on the edge of a pool. I looked at her sitting beside me. Her eyes were bright and sparkling. Her eyelashes fluttered gently.

"What's America like?" she said.

"It's a great country. I have a home, a good job, and a nice car, but tonight ... tonight I feel ..."

To my astonishment, I started to cry. I could almost see myself crying and wondered what had come over me, even *who* I was.

"I want to be loved. I feel no one loves me," I confessed to her. A rush of raw feeling was flowing through me; I could control it but it felt so natural to just let go.

"Will you be my friend?" I asked.

"Sure." She smiled.

"Can I hold your hand?"

She let me. Hand in hand, we walked around the pool.

We talked for about an hour. It was easy because she was a stranger and I knew in all likelihood I would never see her again. After a few minutes I had calmed down and pulled myself together.

"I guess I'd better get back." I wiped the tears from my eyes, feeling somewhat ashamed.

She nodded understandingly. "I'll get someone to drive you back."

"I'd like to see you again sometime," I said.

"Let me get someone." I nodded and she walked away. I sat down on a curb and a few minutes later Amyris and Sasha rolled up in a small car.

"You had too much weed," Amyris said. "I don't think you're used to it." Sasha nodded sympathetically.

The next morning I remembered everything. Before I headed to the airport, I called Amyris.

"I lost it last night. Apologies."

"It's okay. It happens."

Then, after a moment, she said, "Your eyes told us the type of person you are." She suddenly added, "They were always looking around. I could see how you were interested in everything."

How could she be so open? I asked myself. Then again, I thought, *I* had been open with them. Maybe that was why.

I was reluctant to leave. There was something about Asia that was fresh and different. It was as though the people were welcoming the wide-eyed innocent, even if I was eccentric and not one of them.

I knew that I would be back in the East one day.

Back in America, I settled into a predictable routine: work, piano, business trips. Without some dramatic change my life would have continued this way for years. The seasons changed with predictable regularity and my life had a fixed pattern, but external events were about to have a dramatic impact on it.

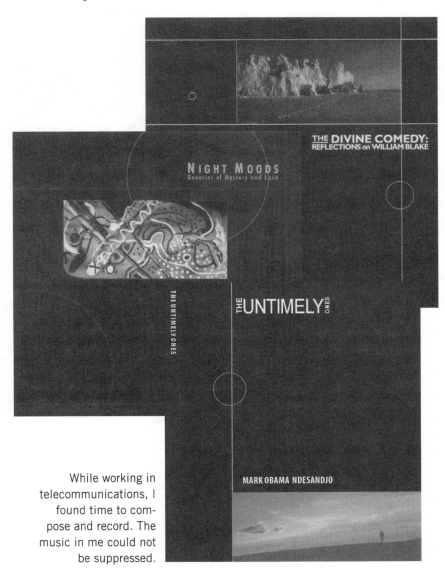

THE **DIVINE COMEDY:**
REFLECTIONS on WILLIAM BLAKE

NIGHT MOODS
Reveries of Mystery and Love

THE UNTIMELY ONES

THE UNTIMELY ONES

MARK OBAMA NDESANDJO

While working in telecommunications, I found time to compose and record. The music in me could not be suppressed.

For a while I was living the American dream, with a nice job, car, and house. I also loved the rush of taking extreme risks.

CHAPTER FIFTEEN

A War Begins: I Look to the East

MUSICAL EVOCATION

Piano Sonata Op. 23 "Appassionata": Ludwig van Beethoven

The LP was old and heavy and the sound scratchy, but the Russian pianist Svia-
toslav Richter's 1957 Sofia performance of this great piano sonata was mesmer-
izing. "The Appassionata" (lit. in an impassioned manner) was composed after
Beethoven had totally lost his hearing, and, like the great Eroica Symphony, was
a statement of independence, an emotional journey characterized by a powerful,
singular melody and forceful sense of line. I heard it first on a somber afternoon
long ago in St. Mary's High School. I had looked forward to lunch breaks, not
only as a reprieve from the rigors of study but also as an opportunity to escape to
Father Cormac's music collection. I would sit there for entire lunches, digesting
extraordinary recordings. For those sixty minutes, as the rest of the school played
outside and the birds sang their songs in the trees and teenagers scratched their
names on water tanks for posterity, I listened to Richter, Gilels, Kogan . . . and
marveled. The stereo system itself was a crude thing, boxed with tarnished wood,
old and antiquated, but with a halo of richness. The wood had a deep, mellow
odor that the room absorbed and dispersed like a rich, aged perfume. Carrying
decades of history, the speakers sat like solid burnished eyes that had seen numer-
ous spectacles evolve below the African sky. I seated myself before this repository
of things musical as one might before a shrine.

It was in this cool, sparsely furnished place that I heard Richter's live
recording. The first movement was amazing. The chords spoke as though from
the lips of the devil himself, and with such a sense of buttoned-up power and

divine fury. The last movement, in particular the coda, was a revelation. Those bruised, scraping chords seemed to touch and crack apart heaven's rafters. Some say that life is composed of long days and years punctuated by brief seconds of extreme ecstasy. For me that performance was such a moment.

"A PLANE HAS FLOWN INTO THE WORLD TRADE CENTER IN MANHATTAN. *There are reports of another crash in Washington, DC . . ."*

I remember listening to the car radio that September morning as I drove into work. It was a sunny, beautiful fall day in Orlando, Florida. As I listened, I remember looking at the blue sky and thinking: This must be a joke.

But it was no joke. Across the country thousands were dying. Two planes had crashed into the World Trade Center in New York, a third had plunged into the Pentagon, and another would soon crash and burn in a barren, windswept Pennsylvania field. At the end of that black day, almost three thousand Americans, including Muslims, Jews, Christians, and other innocents, lost their lives due to a conflict half a world away.

I looked at the other cars around me in the traffic. They looked so normal, tidily clustered together on a busy commute. The drivers' heads were barely visible through streaked glass windows, but their blurred profiles were sharply bent over consoles, imbued with a new tension. They, too, were listening and wondering why all hell had broken loose that Tuesday in America.

Back at the office, a small group of people were clustered around a television set hoisted into one of the open cubicle spaces. Their expressions mirrored the horror they felt at the sight of the smoking towers on the small screen.

"Kill those fuckers!" someone muttered.

I looked at his face, distorted by fear and anger. I looked out the window. It had been such a perfect day. Little did I know then that my life, and the lives of millions of others, would soon change. September 11, while a tragic day for so many, was also a catalyst to action for many more, myself included.

I had been surprised and shocked by the terrorist attacks. Yet, in retrospect, we should have seen it coming. For years many Americans were unaware of the global unpopularity of our foreign policy. We were like people stuck in steel boxes, with no windows but plenty of goodies like TVs and PlayStations inside to keep us distracted. Even my beloved grandmother reflected this cultural unawareness when she would visit us in Kenya.

"I love Kenya but the bananas always have spots on them," she complained. "In America our bananas are perfectly yellow."

In the hush of our office, I said, "This will change America. If we're not careful it will change us for the worse."

A female colleague looked up at me. She was the nicest person I knew at the office, always greeting people with that sweet, southern hospitality. She would smile in the prettiest way. If I was out of sugar for my tea, I could always borrow a cube or two from her. She had never raised her voice in the few months I had known her.

"What do you mean?" she said, her shocked face turned from the TV toward me.

"If we're not careful the government will not stop with the assholes who did this," I said. "They will use it as an excuse to become more powerful and restrict our freedoms."

"Who gives a shit!" she said. "Just let's get those bastards!"

Life would change for all of us because of 9/11. My colleague had changed almost immediately. I would change, too; after all, change was all around me. I had just left Nortel. Faced by a huge reorganization and no longer with my mentor, I had decided to accept another job. EPIK Communications, a small upstart optical services provider located in Orlando, had offered me an executive slot with a higher salary. I had left Georgia for Florida with some trepidation, and it was like landing on the moon in some respects.

Over the next few months, though, there would be an almost imperceptible shift in what it meant to live in America. Something had been lost, perhaps forever. It had to do with the fear, which was everywhere.

The casual optimism and hopefulness that had characterized this great country seemed to vanish or go into hibernation in some secret place.

I felt Americans were now committing a version of the seven deadly sins. They were at a crossroads that threatened their freedom and the sense of invincibility that had nurtured this great land for two hundred years. Patriotism now had become an excuse to spy on our neighbors, particularly those who were different, such as Muslims. Big Brother annexed the Internet, adopting it as its personal fiefdom, with electronic surveillance we would not realize the true extent of for more than a decade.

There would be perpetual war. Military spending would increase in perpetuum, exhausting domestic priorities and justified through alarmist talk of invisible enemies, defined by the US government and the military industrial complex.

There were the 2001 Crusades. We launched invectives against Islam, turning religion against religion, claiming religious neutrality on the one hand, while funding Christian programs and initiatives on the other.

There were the persecuted entrepreneurs. We were diminishing the freedom to invent and invest in new technologies in the face of the marriage of entrenched interests and government censorship. We were messing with the Constitution, passing draconian laws, trying to change even the Bill of Rights in the heat of panic.

Finally, there was a thirst for revenge, and even less understanding than before. We were treating the rest of the world as a victim of—or an instrument for—payback, not a platform for correcting the economic and educational inequities that foster terrorism.

Understandably, the economy went into a tailspin. The economic impact had dislocated EPIK and I was now out of work, quickly running out of money, and deeply in debt. I had choices to make, but I knew my future did not lie in Florida.

Around this time I had laser surgery on one of my eyes to correct my shortsightedness. I looked forward to the end of twenty-plus years of squinting and fumbling with spectacles, contact lenses, and saline solution and awkward fingers splayed across my eyes.

When I woke up the morning after the surgery, for the first time I could see in focus—the black TV, the lamp above my head keeping silent vigil, the shafts of morning light cutting through the cool air. I wondered if my new sight was a symbolic watershed, marking an enhanced outlook, something that would help awaken my spiritual side.

Now, like the Sphinx, I was rising into a new world. On the spur of the moment, I decided to get two tattoos, one on each of my upper arms, of the words γνωθη σαυτον (Know Thyself) as were once written above the entrance to Plato's Academy.

Were all these changes the beginning of a renaissance for me? I wondered.

I was sad, even depressed. As the months passed by, there was a sense of dwindling energy behind everything I did—whether at work or at home. I recalled how inspiration is said to vanish at the age of thirty. I was determined to escape this midlife oblivion. I had always been charging ahead, occupied with jobs and challenges. Now I felt I had failed. *Is this all there is?* I would ask myself.

I felt a growing angst. Often I would flee my house, repelled by its monotony and the mosquitoes and other small animals that seemed to maintain a virtual siege, barely restrained by tons of insecticide and netting. I would take long drives on Interstate 4, away from the cagelike houses whose wire gauze covered entire swimming pools for protection against alligators. In Florida's watery stew, we were all interlopers, and even at the beaches, sharks and fish festered in an uneasy balance with surfers and swimmers. Here rivers of life pulsed and died away, crossed and diverged, ever intersecting in time and space. I would drive for miles along the beach road without seeing any bathers, stopping to swim in the green water and occasionally renting a surfboard. For a brief while I could lose myself in the water and the beaches that were white and smooth as baking powder, or crispy with shell-like fragments that jingled like pennies beneath one's toes.

Flux was everywhere, and I was changing. I was seeking something, and the rush of danger partly filled that need. In my last few months in Florida, I went from swimming to wakeboarding to kitesurfing. Rick, my kiteboarding coach, was a man in his twenties, lean and brown, who prowled rather than walked. His speech patterns were rich with off-kilter words like *sweet kiting, youknowwhatIamsaying,* and *awesome.*

I remember a lesson I had the weekend before 9/11. While standing on the beach, a gust of wind snapped up the kite, and in an instant it was about a hundred feet above my head, barely visible behind the white-hot blast of the mid-afternoon sun, steel strings pulsing in the warm air currents from the Gulf of Mexico. It gently pulled me toward the water.

"Be careful!" Rick shouted at me. "The wire can cut a dude in half!"

My mind snapped back to attention just as another gust briefly lifted me into the air. It was a rush—the rush you get when you lose control, face death, and stay alive. My eyes, now restored, glanced over the gentle froth of the emerald waves. Flocks of birds darted in great, lofty streams like black fragments bursting through a shattered blue-and-white sky, oblivious to the people and buildings below.

I too wanted to fly, and whether it was up or down I did not seem to care. The freedom that came with exploring danger became more attractive. I decided to resume a sport I had tried a few years earlier but had not pursued: skydiving

I remember one Saturday morning it almost all ended for me. The drop zone was surrounded by a spotty array of flat white hangars stuck in nondescript backcountry, with a state trooper office as its only neighbor. Pretty young women were sunning themselves and intermittently staffing the office.

Bob, the jumpmaster, was all smiles as I suited up. Short and brawny, with a big handlebar mustache, he also owned the drop zone.

"We were pioneers in sky jumping. We invented a lot of techniques, like tandem, right here," he said proudly.

We jumped from 13,500 feet and flew through the air at 120 miles an hour.

As I exited the plane, I saw it veer diagonally away from me as I faced upwards. A deafening rush of air and the shock of weightlessness enveloped me. I forgot all distractions and experienced the marvelous rush of both flying and falling. The wind tore at my face and howled in an immense fortissimo. As I plummeted I keeled my arm rightward and tore away from the jumpmaster. When Bob passed me I saw the wind ripping at his cheeks, but he was still smiling.

Then a strange thing happened. I saw the ground, initially a cloudless mass, become distinct as it rushed toward me. Every instinct in my body was screaming at me to pull the cord but I didn't. A random thought went through my mind.

If I die, someone is going to fill out a lot of paperwork for the insurance company.

I had no fear. I wanted to hold off as long as possible. The air howled about my ears like the sound of an ascending 747. I was staring death in the face, but I felt so alive, so free.

Barely 4,000 feet above the ground, I steered my body to the left. I had been in free fall for at least forty seconds. I looked at the altimeter: 3,900 feet, past the danger point. I snapped myself back to attention and pulled the chute strap. It popped open without incident. I spiraled several turns at a mad pace and became delightfully vertiginous. I fell awkwardly onto the green grass, high-fived some other folks on the ground, and let out a whoop.

For a long time afterward, I wondered why I had not decided to open the chute earlier. Was my life so worthless that I could play with it this way? For so long I had been bouncing from job to job, just like from extreme sport to extreme sport, from opportunity to opportunity, directionless. Surely I was meant for more than this?

A few days later I found a tape of Grandmother playing the piano. It had been more than fifteen years since she died. The tape was a little black TDK with the words *Ida* scratched on a yellow label. The music was snippets of Joplin, Chopin, and Fats Waller, played with Ida's unique lightness and rhythmic awkwardness. The music broke forth like the sun through the blush of dawn. It was like the phrase from Rilke:

You must change your life.

I was now starting to look inward, and eastward.

I remembered that discussion with the nun in New Jersey from years earlier. I could hear her voice: "Don't forget us, Mark!"

I realized I had been given a rare freedom. I had a few months to reconsider my life, and I definitely did not want to go back to where I had come from. I was still not sure what I should be doing, but I knew I wanted to help others, to do something like that old nun in New Jersey. Fueled by a passion to do right, perhaps, through my music, I could also help atone for my many selfish acts in my life. Mostly, I wanted my heart to pound with a passion for doing what I loved.

The question was where to go. Then one day I knew.

To China.

I can come up with many reasons why I chose my new direction, but ultimately it was as though there was a voice in my head saying: *It's China, stupid.*

My friends and associates were somewhat mystified when I told them. It seemed out of character for me, they said. But I needed to leverage this angst and get away from the lethargy. I would start anew in a place far from America, far from Kenya. At first I seriously pondered shaving my head and walking across China.

"The toilets are unbelievable," someone told me. "Be prepared."

Others looked at me in alarm, knowing I was a vegetarian. "They eat all sorts of things back there, like snakes and scorpions. And you don't know what's in it!"

The idea of traveling across China in some ways intimidated me. I had a moment of envy and regret one day as I watched a beautiful Porsche dash across in front of me. *Was I up for this?* I admitted to myself that I was afraid of losing my possessions. I also had debts to pay, a mortgage. But I needed to break out of this cycle of boom and bust and turn my life around. I would no longer allow banks and corporations to dictate my life. Charity and culture would come first from now on, everything else would follow. A good friend who went to India to join an ashram had once told me: Follow your passions and you will succeed.

Similarly, China has a saying:

走自己的路让别人去说吧
Walk your own path and let others say what they will.

I had been postponing facing up to the things that really matter. I never had an adventure that committed me to immersing myself in poverty or totally accepting another culture. I was also aware of the dangers of traveling alone in a strange country. Perhaps my apparent courage sprang from innocence. I had never been in a life-threatening situation. Death, with the exception of David's passing, was a stranger to me. I still retained the optimism of youth and the invulnerability of the naive.

I wanted to lose myself in someplace new, to be reborn.

So I knew where I wanted to go, but how to manage it on limited funds? I tended to spend evenings at bookstores such as Borders reading and drinking coffee. On one visit, I was poring through the magazine section when I spotted a bright red periodical on a chair next to me. The word *abroad* attracted my attention. I came across an article that described foreign teachers living and working in China. Soon after, I was hired. I would be an English teacher on salary in Shenzhen, a mainland city close to Hong Kong. I would receive a small stipend, room and board, and, particularly important, instruction in Mandarin.

My real goal, however, was to set up a program in China to help orphans.

A desire to help children runs through my family. It started with Ida and her piano lessons. My mother had also run a kindergarten for many years. Even Granny Sarah Obama had begun an orphanage in Kogelo. Now it was my turn to help needy children. I had donated money and weekends before, but this was on a bigger scale—giving myself over to this goal and changing my life entirely.

I drafted a plan for a program called *Jiao Gei*, giving in Chinese. I would bring donations from Americans to help orphanages in China. I would also set up and direct musical events to raise money for disadvantaged children. I spent weeks making phone calls to Stanford and Brown alumni, and I even contacted the Gates Foundation. People were willing to give advice but no one was willing to provide funds or even a manageable process. The Gates Foundation seemed to be geared toward large corporations and trusts, not individual volunteers. In the end, it went nowhere.

In desperation I tried to drum up publicity and contributions. Before I left Orlando I contacted an *Orlando Sentinel* reporter who expressed doubts I would succeed. "You left EPIK. Why?" she asked. "That must have been quite a compensation package for you to retire on after only seven months."

Then, without a hiccup, she added. "About your orphan project. It's a good idea, but that's all it is."

Although I was dejected I would not let it stop me from going. Before I left for China, I sold my car and gave my most precious belongings to friends for safekeeping. The rest of my things, including my piano, I put in storage. It tore at my heart to leave that piano. It had been my best friend for many years. I ran my hand over its cool, smooth, lacquered brown finish one last time and wondered when, and if, I would see it again. I comforted myself with the thought that if things did not work out, I would soon be back. However, deep inside, I knew that I was changing fundamentally. My life was taking on a new, more hopeful, direction. I would soon be thousands of miles away. For how long, I had no clue. Little did I know that China would become my future and that, in the end, I would not change China. China would change me.

CHAPTER SIXTEEN

The Middle Kingdom: China*

MUSICAL EVOCATION

Liu Yang He (A Folk Tune)

This piano arrangement is a simple folk tune from the villages of Hunan in central China. It is elegant and poignant, and I loved it the moment I first heard it. In my China concert performances, many in the audience connected with this melody. I was surprised to find out later it had been popularized in the 1950s and '60s as a communist song that extolled the virtue of Chairman Mao. Without words, however, the music speaks a universal language free from ideology. In the process of learning it, I took the arrangement composed by Wang Jianzhong, arranged it again, and made it my own. Thus, through its many permutations, my artistic interpretation reflects the changes and allure of the Middle Kingdom, where my life would gain a fresh and moving perspective.

中

THE CHARACTER FOR CHINA, PRONOUNCED *ZHONG*, IS FORMED OF A GLOBE bisected by a vertical line, and since feudal times it's indicated that China was the middle of the world, and the Emperor was its divine representative.

To me, however, this character was not only artistically beautiful but also represented a place that would become the center of my universe, a home for many years. A place whose people and culture refreshed me, providing a platform on which I would re-evaluate my life.

---

* Names have been changed for reasons of privacy.

I flew into Hong Kong with some trepidation. From there I would cross the border into Shenzhen and finally be in communist China. I did not know what to expect.

Would I be allowed to watch TV or movies? Were there certain clothes I had to wear? Would the police spy on me? Would I be allowed to have Chinese girlfriends? To me it was a hazy place; for all I knew, everyone might be wearing green Mao jackets and jailing curious foreigners. I was entering an unknown universe.

"Shenzhen is a good city to live in," the director of the English Teaching program had told me before I left. "It is relatively warm all year around, is situated right next to Hong Kong, and Putonghua is the official government language. It is also an immigrant city, and you will be exposed to people from all over China."

His words were intended to comfort me, but I was ready for anything. After all, I had jumped from ten thousand feet and flipped wakeboards. I had driven jalopies in Kenyan traffic and faced lions so close my camera was out of focus. I had the confidence and naivete of youth, even if thirty-six wasn't that young.

Teaching English was not my principal reason for traveling to China. I had little interest in being a paid instructor. Although the job would help me understand a little of Shenzhen's bourgeois life, I knew I would keep it for a few months at most. Mostly, I wanted to work with orphans, learn the language, and do enough business to pay the bills.

After spending a night in Hong Kong, I crossed the border into Luo Hu, the famous crossing that has served as the entry point into China for millions of people.

After lugging my bags past the gruff border police, I entered what seemed like a cross between a massive concrete obstacle course and a car wash. Vehicles parked topsy-turvy next to the door; policemen, taxi drivers, and hundreds of travelers scrambled up and down endless ramps like a Chinese Escher drawing. Everywhere were posts, pillars, and soggy pools of rainwater. Shenzhen yawned around me like a hot, open mouth.

China had poured billions into its cities, infrastructure, and people. To walk the streets of its newest city, Shenzhen, just more than thirty years old, was to see a place that reached for the stars. The new conference center with its wavelike curves that washed colors of gold, white, and orange over the city at night, the gleaming subway that shot its metal bullets through the city's innards from dawn to late at night, the soaring banks and hospitals whose windows, like encrusted diamonds, sparkled in the electric air. It all said to the world: *Look at Me.*

In all of this gleaming metal and marble, rough stone and wet concrete and loam, clean linen clothes and ubiquitous cell phones, even in the filth and garbage that streamed from the shanty towns to the streams and in the hardscrabble canteens and worker dormitories that leached pain and desperation, there was still the unmistakable rush of hope and promise. There was the belief not only that to be rich was a glorious thing, but also that hard work would always be rewarded.

And there were no harder workers than the Chinese of Shenzhen, who often worked fourteen to fifteen hours a day, six days a week. They worked from four or five o'clock in the morning, when the sounds of cars and buses would slowly increase in intensity, to nine or even ten o'clock at night. From the Luo Hu Station with its brand-new passenger terminals to the Windows of the World theme parks, from Shennan Boulevard to Hong Li Road, from Futian District to Bao'An, they would stream forth in their daily pursuit for wealth. The murmur of a city wakening, galloping, and cantering would throb through high-rise windows and bedroom doors from morning through evening. China was loud, not occasionally loud, but persistently, abrasively, intimidatingly loud.

It would take me some time to understand this jumbled city. On my journey from the airport, I received my first lessons in Chinese curiosity and driving etiquette.

I had taken a red Jetta taxicab and was on my way to the hotel to meet with representatives of the Foreign Language School of Shenzhen.

"Where are you from?" The young, ruddy-faced taxi driver half turned in his seat to face me. I would soon learn that all taxi drivers tended to ask the same question.

I understood and answered in stilted Chinese. (I had mastered a few phrases.)

"America," I said.

"Thank you! How long have you been in China?"

I wondered why he was thanking me.

"Airport. Today!" I said after a long pause, trying to remember the words from my phrasebook.

"Shenzhen very clean. Very nice!" He nodded briskly, and his sudden burst of English was strongly accented.

"Everyplace else is completely disorganized!" he continued.

"Look out!" I interrupted him, almost shouting.

I saw a strange contraption moving up the single-lane highway toward us. The front was a hybrid motorcycle of sorts, and the rear was a wooden cart stacked several feet high with pieces of cardboard and other junk. Two people were sitting on the single seat. The driver's feet strained furiously against the pedals as he barreled toward us. Vehicles dashed by in the opposite direction, honking their horns in impotent rage.

"He's driving the wrong way!"

I don't remember if my Chinese was passable but it did not matter. The taxi-cab driver didn't look fazed at all but neatly zipped by the ramshackle contraption. His swarthy face peered at me in the rear-view mirror for a moment, then he shrugged and barked out, "No problem! Your Chinese is very good!" He gave me the thumbs up.

The cart peddler and our reaction, like so many incidents in China that seemed at first trivial and inconsequential, would grow to symbolize the complexities of modern China and its very newest city, *Shenzhen,* which literally means deep ditch. As we talked more I sensed the cab driver was proud of Shenzhen, even though his friends called it an immigrant city without culture, and many foreigner customers considered it an unremarkable stopover on the way to Shanghai or Hong Kong.

Its sleepy swamplands and villages had endured the dynasties of the Middle Kingdom. Qin faded into Han, Han into Tang, Tang to Song, Song into Ming, and then fast-forwarded though the Republic into Mao's China, or the New China. Through these thousands of years of revolutions and wars, Shenzhen's mangroves stood tall and silent, their burled trunks twisting through the mud like snakes endlessly chasing themselves.

China had changed dramatically in the thirty years since Paramount Leader Deng Xiao Ping, in the late 1970s, ushered in what became the *Gai Ge Kai Fang*, or the opening up of China. On one August day in 1982, he had stood on a Shenzhen ferry, looked out over the green hills of Lianhua Mountain and the quiet fishing villages on the river bank, and declared: "We will build a city here!"

Within months, the construction began.

Shenzhen became a bustling nexus of almost ten million people from all over the country. They came to seek their fortune, to get married, but most of all to be free from the social and economic constraints of their more traditional hometowns. Adjacent to the international port of Hong Kong, the new city was also a terminus for foreigners entering the mainland. They saw a trashy boomtown of polluted skies, criminals, prostitution, excessive development, and cutthroat capitalism. I, on the other hand, saw a thriving, rich, and culturally stimulating home.

Just months after Chairman Deng's speech, the words coined by German visitors in the early days, *Zeit ist Gelt*, became a credo of sorts, translated into the phrase:

时间是金钱，效率是生命
Time is money, efficiency is life.

This motto was erected at the foot of Weibo Hill in Shekou Industrial Zone in early 1982 and became synonymous with the young city, as did the motto "Shenzhen Speed." True to form, the Shenzhen International Trade Building was constructed in 1984, at the rate of three floors a day.

In Shenzhen, Porsches and BMWs crowded the streets next to wicker carts, and Buddhist monks strolled casually through upscale malls. Elderly people danced to Peking opera or practiced calligraphy and *taijiquan* (martial arts) on the sidewalks on Sunday mornings. Laborers chatted loudly in their hometown dialects while minibuses lurched over potholes and blared their horns across Hua Cheng Bai and Ai Hua Road. Beauties from Sichuan shielded their carefully tended alabaster skin from the sun under paper umbrellas. Businessmen from Wenzhou and Hang-zhou screamed into cell phones while hurling spitballs out the windows of their BMWs. Grandmothers liberally let the kids do their business on the bushes or over the drains, occasionally holding babies upside down to gently inspect their private parts.

On evenings, which were dedicated to lovers, couples promenaded hand in hand, in their Chinese slow walk, the meandering and eternal *liu da*. The attitudes and traditions of the immigrants that made Shen-zhen their home wrapped across the city like the skeins of a web, knitted together by the collective memories of five thousand years.

The taxi driver dropped me off at the Landmark Hotel. Shenzhen's Western-style structures were a thin veneer that could barely hide the face of this very Chinese city, despite the best efforts of its Hong Kong and Japa-nese developers. I entered the hotel's gold-trimmed doors. In the lobby, behind the smart new appointments, were the ever-present stares of the locals, observing and judging. A few minutes later, I was greeted by Amy Bell, the resident director of the English program, and her assistant Col-laneet. Amy was a portly woman in her forties, whose red hair loosely swept over a friendly, mobile face. She took seriously the Confucian dic-tum that gentlemen (and ladies) should know much but hold close their real thoughts and feelings. Amy, accordingly, was gregarious but revealed very little.

Collaneet was younger, dark-haired, and almost brooding in her quiet and methodical gestures, as though part of her was someplace distant. Both had put their American lives on hold until their Chinese adventure was over. They would be instrumental in helping me acclimatize to my new life, and I was grateful for that.

We took a taxi to the Foreign Language School, one of the oldest and most respected schools in the city. I looked out the taxi window to see noodle shops, tiny convenience stores, refuse-filled alleys, and vendors hawking massages and shouting "DVDs! DVDs! Movie, movie!" And everywhere there was the color red. Red signs, red clothes, red tassels, and red lanterns. Like a smoldering fire in the Chinese breast, red in all its dynastic and political significance was burned into the body politic, never to be extinguished. These days the ruby red of automobile lights and neon building signs reflected the glowing breath of the modern Chinese dragon.

Even though it was only yards from a busy thoroughfare and a large shopping district, the school retained an air of being set apart because of the huge trees spreading a leafy green canopy above it.

Inside its tall walls, a large central courtyard was bounded by six floors of classrooms and dormitories. Foreign teachers each had their own apartment. After lugging my suitcase into my simple studio, Amy introduced me to the Chinese teachers. As we passed the busy students who milled around us in their blue-and-white uniforms, a short, slender, middle-aged lady came up to us. She wore a dark, tight-fitting dress, and her black-rimmed spectacles revealed shrewd dark eyes. She held out her hand.

"You must be Mark. We are happy to have you."

"Mrs. Hu is one of our secondary-school teachers," Amy interjected. "One of the best!"

Mrs. Hu smiled. She spoke precise, clipped English. "Perhaps you can teach my class tomorrow afternoon? I would like to learn from you!"

"Sure," I said, flattered.

She smiled and walked off. Amy gave me a quizzical look. "You know what this is, don't you?"

"She is being nice, isn't she?" I asked. "Letting me teach her class a bit."

"You don't get it, Mark." Amy shook her head in bemusement. "They want to observe you!"

Thus I quickly learned that, as with all foreigners, I would be an object of mild fascination and constant observation. We foreigners were so different, in our habits and our looks, and an endless source of interest.

The class next day was filled with teenage students, each hunched over a desk as though painstakingly observing its wooden surface. Mrs. Hu and four or five other teachers and the headmaster were squeezed into the back of the room.

"My name is Mark Ndesandjo, and we are going to discuss some topics in English. First I would like to get to know you. I will ask you why

you want to learn English and what your goals are in life. Any volunteers?"
I began.

Some students looked up attentively, others shifted their eyes nervously between me and the teachers at the back. Several remained hunched over, peering closely at the grain of their desk. No one raised a hand, so I asked again.

The girls looked blankly at me. After a few seconds one girl raised her hand.

"My name is . . . I want to learn English because . . . to become more international."

I waited for more, but she just looked back at me expectantly from behind her large glasses.

The rest of the class was growing fidgety. I was losing them.

"Okay, forget the introduction. Instead we're going to play a game called I Spy." I figured this would be a fun way to ascertain the students' English level.

"The game goes like this: I spot something in the room and I tell you the first letter. For example, if I see a lamp, I say, 'I spy with my little eye something that begins with L.' Then you have a chance to guess what the thing is. If you guess right, you get a point and take a turn to choose."

"I spy with my little eye something beginning with T . . ." Hands shot up.

"Teacher!" a student cried.

"Right, your turn. You have to start with the phrase 'I spy with my little eye . . .'"

"I spy . . ." He paused. ". . . something beginning with B!"

Soon the classroom was buzzing with new words. Hands were shooting up, and once-surly faces were now eager.

"The students listen to you," Mrs. Hu said after class. "They pay attention."

"You passed," Amy whispered, and walked off to join Mrs. Hu. Someone tugged on my shirt. I looked around to see a short girl looking up at me.

"Yes?" I said.

"Do you think Chinese have small eyes?"

"What?" I was flabbergasted.

"Is that why you say 'with my little eye.' I don't like small eyes. They're ugly, yes?"

"Don't worry. That's not what I meant."

"Oh, I see!" The girl smiled with relief. "Then you should just say 'I Spy'!" She rushed away to rejoin her girlfriends. I was quickly learning that the Chinese were not just interested in me; they were interested in my observations too.

The English program had more than thirty foreign teachers flown in from the United States and assigned to district schools across Shenzhen's three major municipalities, Longgang, Bao'an, and Futian, where I worked. I received a basic monthly stipend and living accommodations. On Wednesday afternoons we had classes in elementary Chinese writing and speaking.

It was there that I discovered the beauty of Chinese characters. I was still a physicist at heart, and it's said such scientists are enamored of shapes. I was enthralled with following lines and curves with a pen, each sequence and pressure point based on thousands of years of tradition. Before long I hungered to learn more.

"Most people don't want to learn to write. The focus of this class is spoken Chinese and very rudimentary writing. Maybe you should take some more advanced classes," Mrs. Li, our Wednesday Chinese teacher, advised me.

She said it carefully, as if a little embarrassed. She spoke perfect English, and although she may have seemed a little shy, she was all business when it came to teaching. Our test papers were riddled with red marks, but mostly encouraging comments.

"Why not try Shenzhen University? They provide more advanced writing classes."

"Later, later!" I said. "This is all so fascinating!"

Besides attending class, I also learned from interactions with pupils and teachers over meals or during classroom breaks.

"These people are like the Internet," someone said to me. "Whatever you say ends up on the other side of town, almost instantly. There are no secrets here."

"When you can talk easily like Amy, ask for a cup of tea, or make small talk in someone's office, then you will be speaking true Chinese!" an official at the local education bureau told me.

One day I asked for rice at the cafeteria and some nearby students burst into giggles and suppressed laughter. A fellow teacher took me aside.

"When you say *mi fan* [rice] don't forget to accent the fan, otherwise people won't know what you're saying. Don't say *yao fan*. Say *yao che fan*. Otherwise, it can sound like a beggar whining or evoke strange images for the Chinese."

Foreigners were always on stage, and the old hands were acutely aware of this.

One day Amy came up to me in the corridor, looking flustered. "Be careful outside," she said. "There are newspaper reports about some foreign guy who has been groping women in buses."

"So? That happens in every city in the world!"

She gave me an icy stare. "In China it's different. You are a foreigner. It means all foreigners in Shenzhen are suspect. The Chinese are very sensitive, remember. When one of us looks bad, all of us look bad. Don't forget that."

I read the report in the *Shenzhen Daily*, the city's only English newspaper. The foreigner in question was deported after a few days, but Amy's agitated expression was a warning to me.

"You go through phases here," a British teacher told me wearily. "First you love China, and then you get tired of people looking at you and treating you like a pet. Then, finally, you start to hate it here and just want to go back home."

I never reached that level of frustration. I was immensely happy, privileged to be living in this fascinating place; the richness of its heritage had so much to do with that.

"China is not so much a country as a culture," an elderly lawyer who had lived there for almost thirty years once told me.

He was right. The language, art, and customs of China ran like a golden thread through the bumpy fabric of its war-scarred history. The written language, in particular, was perhaps the single most important element, binding together the various dialects of fifty-six ethnic groups and thousands of years of history.

That first week I arrived in Shenzhen, some old American contacts helped me link up with two young Chinese women who put me in touch with the government welfare organization in charge of orphanages.

The women also introduced me to interesting places in the city.

We visited parks and museums and even went on a day trip to Hong Kong. My hosts were gracious, never asking me for anything except that I tell them about the West and help improve their English. In this they were similar to many others I met in Shenzhen. When they asked the inevitable "Where are you from? Why did you come to China?" I would duly rattle off some answer having to do with the culture and business, but would go no further.

It was as though my real ambition was too fragile, and talking about it in detail would damage its potency and luster. How could I tell them that I was a foolish dreamer who was going where his heart told him to go? My decision to come to China had been instinctive, beyond words, prompted by guilt and hope. Like the Maasai tribe of Kenya, who regard photos with suspicion as traps of the spirit, I regarded the articulation of my true dreams as inappropriate and risky, something to be shared with only a few kindred spirits.

When I arrived in China, I thought with my education and experience it would be easy to line up a good job. How wrong I was. In fact, I was in for a rude awakening.

I walked into the lobby of Zhong Xin, China's second-largest telecom equipment company, shortly after I arrived in Shenzhen. Zhong Xin was a formidable competitor I remembered from my Lucent days. I was dressed in business-casual attire, confident I could land a job.

"I'm here to see the president, Mr. Liu," I said. The receptionist looked at me in surprise.

"Do you have an appointment?"

"No, but I called his assistant," I lied.

She whispered to some of her colleagues, rapidly and urgently, and then made a few phone calls. I knew that the chances of getting a meeting with the head of the company were slim, but I would at least get to talk to someone in charge. As my grandmother might have said, it was a gesture full of chutzpah.

A few minutes later three people came to meet me in the lobby, a man and two women. A middle-aged woman peered at me through her rimless spectacles and greeted me in English.

"I am Mrs. Liu, the head of marketing here. How can I help you?"

"Hi, I'm here to see the president. I have a proposal I wanted to share with him about how to improve marketing here."

"May we see it?" she asked.

I pulled out a proposal I had put together to revamp their website, as well as a copy of my CV.

"Mr. Liu is busy right now," she replied, looking eagerly at the manila folder, "but if you show us what you have put together we can discuss it."

The four of us walked into a conference room, and they silently leafed through the proposal.

"This is very impressive," Mrs. Liu's assistant said. Mrs. Liu just nodded and then excused herself from the room.

Taking the hint, I quickly replied, "I think there are many areas where I could help you. In fact, I am looking for work as a consultant . . ."

Mrs. Liu came back into the room.

"Let us arrange an interview with my colleagues for next week," she said. We parted cordially and they promised to get back to me.

On the day of my official interview, a short, quiet-spoken, lanky man greeted me. Mrs. Liu and seven other people were also present. We discussed telecommunications for about two hours.

"We think we can find a position for you," said Mr. Du, calling me after the interview. "I am going to America and need someone here to replace me."

I was overjoyed. Twenty centuries ago the scholar Judah ha-Nasi had declared "the brazen go to Purgatory." No matter. My chutzpah had succeeded.

"You can work with Mrs. Liu. She is responsible for overall marketing strategy here at Zhong Xin."

My next question was critical, but I voiced it without hesitation. "Mr. Du, how much is the salary?"

I needed to earn enough to maintain my house back in Orlando and figured that at least 24,000 renminbi (about $4,000) a month after taxes was the bare minimum.

"I think about eight thousand."

"Dollars or renminbi?"

"Renminbi." This was about $1,300. My heart sank.

"Is that per week?" I said desperately.

"Per month."

I was floored. That was barely more than I was making as a teacher. Granted, it was a job that would put me back in telecommunications, but wasn't I worth paying well?

I followed up with Mrs. Liu and asked her if I could work from home part of the time to pursue other things.

"You must come in every day," Mrs. Liu replied. "No flextime or working from home. It's how we work here. You will work for me." Her voice was polite, but it was clear what she wanted and what she would allow.

I would have no time to spend with the orphans or to develop my own business, let alone to study Chinese. I declined the offer, disappointed. Since arriving, I had seen how the Chinese worked. Often, results were less important than time spent on the job. A manager could be brilliant and finish his work in half the time of another, less efficient person, but the traditional boss would value him less. I believed my time was worth more, and I could not afford to end up exhausted each day. All that work spent in landing an interview, only to be treated like a factory-farmed chicken at the end.

Confident I could find better work, I wrote and mailed my CV to more than two thousand companies in China and America. Not one replied. I realized that my goal of landing a good corporate job in China would have to change. In fact, maybe this goal was not part of my dream, and it was not meant to be.

Meanwhile, I lived a modest life. For months I had to rely on my savings and barely made enough to pay my bills. Fortunately food, clothing, and rent were much less expensive than in America. As long as I kept my needs simple, I could be happy without making much money. I had no house to maintain, in time just a simple rented apartment. I used the bus or sometimes took taxis. I could get a decent cup of noodles with a good conversation in Chinese with the shop owner for about five kuai, or ninety cents.

I was an impatient teacher, and unorthodox in some of my teaching methods. Many of my experiences during my six months of teaching are recounted in *Nairobi to Shenzhen*. In one passage David, the protagonist, is teaching some third-graders:

He swung his legs onto his desk, stood up on the frail wood, and started dancing the mambo. He slowly gyrated his hips and made a swooning outward motion with his feet. He looked at the ceiling as if in reverie. The sea of blue and white before him turned silent, so suddenly he thought they had gone into shock. There was complete silence while he gyrated on the desk feet above the floor.

"Dancing!" He laughed.

The children just looked at him, mouths wide open. The smallest boy suddenly came up to him in a jerking motion, almost as though pulled by an invisible and wanton hand, and tugged at his trousers.

"No! No, teacher David! Don't do that!"

It was as though their teacher had committed a mortal offence. He had once again broken an unspoken code. For some reason he thought at that moment of a scene from the movie Bridge on the River Kwai where the English officer was talking to the Japanese camp commandant. It had been something about allowing officers to do manual labor with the enlisted men. "British officers don't do that sort of thing. It's just not done!" or something like that.

He was an officer in this Confucian system. The students were the enlisted men. They could do naughty, outlandish things. But he couldn't. This first day he had already learnt that the teacher occupies a special, almost revered, place among the Chinese. They are the high priests, schools are their temples, and students are disciples. He realized he had let his trousers down, metaphorically speaking, so he jumped back onto the floor. This time the students were quieter and more obedient. They did not know what to make of him.

I had also jumped on the table one afternoon and gotten the same reaction. I discovered what David had discovered. I was too poor a teacher to make sense of all this. To teach them well required a more experienced and skilled person. The words I'd had tattooed on my arm held special significance here. According to Chinese tradition, rather than Aristotle or Socrates it was Confucius, or Kong Zi as the Chinese called him, who had proclaimed:

自知之明
Know yourself.

I also felt these children in their well-appointed classrooms did not need me. They were sweet and polite when they wanted to be, but there was often something spoiled, even corrupt, about the process, as though learning was often just a ritual and foreigners were just hired help. The Chinese, indeed, have a word for a spoiled young child: 小皇帝 (*xiao huang di*), which means little emperor. A large number, though not all, of the children were noisy, disobedient, and completely uninterested in English. I quickly decided to leave my teaching job, continue Chinese classes at Shenzhen University, and focus on other opportunities, perhaps start a business.

One day I was late for class at the Foreign Language School.

"Mrs. He wants to see you, Mark. I think she is a little angry!"

I walked into the headmistress's office. It was an airy room, tidy and furnished with new chairs and desks. An oversized potted plant stood in one corner. Mrs. He, a middle-aged woman, sat at her desk. When she saw me her expression changed from one of concentration to irritation.

She was older than me, though her face still held vestiges of youth. An occasional rosy tinge to her cheeks, a sudden, arrogant, and impatient flash of her eyes, a few strands of hair that playfully escaped from her tight bun to fall over her eyes—all were slightly appealing hints of better days. Today, however, her lips were thin and hard, her poise rigid and angular, that of a person used to control, one who gives orders even at the expense of friendship or love.

"You were late . . . late!" she said. Her hands clutched the sides of the desk, as if for support.

I took a deep breath. I had thought long and carefully about what to say.

"Mrs. He," I said, "I'm leaving. I cannot continue with this job." She looked at me as though I was out of my mind.

"You cannot just leave! You have a schedule you must maintain."

"No, I'm sorry, I have no time. The schedule here does not give me the flexibility I need. There are other things I came to do in China. I cannot stay."

Her eyes were wide. I had uttered the unspeakable. I had said no. In China, this word has a magical force. In more genteel conversation, it is replaced by "Not convenient" or "I have something else I need to do," or some such euphemism. She pursed her lips tightly, her white knuckles visible against the dark table, and glared at me.

"You Americans! You are . . . you are . . . so lazy!"

I could have told her that I spent four hours a day studying her language, that another two hours were spent looking for jobs, and the rest teaching, practicing piano, and writing. But she would have no doubt just continued on about how "you people" are just interested in an easy life. How I was soft, and thus I could not work there.

I stood and walked out of her office. I didn't look back.

━──◆──━

I had already been in China six months and had started thinking about setting up a marketing consulting business. I had seen the terrible English featured on storefronts and in advertisements all over Shenzhen. From my business background and education, I could understand the huge problems that Chinese companies faced in trying to trade with the West, foremost being the poor quality of their English communication. How could they expect to be professional if their English seemed to be written by a nine-year-old? Everywhere I looked in Shenzhen the English was atrocious.

The slogans on T-shirts were just one example of this. I was on a tour bus and noticed a teenager who clearly didn't speak a word of English. She wore a blue T-shirt with bright red letters reading: Fuck Me Please. When I told her as politely as I could what this meant, she just laughed and continued to wear it. Maybe she thought that no one there except me would understand what it meant.

If the population couldn't follow basic English, I could only imagine how mysterious the complexities of branding and strategic marketing must be to them. I suggested to a friend that we set up a company to provide both professional English marketing and business and sales consulting.

To my astonishment, a few days later my friend David came back to me and said, "Okay, Mark, we're setting up an office in downtown Shenzhen. We'll be ready to start in a few days."

I provided some investment funds and was soon registered for a work permit. My new company, World Nexus, landed its first contract in a matter of days. Before long we had a score of reputable customers. We focused on services such as website design, advertising, and marketing communications. The company would grow slowly but steadily.

However, my modest income from World Nexus could definitely not support my Florida house payments. I rented out my home and tried to get mortgage reductions, but the banks were not interested. My credit record, perfect for ten years, was now in tatters. Desperate, I finally reached someone at the bank via phone from China.

"I cannot sell the house. I have renters, but I need to find a way to lower the payments. I should be able to catch up in a few months," I explained.

"Why are you telling us this now?" the rep asked. "You should have paid on time."

"Before I left the United States I tried to arrange a fast sale, and I called your bank for approval. No one got back to me although I made several attempts to reach you. I lost my job and that's why I am in difficulty. What can I do?"

I spent a long time on the phone to no avail. After being put on hold for more than an hour, I slammed the phone down in disgust. Finally, a few days later, I got hold of a representative.

"Well, we do not lower payments," he said, "but don't worry. Just make the missed payment next month."

"But that's the point. I need to find a way to lower the payments, at least temporarily."

"We do not lower payments."

"Don't you have some sort of program to help homeowners? My credit has always been very good. In ten years of owning homes, I never missed a payment," I pleaded.

"No. Is there anything else I can help you with today?" he asked in a singsongy tone.

I then realized the banks and credit-card companies all had the same attitude about their customers: They didn't care. To them I was just an inconvenient statistic. I maxed out my credit cards, defaulted on the mortgage, and realized the bank would foreclose on the house.

I made a fateful decision. Although I had started to change my life, I'd quickly discovered that I was still in a prison of sorts: debt. I refused to be a slave to the banks and credit-card companies any longer. I would pay them their money, but in my own time, and not at the expense of the new direction my life was taking. As it turned out it would be years before I could start to do that.

Even as I lost my house to the bank, I found another reason to stay in China.

I had fallen in love.

It was almost as if someone from *Dreams of Red Mansions* was uttering the famous phrase:

乐极生悲, 苦尽甘来
Great sadness follows happiness, and great happiness follows sadness.

— ❦ —

Every afternoon I was not teaching or working I would go to cafes and teahouses to learn Chinese. I would carry books and notes and spend hours writing and memorizing characters and phrases. One day I visited a teahouse near my apartment. I enjoyed spending afternoons there. In the center of the lounge was a fountain whose sound merged with the gentle relaxing music of a classical stringed instrument called the erhu.

"What are you reading?" The voice came from behind me. I looked around. It was a woman I had never seen before. From her clothes I gathered she worked there. She was much shorter than me, her lithe body slender and graceful. What attracted me most was her skin. It was pale and very smooth, unlike the darker-skinned Chinese around her. Her elegant profile and the contrast between her light skin and long black hair made her look like a beautiful idol from a 1930s silent movie. Her eyes looked at me with a mixture of curiosity and hesitation.

"Chinese!" I laughed.

"Here, your characters are all wrong. Let me show you." She primly sat down beside me. With a gentle smile she leaned over and wrote down the character in question.

"What's your name?" I asked.

"Xue Hua," she said. It was pronounced SHWAY WA. "Like snow," she added.

I knew that *hua* was the word for flower. In my mind I saw a snow flower, and then it was easy to remember her name.

I began going to the teahouse more frequently. Because the items on the menu were quite expensive and I was very thrifty, every time I went I ordered the least expensive tea or a simple meal for about fifteen renminbi (about two US dollars). On slow afternoons I would walk to the teahouse and study Chinese with Xue Hua, after eating a meal, which she prepared.

The other teahouse staff were friendly, but I could sometimes hear their whispers.

"The foreigner is so strange. Xue Hua gave him some Molly Hua tea and he *ate* the flowers. Foreigners think they should eat everything!"

Once, less charitably, someone said: "He is so black . . . and ugly . . . Look out!"

I didn't care. Xue Hua was different, she was comfortable around me, and I around her.

Then, one day, things began changing. When I walked in, Xue Hua had a frown on her face. She tried to act unconcerned, but I asked her what was wrong.

"The new price is twenty kuai," she told me, frowning. "The owner says that the price is too low and we need to charge you more."

The owner of the teahouse, a young lady who always gracefully crossed her legs, smiled graciously, and could see a foreigner from a mile away, was polite but firm with me.

"I'm sorry, but we must meet our overheads." She flashed her white teeth in an almost-smile.

I disliked the woman's penny-pinching and visited less frequently. A few weeks later my cell phone buzzed. It was Xue Hua.

"Where are you? When are you coming to eat?" she asked.

"I don't like your boss," I said. She didn't reply. In the ensuing silence I had an idea. "Let's go for a bicycle ride."

I still have a photo of that ride we took to the Xiang Mi lakeshore, just a few miles from my apartment. She sat on the back of my bicycle, as young lovers in China do. We sat on the pier and splashed our feet in the water. In a photo from that day, her foot is next to mine, her toe splayed out. She could wiggle it at will and I would laugh because it looked like a big radish. Heading back as the sun set and a red glow seemed to burn up Lianhua Mountain, the feeling of her hands around my waist made me forget about classes, work, banks, and making ends meet. Everything. At that moment I realized I was falling in love.

I invited Xue Hua to my apartment one day and gave her a special gift I had made for her. I took a bowl of water and handed her a red rose.

"What? Why are you giving me this?"

"Look closely." I smiled at her.

"My goodness!" She looked more closely. I had written *Mark and XH* on each petal.

"Now pick them up and drop them in the water," I said.

We dropped the petals and saw them float against each other in the glass bowl.

Xue Hua didn't say anything, but I saw from her eyes that she was moved. It did not take much to make her happy, though she did have moody spells.

Soon we were dating. I learned that she had recently come to Shenzhen from Henan and had taken the teahouse job temporarily until she could get better work. Her parents were farmers and she had been raised in poverty. Like many migrants to Shenzhen, she had a dream of living a better life than her mother and father. She wanted to do something in sales and to set up her own business.

Around August 2002, a few months after I had decided to leave the teaching program and set up World Nexus, I was working and happy. The money I received was meager but at least with two partners doing much of the day-to-day work, I was able to divide my time to please myself, allowing me to still learn Chinese and help at the orphanage.

As I continued to live and work in Shenzhen, I felt as though my carefully laid plans for earning money and pursuing a corporate career were now vastly unimportant. All my ideas of getting a high-paying job had come to naught. I could have gone back to corporate life in America, but it would have meant leaving the orphans and possibly Xue Hua, who even at that early stage I knew would not have been happy in America. I well remembered my own unhappiness when I had left Kenya for America.

I recalled the time when my grandmother visited and wanted to bring one of our Kenyan domestics back to America, to help her around the house.

"Ruthie, I can give her a good salary and a place to stay. All she would need to do is help me around the house. How much I want someone to help me around the house! Sweeping the leaves from the path every morning . . . oy, what a chore!"

Juliana, our ayah, on hearing the proposal, was ecstatic. "*Kwenda amerika mzuri sana!*" [It will be great to go to America.] But my mother quickly talked Grandma out of the idea.

"Ma, she wouldn't be happy there. She would be away from her people and it would be a huge shock to her. You should consider these things!" she gently chided.

"Maybe you're right, Ruthie," Ida eventually conceded. That was that.

I loved Xue Hua and knew she, too, had strong ties to her family and to China. I didn't expect her family to welcome me with open arms, but it was still a shock to hear Xue Hua describe her mother's reaction on first hearing about me. She was horrified to learn her daughter was dating a foreigner.

"You will leave me and go away with him!" she cried. "My grandchildren will not be in China to live with me. I will lose my daughter!" Xue Hua was distraught after that phone call, her eyes red and face flushed.

I did not know what to say. I had enough trouble dealing with my own family, let alone hers. For now Xue Hua and I had each other.

At times, particularly at night in that dream state between wakefulness and sleep, I had strange thoughts, the pictures in my mind encompassing images of my youth in Kenya and my present life in China. I felt that I was in a space that was mine to mold into whatever shape I pleased, with no obligation to my mother, my father, my friends, or even that long-departed-but-ever-present kindred spirit, my grandmother. I could imagine having a dialogue with Ida.

"I've found this terrific girl, Grandma. And I did it myself, with no matchmaker."

"Oy, don't tell me you fell in love with some schmuck who doesn't value you? Young girls these days. They let themselves be treated like toilets. A man comes along, does his thing, and then forgets to clean up!"

"Grandma, how can you say that? If so, it's the guy's fault! It wouldn't be my fault, would it?"

"*Oy vay iz mir!* Of course not. It's always the women's fault. We use men, and then look at the consequences. Here, I have some leftover borscht. Want some? I even have a little gefilte fish that Mary brought me the other day. If you don't like that, we can head to the shop down the road and get a corned beef or pastrami sandwich!"

"Grandma, I think I'm going to marry this girl!"

In my dream, she would come up to me, gently put aside her bowl of red borscht, and look at me so closely I could smell the baby powder on her cheeks and the faint scent of age.

"Well, if you love her . . . that's the important thing. If she has a little chutzpah and cooks you good food, that's something. Is she blonde?"

"No, her hair is black. She's Chinese."

"Doesn't matter." Grandma would give a long sigh. "All the world is going to be brown one day. Just love her, and all will be well. Here, have some matzo balls. Oh, I forgot, you don't like them either!"

And her kind face and wispy strands of ashen hair would fade back into the night, at one with my dreams and the breeze from the South China Sea.

Practicing the ancient art of calligraphy. Here I am writing a Tang dynasty poem at a friend's home. c. 2012

Art Builds Bridges. The proceeds of the sale went to help schoolchildren in Guangdong. c. 2012

Shortly after I arrived in China I met my wife, Xue Hua. We fell in love, and she was a fundamental force in helping me confront my past again. This photo was taken on a trip to Italy. c. 2004

Xue Hua and me admiring the scenery on a trip to the Great Wall. c. 2004

CHAPTER SEVENTEEN

The Orphans and a Cup of Water

MUSICAL EVOCATION

"Vipers Drag": Fats Waller

"Again, dear! I want the neighbors to hear it!"

I remember Ida opened the door to the yard when I played this piece on her Baldwin long, long ago. Forgotten images once again congeal out of the pale smoke of memory: a corpulent blind, black composer playing so fast and hard that the strings break; Ida's laugh when I told her Vipers Drag means smoking marijuana; the faint sense of repulsion when my classically trained ears first heard this piece; and my grandmother's sharp blue eyes, brimming with love and pride. This music has always been about stepping into the unknown, taking risks with a passion. Giving back to the kids was like the stride tempo in my left hand, an ineluctable duty, reliable and persistent, but above all, the sign of a heart pounding within the fogginess of China.

THE SONG DYNASTY DEVELOPED A PHRASE, WELL KNOWN AMONG THE Chinese, which could have fit in Dickensian London as well:

个人自扫门前雪, 莫管他人瓦上霜
Let each person sweep the snow from his own doorstep, and ignore the frost that falls on others' tiles.

Yet, speaking now from twelve-plus years of personal experience, I had known many instances of Chinese warmth and extraordinary graciousness. At worst they were indifferent to me, which was okay, as I was reasonably independent. Yet, because I was a foreigner living in China, for a long time I was not sure about how far civil society among the Chinese, not just between Chinese and foreigners, had developed.

Then, on a balmy summer day in 2008, the Wenchuan earthquake shook China to the core. In a matter of hours, almost ninety thousand people died; millions were left homeless and injured. As if a core of emotion had burst open, normal Chinese citizens spontaneously donated time and money to help complete strangers in Sichuan Province, thousands of miles from their own homes. This was the moment Chinese bigheartedness came into its own.

In Wenchuan, for the first time in a long while, on a massive scale, millions of Chinese spontaneously chose to help strangers in need. The world saw it, too, and was pleasantly surprised.

Although the scenes of generosity that surprised the world were a novel experience for many abroad, they were an outward confirmation of what I had known for many years: The inner goodness of the Chinese was always there—and it didn't need an earthquake to reveal it. I had seen this firsthand at the Shenzhen Welfare Center.

On my first visit to the orphanage in the Meilin District that autumn day in 2002, I got lost. My friend Alicia, a young woman who also had wanted to do volunteer work (even while employed in a backbreaking job), couldn't make it that day. She ended up giving my taxi driver directions over my mobile phone.

Twenty minutes later, I was in front of the orphanage. The grim building stood like a fortress behind huge, dusty trees, surrounded by gray office buildings and depressing apartment blocks. I walked in through the steel doors and was greeted by a young woman with a broad smile.

"Hello, I am Miss Ma. You are here to teach piano, yes?" she said gaily.

I nodded, smiling broadly.

"Come with me to meet the children."

On the second floor, a classroom was crowded with fourteen children aged six to eight decked out in their Sunday best and standing next to an upright piano.

"Hi!" I said and waved my hand.

"Hello!"

The roar they gave was like an express train. Startled, I almost dropped my bag. I instinctively moved toward the piano and sat down. I beckoned to a little girl sitting in the front row. She was swathed in a huge parka even though it was sweltering outside and there was no air conditioner. Her head was turned up sharply and her wide eyes looked at me expectantly, her mouth half open and hands resting on her crossed legs.

"You want to try to play piano?" I asked her.

She hesitated, as if not understanding. A nanny chided her gently and nudged her toward me. I lifted her up on to my lap. She was as light as a feather.

"Here, you hold your hand this way!" I said in halting Chinese.

I placed her hand on the middle C and pushed down. As if on cue, other children stood up and gathered around the piano. Soon it was quite crowded. Some tried to push away the girl, but she was now determined to stay on my lap. Not knowing what else to do, I decided to play a Chopin impromptu.

There was only one problem. The little girl did not want to leave my lap. She continued to look up at me with those expectant eyes. After much coaxing she retook her seat. I awkwardly played the Chopin.

Back in the United States, during my work at Nortel and Lucent, I had comfortably given talks on stage to hundreds at a time, but there was something intimidating about looking at a dozen expectant young faces. When I finished playing, everyone clapped politely. I gave lots of hugs and high-fives.

I wanted to see more.

"Can I see the babies?" I asked.

"Of course!" Miss Ma responded.

"Good-bye!" I said, waving to the kids.

"Good-bye!" the class roared back.

When I stepped into a large room on the fourth floor, I was overwhelmed by the sudden calm. It reminded me of those nights long ago in Kenya when everything, even the bright moon shining through the window grille, seemed to be shrouded in silence. Yet in this place it seemed inappropriate. There were about sixty cots arranged in neat rows, each holding a baby. Cylindrical neon lights overhead harshly illuminated the green-and-white room, and occasionally they buzzed as if to rouse the unnaturally quiet inhabitants below.

"Do they stay here all day?" I asked. One of the ladies nodded. I remembered what my mother had told me about children long ago: "They need stimulation. Their minds are like blank pieces of paper. They are always absorbing what is around them. That's how they learn."

I walked over to one of the cots. A baby's rubicund face looked up at me. It looked sad. I grasped his hand instinctively.

"How are you, little guy?"

His big black eyes looked back at me, refusing to let go of my little finger. At that moment the child and I were not thinking of America or China, capitalists and communists. Nor were we thinking of black and white, or yellow and brown. Our connection was something like music, beyond words, at its core about being human. I gently pulled my hand away.

"Is there anything you need that I can buy you?" I asked Mr. Wu, one of the teachers.

"Some DVD players would be nice, for the children to watch movies, as well as baby food, and ceiling fans when it gets hot," he said.

Before I had left the States, some of my EMBA buddies at Emory had helped gather donations. I sold my piano CD, *Night Moods*, which I had stacked in my house and raised a little money to buy items for the orphanage when I arrived in China.

One of the first signs I recognized when I was driven into Shenzhen was that of a major American company. I believed that many such companies would gladly make contributions to the orphanage, especially this one. I called up the general manager, fully expecting him to make contributions in kind. A deep Midwestern baritone answered my call.

"I'm Jack, how can I help you?"

I explained that I had just arrived from the United States, planned to make a small donation to the orphanage, and hoped his company could do so in kind. I had had no luck drumming up corporate contributions from foundations and companies back in the States, but in China it should be different, I thought. After all, we were Americans, and we wanted to make a good impression.

"Actually, let me have you talk with Mr. Chen. He handles such matters."

I sensed an imminent brush-off.

"Well, perhaps you can explain to him first?" I suggested, not wanting him to just pawn me off on someone else.

"Sure." After a few minutes on hold, another voice came on the line, this time speaking in somewhat-halting English. We exchanged a few pleasantries.

"We really don't give out things," he suddenly said. "We cannot help you, I'm afraid." Then, as if to be more courteous, Mr. Chen quickly added, "But if you want to buy the DVD players from us, we can help arrange the logistics."

Logistics? What logistics? I thought. It's just two DVD players. Disgusted, I thanked him for his time and hung up. I was particularly disappointed because this company was seen by locals as typically American, and its power and reach represented the United States, for better or for worse. To this day I remember a comment made by a fellow Chinese teacher:

"I used to work there. I thought it was good to work for an American multinational. But they worked us very hard, for very little pay. I had no time for my family. Very hard."

I called my business friend, David, who had a car, and though I felt I was giving money to a robber baron, we went to the company's store because it had the lowest prices and bought two DVD players. The orphanage director was delighted with the gifts and gave me and David a little plaque I have kept to this day. My help wasn't much, but it was a start.

I began to go to the orphanage regularly. Most every Saturday I would hop on the clattering green minibuses that bumped, squealed, and careened over the busy residential streets from Futian District to the relatively deserted junction in Meilin, where I would hop off.

I would walk past the Toyota dealership with the huge mangrove tree that still loomed over the entrance, its bark cloudy from the dust of passing cars.

I would pass mom-and-pop grocery stores whose black cavelike openings revealed pots and pans and household wares, cigarettes, and freezers filled with ice-cream bars and cold drinks. Middle-aged men would lounge against doorjambs, clutching flaccid cigarettes and sometimes casually rubbing ample, exposed bellies.

I would cross the impossibly high and ugly overpass over the clusters of honking cars,and descend the other side into the quiet street lined with huge trees. Occasionally, the wind would rattle the awnings of a nearby Muslim restaurant.

At my first lesson, five students and a teacher clustered around the piano.

"Here, have some water." The youngest student, a beautiful girl with long black hair caught up in a simple pink plastic barrette, handed me a small paper cup.

Because I was already starting to play, I just nodded as the teacher took the cup and placed it on top of the piano. From then on, there would always be a cup of water for me at every lesson.

In China it is considered polite to offer a guest something to drink. For the well-off, it is tea. In humbler households, it is water. Always, the cup is offered with a smile. The tea or water is often not consumed but lies on the table like a silent souvenir, a flower of friendship.

One day, perhaps because I played the piano too hard, the cup tipped over and spilled on the keys.

"Dui Buqi!" I apologized. Everyone laughed good-naturedly, and the lesson continued. However, after that I stopped getting my cups of water. Eventually I forgot about this ritual.

I had almost a dozen students those first few years, ranging in age from five to eight. There was Luo Ming, the beautiful little girl who always dressed herself in rouge and makeup, and who refused to eat the apple pie I once gave her until she was alone after class. There was Fu Xin, the tall lanky teenager who quietly practiced the Bach Inventions and never voiced the frustration he must have felt playing these challenging pieces.

I particularly remember the little eight-year-old boy with tousled hair and huge hands that produced beautiful sounds. I do not even remember his name but will never forget the sweet smile on his face and the way he bent prayerlike over the keyboard. He didn't say much, until he started to play. I taught him only a handful of times, over the space of a few weeks. Each time he would pore over the keyboard, as if searching for an answer to a question or riddle. Seconds later, he would arrange his hands over the keys, toss back his hair, and play the piece perfectly. Then a slow smile would spread across his face. It was gentle, pure, and unaffected, the celebration of a eureka moment.

One day, as I walked through the orphanage gate for another lesson, the boy was nowhere to be found. I assumed that he had a class or perhaps did not feel well, for he always looked sickly to me. After a few weeks without seeing him, I questioned one of the teachers. She looked at me with a puzzled expression.

"Oh, you didn't know? He had to go to America for an operation. He didn't make it."

"He died?" I said, shocked. I wanted to make sure I understood what she was saying. She nodded.

He didn't make it. The words pounded in my mind. He had been so sensitive, so gentle. Now he was no longer with us. So fast. So sudden. And I could not even remember his name. How many nameless children were there out there who would pass through my life briefly, to be instantly forgotten? I remembered his spadelike hands, gangly and knotted, yet beautiful instruments of sound. His shy, bittersweet smile still lingers in my mind. That day I felt as though someone had punched a hole through my stomach.

And then there was the story of Bao, my orphan student.

"I have something to tell you, Mark," Bao said to me once before a piano lesson. I had been teaching him for six years.

That day he seemed more diffident and reserved than usual. I could see his brow wrinkle as he carefully selected his words. Little did he know that words are like feelings, they can be controlled only so far, particularly when they must express a story like his.

"My mother died last week." He paused, as if to draw breath. "It was right before the dragon boat festival."

Bao's mother had adopted him after finding him in a latrine, abandoned by his natural mother. I remembered she had been very sick recently and that Bao had been worrying about what to do. Now she was gone. She had left this boy and the district of Longgang, China, for another place, another world

He had sometimes mentioned her to me in passing. I had long wanted to know more about this mysterious woman who had brought him to the orphanage more than a dozen years ago, but I had never probed deeply.

I sat down. He did too. Evening was drawing in, and the room was already a little darker than when he had entered.

"Was it painful for her? How did it happen?" I asked.

"She died in her sleep. I don't think it was painful. We took her body to her burial place. We were about eighty to one hundred people. She had so many people who loved her. . . ."

I nodded, forced myself to be quiet and just listen.

"Look!" He showed me a photo. It was a black-and-white, fuzzy shot of a woman holding a baby, with a second woman standing beside them. The grainy quality of the photo looked like that of newsprint. Indeed, the two-by-three-inch print was cut from a newspaper, laminated with plastic.

"I've had this for almost twenty years. That's me," said Bao, pointing to the baby.

The woman holding him was in her thirties. Her tousled black hair swirled about her smiling face like a small tornado. She had thin lips and a broken tooth, but nothing could detract from the happiness on her face. The baby had a high forehead and a bewildered gaze. What looked like a blemish on the photograph was a large gash on Bao's lip. His small patch of curly hair waved in the breeze. The other woman was in profile, standing off to the side, looking at the two of them.

"This was a newspaper article written days after she found me. I had been placed in a box beside the refuse in the latrine. There were about four hong bao [red envelopes] in the box with me, with about ten kuai [about two US dollars] in them. She told me: 'You were smaller than a cup.' They couldn't believe I was still alive. I had a cleft lip and was very sick with fever."

Bao handed me a small object. "She gave me this before she died," he said.

It was a jade disk, about an inch in diameter with a hole in the center. Other than a smudge of green, it was perfectly white.

"She gave it to me . . ." His face was composed but his voice trailed away.

"You were a lovely baby," I said, looking at the photo.

"I had a terrible fever and they took me to the hospital. The whole village came when she found me, including the village chief. The hospital took one look at me and said my fever was too high, they couldn't save me. But my mother took me home and used a special acupuncture needle. She poked me in many places to control the fever. Look."

Bao pulled up his shirt and showed me his thin, white stomach. Curving across his skin like the fins of a submerged dragon, I saw about six or seven small lumpy scars, each about an inch long.

"This is what she did. It saved my life. Even the hospital did not know what she knew. In the village they have their own ways to treat illness. Later, she took me to the hospital and they gave me an operation for my lip."

"Why did your natural mother leave you?"

"Because of my cleft lip. I would always be ugly to her," he said matter-of-factly. I couldn't tell if he was ashamed or sad.

We were silent for several seconds. I could hear the children preparing for dinner. I looked out the window into the gloaming. Not long ago, it had been easy to open them and let in some air when it became too hot. Now bars had been installed on the window frame. They gleamed like chrome on a new car. I saw Bao's face reflected in the metal. It was a little more pensive, and moisture glistened in his eyes.

"When I was three she brought me here to the Welfare Center," he said. "I had six brothers and sisters, so financially it was very difficult for my father and mother. 'I wanted you to get a good schooling,' she told me.

She was right. If I had stayed I would never have gotten the schooling I received in Shenzhen, and there was so much I would not have known."

I nodded.

"You know, the government gave them two hundred renminbi (about $32) per month in baby milk powder."

"Why did she decide to take you in? What was the biggest reason?" I asked.

"It was because it was the right thing to do. She couldn't understand how someone could leave behind a baby. She loved me. She told me that she was crying so hard when she came to Shenzhen, she didn't want to give me to these strangers, but she felt she had to. You know, Mark, she saved my life and now I want to help others, because she helped me."

I hugged him. I had never hugged Bao that way before. It had always been a high-five or a light embrace. I held him—tightly. I looked at the teenager who had lived in this place for more than seventeen years. Seeing the tears in his eyes, I found it hard to speak.

"She gave you her love, unconditionally. And she didn't ask for anything back," I said, my voice almost breaking. "This is what a good person does. She was your true mother, and she will always be around you."

He nodded.

"The second thing is that I have decided to join a company," Bao said, and he went on to describe a new venture he was joining, to provide management training to companies in Shenzhen. We talked for a few minutes more, and then we began our piano lesson. This time he played the Chopin Andante spianato from beginning to end, better than I had ever heard him play.

Yet the music that day seemed peripheral, as did his talk of business.

I was proud of Bao. He represented a China that combines grace and charity, culture and self-awareness. He was finding his way, and perhaps I had helped a little.

The students' and teachers' attitudes toward me changed over the years I visited the orphanage. The fine clothes and party hats of the first few days eventually vanished, to be replaced by hoots of greeting and high-fives, T-shirts and hot pants. I was treated less like a potentate and more as a regular guy, a *lao bai xing*. I could freely come and go.

When I looked at the building's broken mirrors and leaking pipes, I would sometimes get depressed. Then I convinced myself that my music was helping to color the memories of children in this place, turning them from dark to light.

When I taught late into the dusk, sometimes I would hear a huge rumbling from the floor above, like the sound of a train rushing through a tunnel.

"What's that?" I asked one day.

"Oh, it's just the mice," my student replied.

"What? There must be thousands!" I said, alarmed.

"Don't worry, Teacher Mark," someone said. "When we serve dinner they rush from one side of the building to the other. They are just looking for food."

There was no horror on his face, no alarm, just a quiet acceptance of the way things were. It was as though all of them—staff, students, mice, foreigners—were living in one stable ecosystem, day after day, year after year, without complexity or angst.

"Haven't you tried to get rid of them?" I persisted.

"Yes, but no luck. It's okay. They don't hurt anyone," came the Buddha-like response. Their often squalid living surroundings did not dampen the energy and aspirations of these kids.

At a talk with young eighth-graders, I asked the children what they wanted to be when they grew up.

"A teacher!"

"A doctor!"

"The president!"

Then a little boy pumped his hand up and said, "I want to be a VIP!"

The staff there was amazing. The teachers took great care of the students, despite their limited government-allocated budget. They became my teachers too.

"Please do not take photos of the children." I was told. "People in the past have done so and have written bad things about our orphanage."

I wound up spending an hour or two each week teaching orphans. In the meantime, my grand initial goals fell to earth with a dull clunk. For now there would be no foundation, no series of concerts sponsored by Bill

Gates. Instead, every Saturday afternoon at about two o'clock I would call Mr. Wu, the patient and wise orphanage piano teacher, to set up a time for me to arrive at the orphanage.

If I was a little late he would call me and urge me to hurry up. I was grateful for his advice and coaching. We both knew we were dealing with children whose deprived, disrupted lives required examples of constancy and commitment.

"It doesn't matter if you see them many times," another volunteer advised me, "or just a few: The key is to turn up regularly and not give in."

My own journey was aided by these children whose actions and questions made me examine so much of what I had previously taken for granted.

"Will you remember piano when you grow up?" I once asked little Luo Ming. She nodded her head and smiled.

I looked at her brow, furrowed in concentration as she played, and realized that even if she forgot who first taught her, I would still be content if she continued to enjoy her music.

"Here's some water, teacher!" Someone placed a paper cup on the piano.

"Why did they keep giving me water, even though I never drank it?" I later asked a friend.

"*Shan Shang Ruo Shui!*" he replied, as though the answer was evident.

I later learnt that this phrase is very old and very popular:

上善若水
Charity is like water, it spreads.

Maybe the water I had spilled had touched her life, and would, through her, spread further into the world.

———

I had been to so many places, experienced so much, and although the journey was continuing for me in China, there were moments when I felt like a child again. At other times I could see events in my past from a fresh perspective and finally understand their meaning. It was as though their stories, like mine, were about how love and music had shattered the shell that enclosed our understanding of what it means to be human and to become part of something bigger.

The experience of teaching the orphans was my long-lost redemption for my American sins. The guilt that had always lingered after Stanford, and the memories of my cruelty and selfishness that had characterized my relationships with women, became less onerous after each lesson. It was as though I was developing wings that enabled me to soar and make my burdens immaterial, even as my soul was linked to these children by a magical chain. Charity redeemed me in my own eyes. To give selflessly was such a wonderful gift. To see charity spread like water was even more precious. How right that nun had been!

The newness of China was forcing me to re-evaluate my life: why I had come here, what I had left behind, where I wanted to go next. Many of these questions had no ready answers, and insight would come to me only years later. But to reach this degree of introspection I had needed a fresh start, which Shenzhen generously gave me.

In 2011, my brother Joseph and I visited a school in the Nairobi slums, where he raised money to help the kids and pay the teachers. Shortly after, I arranged for UPS, the city of Shenzhen, and the American Chamber of Commerce of South China to donate sports and art supplies to the school.

My first visit to the Meilin orphanage in 2002. I was impressed by the dedication of the staff. Some of the kids cried when they saw this strange foreigner!

A 2009 Shenzhen charity concert with the pianist Chen Sa raised more than thirty thousand dollars for the Meilin orphanage, where I have taught kids to play piano since 2002. Some of the money was also used to buy art supplies for kids in Kenya. At the concert, the city of Shenzhen honored me as Image Ambassador for the work I had done with orphans.

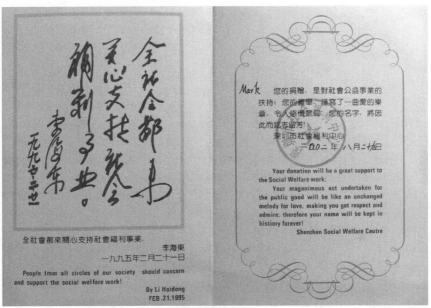

全社會都來關心支持社會福利事業.

李海東
一九九五年二月二十一日

People from all circles of our society should concern and support the social welfare work!

By Li Haidong
FEB.21,1995

Mark 您的捐贈，是對社會公益事業的扶持；您的義舉，譜寫了一曲愛的樂章，令人感懷景仰；您的名字，將因此而銘志留芳！

深圳市社會福利中心
二〇〇二年八月二十五日

Your donation will be a great support to the Social Welfare work:

Your maganimous act undertaken for the public good will be like an unchanged melody for love, making you get respect and admire; therefore your name will be kept in histiory forever!

Shenzhen Social Welfare Ceutre

With a donation from my Emory University EMBA classmates and proceeds from CD sales, I bought some DVDs and other items on my first visit to the orphanage. The director gave me this certificate of appreciation. c. 2002

CHAPTER EIGHTEEN

On Love and Dreams

MUSICAL EVOCATION

The Revolutionary Étude, Op. 25 No. 11: Frédéric Chopin

Many call the Op. 10 No. 12 Étude by Frédéric Chopin the Revolutionary Étude. To me this description is more suited to another of his compositions, Op. 25 No. 11. A simple tune starts in the right hand, pensive and unsure. Then the keyboard explodes with a thunderous accompaniment from the left hand and a dazzling cascade of notes from the right.

In the years from 2004 through 2008, the world began to claw back hope and confidence after an interlude of fear and panic. In the 2008 US presidential election results, the American architects of the Global War on Terror failed to rally people through fear and were defeated by optimism and belief in the better angels of humankind—an overdue revolution of sorts. On a personal level, I finally found the courage to reconcile myself to the family I had rejected, starting with a long-overdue reunion in Washington, DC.

DURING A RECENT DISCUSSION WITH SOME CHILDREN AT A PRIMARY school in Singapore, I suggested a game. I proposed giving each of the twenty-six letters of the English alphabet a number: A is 1, B is 2, C is 3, and so forth. "Find me a word whose letters add up to one hundred," I asked. "It has to do with dreams and success."

While the children were thinking, I reflected on the power of dreams. I believe they are about the future and our individual potential to carve our own path. It was such a dream that led me to China: a dream that I would start a new life there, based on learning the language and making a difference. The city I chose to live in, Shenzhen, is a boomtown, a place that is part of the future of China, but it also has its feet rooted firmly in tradition.

The traditional Shenzhen is still there: all you have to do is look behind the glimmering new skyscrapers and fancy shopping malls. At the gas station on Lian Hua Road, next to the near-bankrupt massage parlor whose gray, neon-lit walls always seem to be on the verge of collapsing, and where the new subway station has turned the area topsy-turvy, you come across Jing-tian Road almost by accident.

At once there is a hush in the air, as though the street is bestowing a silent benediction. Tall, leafy mangroves still line both sides of it.

Walking up the gentle incline, you may see a family playing badminton in a small park across from a woman sitting in her idling, brand-new white Honda. She leans out of her window as she chats with a friend though her mind is really focused on showing off her beautiful car. Elsewhere, you see the *liu da*, or slow walk, of grandparents as they meander behind their grandchildren. When you cross the intersection, branches from the trees dip down precariously so that the leaves feel like they may touch your head.

About five years ago, after a busy work day, I returned to a street that just that morning had been lined with thirty-year-old cypress trees. Barely *eight hours later* it was a naked patch of concrete, punctuated at regular intervals by large gaping holes where the trees had been torn out. I complained to a Chinese friend, who replied, "Don't worry, it's just development. It's good for Shenzhen."

I wonder: *Does Jing-tian Road face that future? I hope not. I believe that in the future China, the current Shenzhen disposition will become more relaxed, more traditional.* "Time is money" will become "Time is precious but can be shared with strangers." Or, in the words of Confucius, "Don't just treasure the water, treasure the mountain; don't just move, but be still; don't just enjoy, but preserve."

So perhaps by the time the kids of today's Shenzhen grow up, there will be a change in the current attitude toward growth at all costs. Perhaps they will begin to ponder over some questions: Do they have a wholesome life based on a quality-based economy and social responsibility? Or are they just living to pursue a quick yuan? Will they begin to stop and check out the blue skies, and will they be able to safely drink water directly from the tap? Will they have more time to be with loved ones, help others, and walk where the branches of trees gently touch overhead?

The scene on Jing-tian Road mingles the ancient Chinese respect for the environment with a timeless sense of repose. It is a wholesome life, rooted in the past, experienced today, and, I believe, should be part of that future.

To learn Chinese calligraphy was one of my dreams. Little did I know, when I started taking lessons, that writing Chinese would help me discover where I was going.

"The first stroke goes here . . ."

As I listened to my teacher's voice, his southern accent somewhat high-pitched, using the tip of his tongue, I gently moved my brush laden with black ink over the sheet of Xuan paper.

"What does this character mean?" I asked him as I traced out each of the eight strokes that made up the character 永. I had come across it before, but I was sure my teacher had his own opinion.

With a gentle smile, Mr. Li said, "It is *Yong*. In Chinese calligraphy (called 书法 *shufa*) it is probably one of the most important characters . . ."

"Why?" I interrupted him.

He looked at me, his eyes wide as though he couldn't believe his ears.

"Why? It involves all the basic strokes used in calligraphy . . . *Pie, Na, Tie, Zhou, Heng, Shu, Gou, Dian*."

What he didn't tell me, for he did not know English well enough to translate it, was that *Yong* means forever. As with most things in China, knowledge is acquired slowly and patiently. Here wisdom seeps into you, at its own tempo.

I had been seeing the beautiful artworks of Chinese brush calligraphy everywhere I went in China. I'd read schoolchildren and parents spent hours perfecting their writing strokes. I could write a little but wanted to know more. I was fascinated by these paintings whose thick strokes of black ink converged on each other, a two-dimensional duet of white and black forces, occasionally in harmony, at other times a perfect storm of motion.

Before I left America, a good friend advised me: "Mark, when you go to China, learn something unique that you can bring back with you. You will always remember it."

I had lost touch with her but remembered her words.

With Xue Hua's help I put up a sign on the gate of our complex, where passersby could easily see it.

Foreigner wanting to learn calligraphy is willing to teach
English in return for lessons.

Mr. Li was a short, bubbly, and effusive man in his thirties who worked a day job in the construction field but was an avid and accomplished calligrapher. His wife saw the notice and quickly contacted us. She told Xue Hua her daughter wanted to learn English and her husband was a fine calligrapher.

I decided to visit them in their simple, modern apartment a few blocks from ours.

Mr. Li took out his long *mao bi*, or ink brush, dipped it into the thick black ink, and gracefully swept his arm over the yellowed paper, his wrist, hand, arm, and body almost dancing to the curving line streaking across the paper. It was as though that first stroke created something, a place where the simplest and most profound polarities co-existed, like yin and yang, being and nothingness. From that moment I knew I had started a lifelong pursuit. I would visit Mr. Li every Friday, learning calligraphy and discussing Chinese culture with him half the time I was there and teaching his daughter English the other half of the time.

Glistening beads of sweat dribbled down his forehead as we sat together in the humid apartment.

"*Shufa* is a unique and rich art," he said proudly as he took a long draw from his cigarette. "*Huying*," he continued while pointing to someplace in midair, "is the smoothness of motion between the beginning and the end." Putting away the cigarette, he reached for the brush, carefully, as though it was made of thin jade.

"*Shufa* is more than three thousand years old, and it has influenced the art of many other countries. Look at the tools."

He pointed to the objects neatly arranged on the table, all the while grasping the brush as though it was an appendage of his hand, frequently making a few strokes to illustrate a point.

"Yellow practice paper and the more expensive Xuan paper, if you can afford it. It's about two kuai (about twenty cents) a sheet. Here's the soft hair brush and black ink. You may also need a dish or two and an ink stone. Although Chinese has more than forty thousand characters, it only uses eight basic strokes. However, because of the softness of the hair brush and the thousands of ways to interpret each character, it is quite difficult to master the *huying*."

He picked up the foot-long brush, dipped it carefully in ink and water, and wrote some characters, all the while explaining. "If the stroke is too fast, the result is an ugly white gap," he said. "If too slow, the ink bleeds over the paper." His body seemed to dance as his hands masterfully blended the brush's speed, direction, and pressure.

Yong not only had eight strokes, but each stroke had a specific beginning and end point, and the strokes had a precise order. I would learn that, even if the final character looked the same, if the correct sequence of strokes was not followed there would be something obviously off-kilter about the final artwork.

Even as I was entering my late thirties, things were coming together in a sequence of actions, like the strokes of a brush.

※

When you visit distant lands, fall in and out of love, experience pain and rejection or happiness and success, and in particular when you are alone, it is easy to take refuge in books. I remember being a child at Mrs. Taylor's nursery, pestering my teachers for the newest volumes. They were simple books bought in bulk; stories that seemed trivial, about dogs and their masters and girls learning to skip, but I loved to read them regardless.

Shufa impelled me to learn my new language even more assiduously. I studied Chinese four hours a day—a practice that would last for years. First there would be an hour of memorizing characters, followed by some reading. I would then listen to tapes of spoken Chinese, and finish by writing with a pen and then with the ink brush.

Around 2003 I started reading *A Dream of Red Mansions* (also known as *Story of the Stone*), next to Chairman Mao's red book, arguably the most famous book in China and its greatest novel. I was determined not to read the English version. I learned long ago that the best understanding of a work of art, whether music or literature, follows from hearing or viewing it the first time without another's interpretation.

It took me a week to get through the first paragraph.

"No, no!" a friend told me when I asked him to explain a particularly difficult section. "You're reading the wrong type of book. Everyday, simple Chinese from the newspaper is the best thing to learn."

"This text is too hard," Xue Hua agreed.

I ignored them. I had always believed that setting oneself a difficult, nigh-impossible, target inspires one to excel.

The book's language is dense and peppered with aphorisms and classical sayings, hundreds of poems, and thousands of little-used characters. However, the direct speech was readable, and with the help of a good dictionary I managed to plod through it all. My tempo picked up and, though it would take years, I finally finished it, having read through what I considered the original work, consisting of eighty chapters and more than 450,000 characters.

Over the years I read a number of fascinating Chinese classics, including scores of short stories, texts, novels, and literary classics such as *To Live* and *The Thirty-Six Stratagems*. Yu Hua's *To Live* is the story of a man born into a rich family before the Communist Revolution. He gambles away all his money and eventually loses his family in the years of turmoil. In the end he finds peace as a farmer. It is as though he has discovered that the secret to life lies in eliminating the urge to have and to possess, and instead enjoy its simpler aspects. *To Live*, though a contemporary novel in its unrelenting and frank storytelling, made me think of how the Chinese, for all their Confucian ideas of stability, are fascinated by extremes, whether in dramatic spectacles or the limits of what people can endure.

But *A Dream of Red Mansions* was the greatest challenge. In its own way it helped me come to terms with my relationship with my father and the family I had left behind in Kenya, and it was a key factor in the completion of my first book, *Nairobi to Shenzhen*.

A Dream of Red Mansions is about four great families of the eighteenth-century Song Dynasty. It spans the lives of many characters, including a young noble, Bao Yu, and the women that surround him. Like Tolstoy's *War and Peace*, it explores the themes of young love, the tyranny of family and class, and other complexities of feudal China, all the while drawing upon the richness of the Chinese language. However, unlike Tolstoy's expansive masterpiece, it does so within the physical confines of ancient Nanjing's boudoirs, placid gardens, and imperial homes. What became an intellectual challenge slowly morphed into an exploration of the similarities between cultures. I saw in Bao Yu and his relationship with women, particularly his grandmother, something that reminded me of the strong women in my own life.

I also saw in the brutality of his father some glimpses of my own bitter past.

There is one scene in *A Dream of Red Mansions* in which Bao Yu is savagely beaten by his domineering, autocratic father, Jia Zheng:

"Gag his mouth. Beat him to death," he commands his vassals.

Too frightened not to comply, two vassals hold Bao Yu facedown on a bench while a third lifts up the flattened bamboo sweep and begins to stroke him with it across the hams. After about a dozen blows, Jia Zheng, not satisfied that the young man was hitting hard enough, kicks the vassal impatiently aside, wrests the bamboo from his grasp, and, gritting his teeth, brings it down with the utmost savagery on the places that had already been beaten.

In another passage, Jia Zheng's mother, shocked at her son's cruelty, exclaims:

"And you say you've been punishing him for the honor of the family, but you just tell me this: Did your own father ever punish you in such a way?—I think not."

It reminded me of my own father and how domestic violence is passed down from generation to generation. I also thought about how these things are rarely discussed outside the family, and, if they are mentioned, many cultures tend to excuse them as normal; even something as abhorrent as beating one's wife is justified as being for the sake of "honor."

After I started working at AT&T, I had started writing an autobiography before giving up. I had tried to write about my early childhood, and in particular about my father, but with no good memories of him I had shelved the project. It was astonishing. I couldn't remember even a small virtue, like him giving me pocket money.

Only now do I remember one event that came close to proving my father cared for me. We were at the Jacaranda Hotel, a popular watering place with locals. While my parents sat at the bar, I played on the rocking horse. I needed coins to put in the slot. I went to Obama Sr. to ask him for a shilling. I don't remember why exactly, but the expression on his face frightened me. I turned to my mother instead.

"Mum, have you got a shilling?" My father looked at her sternly.

"Make sure you have enough for the drinks," she said to my father as she gave me the shilling.

That was the closest I came to remembering my father ever being kind: that he allowed my mother to hand over a shilling for my rocking horse rather than spend it on whisky.

—◦—

While in Shenzhen, I started to work on my novel, *Nairobi to Shenzhen*, more intensively than before. My burgeoning admiration for China, its people, and my new life were impelling me to move forward, letter by letter, word by word.

I remembered my mother's observation: "Your father was abandoned by his mother when he was very young. I think he ran away from home afterward. When children that young lose their mother, it affects them for a long time afterward."

Could I start my book with such an observation? Could this story hope to explain my father's demons?

"His mother ran away to Kendu Bay," a relative told me years later. "He was left to live with his father, and then ran away after her. I do not know if the bridal dowry was returned, if there was a divorce."

To my father, then a child who had lost his mother, such distinctions would have made no difference; the situation likely devastated him. For the first time ever, I felt sympathy for the boy he was. I could feel a little of what he might have felt.

Barack Obama Sr. and his sister fled the home of their stern, imperious father to seek out their young and beautiful mother.

"I cannot say why he ran away from his home," an uncle cautiously told me years later, almost as though his words danced on the edge of impropriety. "But why would a child leave his home? You think! You guess!" He would say no more.

Half-starved and filthy, young Obama, then barely seven, and his sister were found on the road to Kendu Bay days later. I imagined the scrawny girl and boy searching after love in the wilderness, among the windswept roads and scrub vegetation of Kogelo, next to the silver lake. Then I understood how this story of abandonment, like a boomerang, had recurred and recurred in the lives of my father's children: There was Bobby (Malik), who had cured his alcoholism and drugs by turning to Islam; there was Rita (Auma), whose blinding love for the men in her life was itself a rebound from the isolation of her early years. There was George, who ended up accused as a petty criminal in Nairobi's ghettos. I had retreated into solitude and later denial of who I was when I could not protect my mother against domestic violence.

And then, of course, there was Barack Jr., who never forgot the one-day meeting with the father he had fantasized about. It could be said that every one of us siblings, and even Barack Obama Sr. himself, had lost a parent, either to drink or through abandonment.

In Luo tradition, the sun represents riches and the moon represents love. At night the sun steals back through its secret path in the forest. One who sees the sun in the evening, the elders say, is blessed. These two children, however, looked up and saw a moon without love, and when they looked down, there was only the blighted landscape of nighttime Kogelo.

Mother, where are you? my father would have thought many times. A lion's roar or a hyena may have answered his plaintive cries. I felt my father lost his capacity to love somewhere between the boulders of Maseno and the steely moon in the night sky.

———

In July 2004 Barack Obama was on his way to becoming a US senator from Illinois, and he was chosen to give the keynote address at the Democratic National Convention. A friend and I drove to nearby Guangzhou to see the convention on television, an event organized by the American Chamber of Commerce of South China. It had been the first time I had seen my brother on TV. I thought his keynote speech a little long-winded, but my American sibling was full of energy, and two sections of his talk resonated particularly with me: the part about red states and blue states and the part about hope.

In that crowded room others must have overheard me discussing Barack with my friend. Someone interrupted us: "He's your brother?"

I replied, loud enough for others to hear: "Yeah, he's my brother!"

Not one to name-drop, I at once felt a little embarrassed and did not say more. But inside I felt a momentary, but real, pride, a warm glow that I had rarely associated with my Obama heritage. I was unusually pensive on the ride back to Shenzhen.

I remembered my mother's weathered, lined face and her resilience all through those painful years. The glimpses I'd had of her pale body fleeing into the night, the muffled screams and thuds, and the Janus face of my mother and my African brother limned against the full moon also flashed through my mind. I thought then of Barack Jr.'s book *Dreams from My Father.*

I had never read his book in its entirety. My excuses were, first of all, I thought the writing a little too self-consciously simple, too guarded, perhaps even boring in places. Second, he had treated my mother unfairly and misquoted her in several instances, probably because, as she pointed out, "he didn't know the true situation either." (One day I would read the book in its entirety, but only after I had at least completed the general outline and content of my own book.)

I considered my brother's rise, and memories of Woodley and Alego surged back to me like water through a cluster of boulders, violently and without order. The rock that covered the face of my hermit's cave was starting to crumble.

While I was proud of my brother, another feeling was swelling inside of me: one of injustice. I so wanted to surpass this part of me who lived across the Pacific Ocean. I so wanted to go further than him, but I now realized that he was leaving me far, far behind.

I felt I had no laurels to rest on, that my life up until this point had been a failure. I remembered my grand ambitions of one day being a Nobel Prize–winning writer or scientist, or of making great music and becoming a famous performer. My childhood precocity, adopted to win smiles and praise from my mother and her friends, had fused into my identity, right through my failed attempts to sell my manuscript of what would become my first novel and my music. This striving for greatness had always been part of my DNA, and each time, due to my own failings or even plain mediocrity, I had tumbled. It would take nothing less than the unlikely rise of an American president to lift me from my cloudy limbo.

But I did not realize this at the time. Instead, I was angry at my estranged brother. *It's not fair! I thought. You looked down on me for telling you the truth! You did not want to listen!* For a brief moment, I realized with a sense of shock that I wanted to write about my father to spit in Barack's face, to force him down from his pedestal so that he might see the truth. Then, in the next moment, I was ashamed at my own selfishness. But no matter how I tried to forget or to mute my anger and my pride, words and sentences were forming in my mind, and it was as if a spigot had been turned on. All the thoughts of my father and of my estranged family that had accumulated since I came to China started pouring out of me in a torrent of words.

I drew inspiration from D. H. Lawrence's *Sons and Lovers*, in which the author masterfully describes the relationship between a star-crossed mother and her son.

My mother had always seen me as a survivor.

"You'll be fine, no matter what," she once told me. To her I was a rock, strong and self-reliant. Even Barack had alluded to this in his book.

Yet Ruth was the real rock.

Ruth Beatrice Baker had survived. So had I. But at what cost? I felt a tremendous sense of compassion for all the hurt she had experienced. There was also guilt, however irrational, that I had not been able to protect her when she'd needed it. To my mother, a supreme pragmatist, the dark and gloomy memories of Barack Obama Sr. were not worth a second thought. She went to her kindergarten, as she did every day, and left those memories in the past.

But for me, no matter where I turned, there was no peace. Everywhere I looked there was Barack Jr.

Every night I would see him on TV or on the web, particularly after he'd announced his candidacy for president in 2007. It was as though I was in a hall of mirrors, but the faces I was seeing were of four people: Barack, my father, my mother, and me. Every so often they would blend and merge and then break apart as if viewed through a shattered prism. I remembered that conversation my brother and I had had so many years ago. As I did so, I asked myself more and more questions. Had I acted wrongly then? Why had I shunted the Obamas to the back of my mind? And why was I dusting off these memories now? I thought of my brother David again and the dream where I'd asked him if he loved me.

For the first time in years, tears flowed down my cheeks. It was as though something hard and obdurate inside me was finally being dissolved.

Soon the 2008 US presidential campaign was in full throttle. I would follow my brother's progress avidly. He was a dreamer, like me, and believed he could achieve the near impossible. His convention speech had given him a unique platform. However, my pride in his achievements was mixed with fear. I believed aspects of my life, if publicized, could hurt him. I lived in China and many might think I was a communist or a capitalist killer of American jobs. In addition, my moral weakness at Stanford and carelessness with money might be used to taint him in the eyes of millions.

I don't remember what made me finally contact Barack. Perhaps it was the ubiquity of his presence. Then again, I was older, more confident, and more secure in my views; I was driven by a need for closure and acceptance, but I also felt guilty at being so far removed from him while he faced his greatest challenge. I wanted to move on with my life. Any hope of my leading a quiet existence in China would soon be over, perhaps forever, and before that happened I felt I should try to make my peace with him. Bloggers and others were already full of speculation about our relationship, most of it negative.

Almost every one referred to the following passage from Barack's *Dreams*:

> *For the briefest moment I sensed Mark hesitate, like a rock climber losing his footing. Then, almost immediately, he regained his composure and waved for the check.*
>
> *"Who knows?" he [Mark] said. "What's certain is that I don't need the stress. Life's hard enough without all that excess baggage."*
>
> *. . . Outside we exchanged addresses and promised to write, with a dishonesty that made my heart ache.**

Does he still harbor bad feelings toward me? Does he hate me? I wondered.

It had been more than a decade since we had last met, in 1993, in San Francisco. It had been a brief and poignant meeting. I had been working at AT&T and was in my car ordering french fries—my favorite—in a McDonald's drive-through on Van Ness Avenue when my cell phone rang.

"Mark, it's Barack! How are you?"

I was shocked to hear from him. The last thing I had expected was a phone call out of the blue.

"Barack, how are you? Where are you?"

"I'm in San Francisco. Just briefly. Can we meet?"

His voice was deeper than I remembered. It was also a voice used to commanding people. I couldn't refuse.

We met the next day for lunch at Tommy's Joynt, a well-known eclectic haunt off of Van Ness.

Barack smiled as we walked in, looking at the plaques and photos that covered the walls and ceilings. "Why did you pick this place?" he asked.

* Excerpt from *Dreams from My Father: A Story of Race and Inheritance*, Obama, Barack. Times Books, New York, 1995.

Tommy's was a haunt for hippies and left-wing progressives, a place that proclaimed its countercultural attitude with memorabilia and cartoons plastered over the walls.

I looked at him. He was wearing almost the same clothes he had worn back in Kenya. *Doesn't he ever change?* I wondered. In a plain light-colored polyester shirt and black trousers, he looked simple, unassuming, characterless. He seemed taller, though, and his hair was shorter.

"I like it, it's got character," I said, trying to sound confident. Inside, I was a mix of emotions. Barack was determinedly matter-of-fact, his expression unreadable. He walked with his head slightly bowed, as though he was both pondering and a little ashamed of his height. We sat at a table covered with checkered red plastic, in a quiet area.

"So what's up?" I said casually.

"I was in the area . . . business," he said. "I just wanted to meet you and see how you are doing."

He looked at me with those unforgettable big, brown eyes in which I thought I detected a hint of warmth. He seemed humbler, less arrogant this time than he was back in Kenya, less in control of the situation. I remember how diffident my stepfather had been during our family trip to the States. Accustomed to a strong, confident Simeon, my mother and I had been perplexed by this meeker man. "I don't like it," she would angrily tell me.

Now Barack was here in San Francisco, in the USA, his home, and yet even he seemed to have shrunk a bit. Was this cautiousness an African-American thing? Or was it that Americans swaggered a little more on the world stage, when they were away from home?

"I'm fine," I replied. "I have a great job with AT&T. Making lots of money. And I love San Francisco."

"Have you been back home?" he asked.

"Of course," I said.

He was silent for a moment. I knew he wanted to talk more about Kenya, perhaps to say that he missed being there, but I wouldn't go there, remembering the discord of our last meeting.

"I wish we could see more of each other," he said suddenly.

I wondered where he was coming from. We hadn't talked for years, and now it was like a different, warmer Barack was sitting before me. I couldn't shake off the feeling that there was something he was hiding, something that I too was hiding and could not share.

Rock and roll played softly in the background. We didn't say anything for a long while. It was as though we had so much to say, but the ice was so hard to break, or the bottleneck too narrow to release our pent-up emotions.

I knew Barack was gently pushing me to go back home to Kenya, or to change my life in some way. He was once again the professor, didact, lawyer, and moralist, and I was the prickly porcupine high on caffeine.

"What are you up to these days?" I asked.

"Some legal work," he said. "In Chicago." Barack was working then at Davis, Miner, Barnhill & Galland, a law firm specializing in civil rights and neighborhood development. Chicago seemed so far away, in my mind a modern Rome associated with tycoons; lofty, weather-beaten buildings; and stills from gangster movies.

I shrugged.

"Maybe I'll go there on business some time."

We were in a circular conversation, a place that refused to go deeper. It was like déjà vu. I was comfortable with that. As for Barack, he didn't want to talk about himself.

"Do you like San Francisco? Are you going to stay here?"

There it was again. That implicit reference to Kenya. To my brother, Kenya would always be a romantic place, one that, in spite of its flaws, had accepted him and offered him family and happiness. It seemed sometimes that Barack forgot I was American. I hadn't grown up in America, but my mother was American, too, and I was a citizen. Yet to Barack I was an unfaithful Kenyan. I wasn't angry, just a little irritated. I wondered why he didn't live in Kenya. I tried not to show it.

"I'm fine, and happy. No problems. I'll probably stay here," I said without much conviction. In fact, I was lying. I didn't like sales and felt like a fraud for saying I did. I loved San Francisco, but constantly wondered if I would be let go from my job.

I wanted to be away from this older brother who at that moment was something between a rabbi and an auditor.

I do not remember much of our conversation; I forgot about it soon after. I remember I paid for lunch, and we shook hands somewhat formally and went our own ways—again. I later learned that he was writing his memoir, *Dreams from Our Father*, at the time. Perhaps he had been interviewing me again for the book, reconnoitering my mental landscape. During our meetings he had never once mentioned anything about a book. On the other hand, he may have just wanted to say hi, and that's what I prefer to believe. *In any case, I don't need him,* I thought. *I can manage on my own.*

Almost two decades had passed since that meeting in San Francisco, a period that would separate our lives immeasurably, and out of the gap we would form vastly incongruent destinies.

It was my mother who finally linked me with Barack—through my sister, Auma. It was an ironic turn of events. After David's death my mother must have blamed Bobby and, implicitly, other Obama relatives. For thirty-plus years, to my knowledge, she had never spoken with Bobby. However, time heals all wounds, even the death of one's child.

"Mark, you don't know what it is like to lose a child," she once cried. "It's like losing an arm. It will never grow back. The pain is so deep."

This woman who had the most reason to hate the Obamas was the link that brought our family back together. My dear mother had found the grace and fullness in her heart to reconnect with Auma. She had been communicating with my sister for some time, and she gave me Auma's e-mail address. When I finally wrote to Auma, I didn't know if she would reply to me, but a few days later she e-mailed me a short note. She was happy to hear from me and provided her phone number.

"Everything has its time," she said to me when I called her. "We knew you would be back."

At last, I e-mailed Barack.

I had no idea how my brother would respond to my e-mail. I knew I was doing the right thing by reaching out, regardless of whether he reached out too. If he did accept me, then it would be in spite of political blogs, his own memories, or family conflicts. I would face him directly and let him know in my own words that I supported him. I refused to be a distant, estranged entity fashioned out of media sound bites and made-up blog posts.

The era was rich with hope and optimism that extended across the Pacific and the South China Sea. But would Barack feel the same way? Would he want to communicate with his long-estranged brother? Within a few days Barack e-mailed me.

Mark,
I hear you've been trying to reach me. I've been a little busy traveling but I hope we can meet sometime.
Best regards,
Barack

When I received his note, it was as though a link that had been broken was connected again, a ragged, broken circle was now looped back into itself. There was no anger or guilt or mistrust in what I read. It was the language of a decent man who didn't hold grudges. I was very happy. The warmer brother I missed had returned.

When I started communicating with Barack, I e-mailed him a brief translation of Sun Bin's *The 36 Strategies*. This two-thousand-year-old classic is globally less well known than *The Art of War* by Sun Tzu, but it is equally famous in China. During the campaign to defeat Hilary Clinton, Barack needed all the tools at his disposal. *Why not help him a little?* I thought. I do not know whether he used my advice or not, but his team undoubtedly used certain strategies to clinch the nomination. Like Strategy No. 6 for instance:

声东击西
Feint to the East, and attack in the West.

This was used when Clinton was led to focus on capturing big states, when in fact the Obama campaign's micro-targeting of electoral districts was the most critical, and successful, strategy of his campaign.

Then there was Strategy No. 14:

借尸还魂
Revive in a new guise.

Barack and his team had proven flexible enough to change when the situation warranted it, such as putting aside the "nice guy" image to directly attack Clinton in Ohio and Texas. As the Chinese might say, the lamb had turned into a dragon.

Our dreams had been about reviving ourselves: outwardly in new guises, but inwardly forged through long-dormant, but smoldering, convictions. Sudden events like 9/11 and, in Barack's case, perhaps the Iraq War, which he vehemently opposed, only motivated us further to strive to make a difference.

This 2011 *Nairobi to Shenzhen* book signing in Shenzhen, organized with Sheraton Hotels, raised about $35,000 for children in disaster areas around the world, including China, Japan, and the Philippines. UNICEF distributed the money.

In concert in Guangzhou in 2011. Together with the American Chamber of Commerce of South China and other performers, we raised about $150,000 to save many kids with chronic heart disease at the Guangzhou Children's Hospital. A sold-out crowd of more than fifteen hundred people attended this Guangzhou concert.

CHAPTER NINETEEN

New Directions and a Special Gift

MUSICAL EVOCATION

Polonaise in A-flat major, Op. 53: Frédéric Chopin

The aptly named "Heroic" Polonaise is about grasping fate by the throat. It thunders, roars, and stretches the fingers to the utmost. I marvel at how Chopin, with his somewhat frail physique, was able to grasp such massive chords—but he did, and brilliantly. At its core, its powerful themes and structures reflected my new life in China. My odyssey of self-discovery in some ways mirrored the political journey of a sibling who lived across the Pacific and who was engaged in a momentous race.

IN 2005, ABOUT A YEAR AFTER THE CONVENTION SPEECH, I LEFT WORLD Nexus and accepted an offer to work as a marketing consultant with one of our customers, a battery-manufacturing company based in Shenzhen that was impressed with my work. The job would be low profile. I would give the firm a strong brand image and a global marketing team. Although World Nexus had been successful, one of my partners had decided to spend more time on a barbecue business he started. To this day everyone believes I am the owner, or co-owner, of this business, yet I never had such a role. The only time I visited the premises was when I was there for a casual party where I played a tune on an electronic keyboard, spoke some bad Chinese, and tried not to get drunk. Nevertheless, the owner kindly credited me with giving him good suggestions, although I feel my advice was minimal.

I maintained and defended my low profile. I loved my privacy and avoided telling most people that Barack was my brother.

"Your brother is the senator, right?" a friend said to me once. "I remember you told us you were very proud of a relative in American politics. It's Barack, right?"

I nodded quietly, hoping he would keep his voice down.

"He has lots of potential!" my friend said in a loud baritone that could be heard down the office corridor.

Otherwise, things were quiet, until Roger Cohen wrote his "Obama's Brother in China" column in the March 17, 2008, *New York Times*, which quoted Auma:

"My daughter's father is British. My mom's brother is married to a Russian. I have a brother in China engaged to a Chinese woman." Cohen then went on to reveal more about me. He ruefully opined that the Republicans would dig up dirt on me to hurt my brother, all the while apparently blissfully unaware he was the one doing just that.

I could already imagine the headlines: Obama has a brother in China! Hear the whisperings about a polygamous father.

I was furious at Auma.

"How could you have told this reporter about me and my girlfriend?" I asked her. "Now they'll drag us into these political games. You don't know what a sensation these things are in China. We won't even be able to walk down the street!"

"I'm sorry, Mark, truly sorry," Auma said. "I mentioned it so casually. He seemed like a person I could trust. I will not give him interviews anymore."

But it was too late. Even though my consulting up to then had mainly focused around such innocent topics as marketing communications and developing company websites, I knew the Republicans could cast this in a negative light, as indeed they eventually did with a highly inaccurate 2008 attack piece in Rupert Murdoch's *Times of London*.

From the time my brother announced his candidacy for president in early 2007, I suspected my life would become an open book. The quiet, peaceful existence it had taken me years to develop in China would change into something raucous, crude, and even vicious. While part of me was proud of my brother, another part was furious with him for involving me in this circus. He could at least have let our family know of his plans in advance.

Then my attitude slowly changed. I had seen where America had gone. There was a pervasive sense of fear all over the country. I remembered how on visits back home to America there was always something heavy and oppressive in the air, especially at airports. Grim men with machine guns and dogs lounged next to subdued passengers lining up for coffee at Starbucks. Newspapers described a government full of corruption and profligate spending, cover-ups of torture, and the world's view that America had perhaps lost its way and thus could no longer command the respect it once did in the world. I had left in part because the hope and optimism that had once characterized the national spirit seemed to have vanished, and moved eastward.

But now Barack and his team were slowly changing this concentrated American angst. There was a movement of millions of people from an atmosphere of fear toward one of hope, exactly what he had described in his breakout speech at the Democratic Convention in July 2004:

Hope. Hope in the face of difficulty. Hope in the face of uncertainty. The audacity of hope! In the end, that is God's greatest gift to us, the bedrock of this nation. A belief in things not seen. A belief that there are better days ahead.

These were no idle words. My family thrived on hope. My grandfather had worked for years as a domestic in the hope that his son would go to university. My Lithuanian grandparents had fled pogroms in the hope of living in a free America. My mother had eloped to Kenya in the hope that she would be with the man she loved. My father had hoped that Kenya would evolve from nepotism and tribalism to something greater. I had hoped that I would write a great book and make music. Barack had hoped to make a difference in people's lives through politics.

My anger was slowly morphing into pride. What an amazing achievement it would be for Barack to become America's president! Although I suspected he did not see it that way, the election of a black president would be a revolution in itself. I had often ignored racism at my peril. I really did not care if people thought of me as black or white or liked me for it (or not), perhaps because I never saw myself as one or the other. My attitude and subsequent unwillingness to anticipate the consequences of racism had hurt me before, but my racial identity simply was not innate. What I wrote in *Nairobi to Shenzhen* about the protagonist David could have applied equally to me:

I was born black, raised white and absorbed yellow.

In addition, the message Barack was sending out about the power of hope and optimism over terror and fear was, in my opinion, more important than whether he was white or black, or whether, as he put it, he had strange ears that some people disliked.

Barack had at last achieved greatness, and in doing so he did not try to constrain me or make me feel inferior. On the contrary, he would free me, particularly through my writing, to be honest with myself, to reach into a better part of me.

My story was thus tied to his, and my future would in some sense be determined by his. We were brothers linked by an invisible chain that would not become apparent until years had passed. Now Barack had eclipsed me, he was no longer conscious of me, except in an abstract, formal way. I was to be his invisible brother, a muted shadow that sometimes appeared to greet him on foreign trips. On the other hand, every action I now took, whether I liked it or not, was going to be contrasted or compared to his.

"Live your own life," he told me once. "Reporters will always be looking for more information from you. If you ignore them they will eventually leave you alone."

It was easier to say than to do. How could I live my own life when my identity henceforth, in the public mind and even my own, was linked to his? Nevertheless, I was determined not to be bitter. I had witnessed bitterness in others, in my father, other family members, and among friends and acquaintances I had known throughout my life, and I had seen that it works like acid, eating people away from inside. I would try, though with halting steps, to find my own path through this maze of perceptions, and to do so I would learn to focus on the simple but important things that defined me: family, music, self-expression, and charity to others. To do so, however, would require a blinding, painful honesty. In time this passage or odyssey toward self-realization would reach certain markers, such as my novel and this memoir. *Nairobi to Shenzhen* was a start, though its flaw was that its contours were blurred by the devices of fiction.

I tried to continue my anonymous and low-key life, with no connection to the Obamas other than my avid reading of news of the campaign and occasional calls and e-mails to family members, including Auma and Barack himself. Then one night everything changed.

It was because of a dream.

It was the time of the debates with Hilary Clinton. I had read reviews that criticized my brother's performance in the first debate. I, on the contrary, thought he did brilliantly. I sensed in the news reports an attitude of doubt, even hostility, toward him. It was as though a huge mental adjustment was taking place in the minds of millions around the world, but it was a reluctant creaky motion at first, constrained by vast forces of inertia and deeply ingrained attitudes and expectations. I went to bed late. Then, around two in the morning, I woke with a start.

Just as a dream had made me go east, it was a dream that finally made me see my brother again.

Dreams and Observations had been the title of the memoir I had left unfinished.

Dreams from My Father was the book penned by my famous brother. My mother dreamt of eloping to Kenya.

My father dreamt of Harvard. I dreamt of China.

It is as though my family feels a peculiar attraction to this shadow world. Perhaps it is because dreams are about the places where rules do not exist, and unspoken wishes and feelings can prevail.

My dream about my brother was vague and unformed, parts of it terrible, but it led me to act in the real world.

I dreamt I was falling from an airplane—the world stretched out below me, magnificent in its sweeping and impassive beauty. At first I was scared. Then the feeling of rushing wind and the warm bright colors rushing up toward me cheered me up. I began to enjoy this mortal fall. My head was now turned up toward the sun and the back of my head felt the cool air rush past. Then there was a shuddering feeling—as though my head lay on a vibrating pad. This palpitation seized my whole body. I knew then that my head had smashed into the ground. There were no sensations of pain or regret or fear. It was almost like a habitual event.

Then the scene shifted to a vast, treeless landscape, where Barack and I were side by side. There was no one else visible, yet we nevertheless had the sensation of thousands of people around us. We were walking slowly, discussing something, when suddenly I sensed a violent motion. A blurry, hard, brown object passed by me and struck Barack. He had been shot.

I struggled to wake up from this dream. I sensed that I had indeed woken up and was in my bedroom, standing over my bed. Comforted, I turned back the covers as though about to prepare for bed. And a bloodless face appeared before me. Its eyes were red and I realized that I was still asleep after all and could not escape. The terror was very real. I was overwhelmed by it. I struggled to wake up, and the juddering and pounding in my head commenced again. The feeling of dread and guilt was so strong that I woke in a sweat. I opened my eyes and saw what seemed like a huge white cloud. With a shock I realized it was my wife's concerned face.

After I recounted the dream to her, Xue Hua urged me, "You must go and see your brother!"

—◆—

To My Snow Flower
Once, a spoonful of love spreads honeylike
Into cold cracks of a universe becoming
Vast golden, a shimmering lake.
A shared sweet look, a laugh, caress,
Your naked body in the moonlight.
Shared secrets, loving you, my bashert.
Ever my other self, be true.
This is you, my love.

Xue Hua, whom I married in mid-2008, had helped me confront my demons before this. At various critical times in my life, she had given me insights into myself that I would not have had otherwise. In time she would encourage me to pursue my writing, even though we knew that it would hurt people in our family by reawakening memories that had long been forgotten or suppressed. In love and gratitude I wrote "To My Snow Flower" for her.

The morning after the dream, I bought a ticket to America to see Barack. I knew he would be in Austin, Texas, in a week to debate Hilary Clinton. Once there I would find a way to get in touch. I purchased a plane ticket using money I had been saving to buy a piano. I had longed for my own instrument but spent the money without regret.

Barack had no advance notice I had arrived in Austin. I stayed with my younger brother Joseph (Simeon and Ruth's son) and Joseph's wife, Dora. She contacted the campaign and, once they knew who I was, they let us in without difficulty. We found ourselves in a small anteroom in an Austin concert hall, waiting for him to arrive from the debate, which had been held in a separate location nearby. There were a few other sponsors waiting to meet him personally. We chatted casually among ourselves, but I had only one thing on my mind: reconnecting with my brother.

It would be the first time I had seen him in many years. The scene had been playing over in my mind for days. What would the meeting be like? How much had he changed? Would he even recognize me?

He loped into the room with his legs taking long wide strides, his head held high, his right arm almost set into an optimal ready-to-shake-hands-ninety-degree position.

"Good to see ya, everybody! How're you *DOING*!"

I thought he wouldn't recognize me. It had been almost twenty years, after all, but he walked straight toward me, his eyes opening slightly in that ambivalent moment between hesitancy and determination.

"How're you doing? Good to see ya. How've you been, Becky?"

The voice was resonant and deep. Later I thought the words had sounded sort of dry and cold, probably from having been repeated a million times in the past year. At that moment they were directed toward me and yet belonged to everyone present. And who or what was Becky? It sounded like a woman's name. Did he mean Back East or something else? Had he confused me with a woman he had met? Or was this some local term of endearment? We hugged. For the first time he drew his left arm from his pocket and patted me on the back. His eyes were open wide, and he seemed surprised at the hug. He looked at my hair, and with a quick motion he swept up a finger to brush his upper lip.

"Hey, you have that old mustache thing! Your hair's shorter. The last time I saw you, you had a big afro!" For some reason it made me very happy that he remembered such details about me.

"What's this?" He reached out to touch my face. I don't remember if he succeeded, but, always sensitive to people touching me, I dipped my head and laughed nervously.

"So did you!"

"No, no. I just couldn't afford a haircut." He smiled. We laughed, and he greeted Joseph and Dora.

For some reason the memory of that first encounter in Nairobi—it had seemed so unimportant in the intervening years and did so now—did not recur. It was as though the new enthusiasm in the air had melted away all negative thoughts. Barack was relaxed and smiling. He was far mellower than the last time I'd seen him. We had hugged—something we had never done before. That night in Austin, it felt as though the ice between us had been broken.

He looked older than in the pictures on TV and the Internet. Those types of photos always exaggerate beauty or ugliness, depending upon the slant of the story and the partiality of the editor or photographer. Up until recently the press had loved or admired Barack. The photos were almost always of him smiling, photographed from below to make him seem something of a charming Wunderkind or benevolent colossus. But the line scored from his nose down to his lips was deep, and the wrinkles around those big brown eyes couldn't hide the ravages of forty-seven years. Yet his skin was luminous; his smile big and genuine. Like me, he had lines on his face. Like me, he had wrinkles around his eyes. Like me, he held his head high. Unlike me, he was the man who would be King.

Feeling that I had to connect with him more earnestly than before, I had prepared a scroll of calligraphy as a present. With it I'd enclosed a note that I hoped he would read one day—when he had a rare, quiet moment.

Thursday, 21 February 2008
Dear Barack,

In case we have no time to talk I wanted to give you a brief explanation of this small gift. While living in China I've studied the art of calligraphy and felt it would be appropriate to give you this very personal present. I wrote the characters myself using the traditional black ink brush called mao bi (hair writing brush). The characters are read from right to left, hung horizontally on the wall, and are (written in phonetic Mandarin):

天涯咫尺 *Tian Ya Zhi Chi*

The expression literally means "Heavens Apart Yet Just A Few Inches."

There are two interpretations. The first is: Two relatives physically close together yet spiritually poles apart. Conversely, the second is: Two relatives physically far apart yet spiritually close together. Depending upon the situation you can adopt either the first or second interpretation.

From my point of view I consider the two of us, linked by the same father, as in some ways very close and yet in others very far apart. For example, I realize that you were born with a profound gift for bringing people together, a talent I never had. So in this sense we were far apart. But I also remember reading a newspaper article that said in high school you loved Nietzsche and Freud. And I believe it also mentioned Jean-Paul Sartre. These men, along with Plato, were my idols in high school. I read La Nausée for breakfast, Beyond Good and Evil *for lunch, and attempted* Totem and Taboo *or* The Symposium *for dinner. I thought this [similarity in our reading] an amazing coincidence. It seems as though there are some things that siblings subliminally gravitate to that are independent of nurture. So in this sense it's like we were far apart physically yet close spiritually. My tendency has always been towards music and art. Perhaps you had this proclivity too?*

Many such examples popped through my head and they were prompted by the tremendous coverage you're getting (particularly recently) from TV, the Internet and just word of mouth. Thinking of you again and again, there were so many strong feelings that I could not resolve. And then, about the time I started reading more about you, a good friend reminded me of a saying in Chinese. Basically it goes like this.

In the great moments of your life you may not remember the names of all those around you, but you will indeed remember the names of those who were not around.

So, my wife said, maybe you need to go and see your brother. And like so many women in our lives, who, as Schopenhauer sensed, have a profound understanding of the unseen rhythms, she articulated what I had been feeling but had been unable to express in actions or in words. So a few days later I decided to come to Texas to see you. In many ways I feel that you are passing through a great moment, a moment charted by destiny, and I want you to know that I support you totally in your great endeavor.

The art of hand-brush calligraphy dates back 4,000 years and is unique to China, although the technique was early exported to other Asian countries like Japan and Korea. The characters on such paintings are circumscribed by smaller characters that form a dedication. The dedication I wrote to you is:

To my brother Barack who is in my heart (right side) From his younger brother Mark (left side)

Please excuse some of the ink marks on the back. This is normal for calligraphers and the marks should not be visible from the front.

Barack, I am so glad that we were able to meet, if only for a few minutes. And even if we were not (I am writing this the night before I head to Austin to try to meet you), I hope you accept this gift and realize that I came just to see you and tell you face-to-face that your brother is no longer poles apart but is a kindred spirit. If there is anything at all that I can do to support you while I am living in China, let me know.

Love,
Mark

"I wanted to see you and tell you that I completely support you!" I said to Barack.

He looked at me. I looked back at him. I don't remember exactly what he said but what more was there to say, really?

"I have a small gift for you and want to take some photos. Is it okay?"

"Let me circulate. Wait here and we'll talk."

He gestured to the side of the room where Dora, Joseph, and I could wait.

I noticed how good he was at directing people to do things. It was as though he would choreograph the positions of guests in that small room, organize the photo sessions, close in on the handshakes, and make eye contact exactly where and when it was needed. He worked the room like a political ballerina, almost floating, his lanky body ever gaining on the endpoint. Barack in motion was like a melodic line that sees the end note even as it is sounding the first.

But he is so impenetrable. At our first meeting many years ago in Kenya, his thin young face seemed completely humorless, his smile dry and forced. He was so earnest about understanding me that he was boring. I thought he looked a little ridiculous in an afro haircut—even though, as he had just reminded me, I had had one too.

In this Austin meeting and others, I would slowly begin to understand my brother. Barack is not effusive in his emotions. Like most politicians, he is careful about what he says and he can keep a secret. As he must, he compartmentalizes his life into the private and public spheres. His feelings are not easily shared. And as easily as he moves among social circles, his inner self is like the Maya's Veil of Vedanta philosophy. One can peel away each veil from Maya's face, and yet there is always another. All seems to be illusion. But the inner Barack, however undefined, is solid. Some speak of his Midwestern values and strong sense of confidence. While there indeed is something of the Midwestern temperament about him, which makes him coolheaded and discreet, succinct and direct, he remains an enigma. His values derive from this ineffable core, but because we all want to know more about the personality (what people see) rather than the inner character (what he feels), his enigmatic side serves him well.

It is sometimes easy to conclude Americans don't particularly like deep people. Anti-intellectualism, for example, really took off in the George W. Bush era. I sometimes felt many Americans tended to dumb down those who are profound. To them, such people are elitist. They are private-school Yankees and stuck-up liberals. So it is perhaps just as well that Barack's inner core remains his own private concern.

His character is deep, as it has had to be to resolve his feelings toward our brilliant, alcoholic father. For what Barack Jr. did not see in Barack Sr., but I did, was the perfect confluence of drink, oratorical brilliance, lust, mathematical precociousness, domestic violence, charisma, and megalomania. Barack Jr. writes about it, but he never experienced being on the receiving end of the drunkard's tirades. I speak ill of the dead, but their influence endures. Can we afford to ignore them?

Barack has brilliantly resolved two psychological aspects that influence his relations with others: the management of others' expectations (his personality) and the channeling of his demons into an inner peace (his character). What else could he be but an enigma, even to his blood brother? So while my eyes welled up that evening, he remained somewhat aloof. Those who witnessed our meeting told me afterward that he was very moved, but I didn't see it. Then again, for Barack, confessions of the heart are likely a private matter between him, Michelle, and Jesus.

I held my calligraphy in front of him. "This is your name in Chinese," I told him. "Maybe it's the first time you've seen it spelled in Chinese characters."

"It's beautiful," he said. "How do I hang this? Vertically? Or this way?"

I gently corrected his hands downward. "Horizontally."

We took some photos, chatted for a few more minutes, and then he left to address the cheering crowd outside.

I met some other people at that reunion. I had seen a huge black guy looming over Barack as he worked the crowd, always just behind him. I thought he was one of the secret service men, he was so huge. It turns out this was Reggie Love, Barack's "body man" or personal assistant, who worked with him until 2011.

"Please, please take care of my brother," I entreated him as we parted. "There are so many nuts out there!" And I pressed his hand. Reggie didn't smile but his eyes told me he understood. I immediately felt better.

As we were heading out, I bumped into a short, stocky woman who graciously smiled at me. In the happiness of the moment I took a photo of myself with her and another woman. She gently protested but I insisted, I so wanted to capture every moment of that day. I learned afterward that this fine woman was Valerie Jarrett, who has long been my brother's close counsel and evangelist of sorts.

Later I would remember certain facts about seeing my brother again. He had hesitated that moment we hugged. He had asked me no questions about what I was doing or what the rest of the family was up to. Perhaps he had forgotten my name? He now existed in such rarefied air, what could five minutes with a person who hadn't reached out for so many years mean to him? I could sense the suspicion in him. Could hear the questions he must have asked himself: Why did he come now? Perhaps he came just because I am running for president? What is his hidden agenda? No one I know has said anything particularly good about him, or particularly bad. Who is this man who calls himself my brother? Why so long apart? Give him a smile and a hug and then forget him and save the world. Perhaps this was the real Barack.

But I prefer to give him the benefit of the doubt: to view him as a magnanimous man who believed I had no hidden agenda. Bitterness and cynicism are the preserve of old men and the past. Then there is the country of young men and dreamers, who trust and believe in the better angels of a man's soul. Time will tell.

So close and yet so far apart.

Barack Obama and me meeting in Austin, Texas, in 2008 during a campaign stop. The last time I saw him had been in San Francisco during the mid-1990s. I visited Chicago a few times after that but was unable to connect with him. At this meeting he was surprised to see his name in Chinese. "How do I hang this? Vertically? Or this way?" he asked, and I showed him. The calligraphy roughly means: So physically near and yet so far apart, so physically far apart and yet so near.
(PHOTO: DORA ZEPEDA NDESANDJO)

In our Austin meeting with Barack, my younger brother Joseph, and his wife, Dora.
She is a big fan of Barack. "Even after meeting so many people, he remembered
details about my wedding preparations," she said.

CHAPTER TWENTY

The New America Has Arrived

MUSICAL EVOCATION

The Moldeau: Bedřich Smetana

This orchestral work of approximately twelve minutes' duration by the late-nineteenth-century Czech composer Bedřich Smetana describes the great river that runs through Eastern Europe. The power and force of the water remind me of the overwhelming pride that I felt when Barack Obama was elected president of the United States, and I sensed the great movement of millions from an atmosphere of fear toward hope.

I remember the first time I heard this recording, in a sun-drenched room in a Nairobi high school, during a lazy lunch hour. The LP paired this work with the "New World Symphony" by Smetana's compatriot Antonín Dvořák. The music starts with the flutes, piccolos, and other woodwinds evoking the spring waters that trickle down the mountainside. Then, as the rush of water picks up momentum, more and more orchestral instruments join in, and an immense wave of sound culminates in a marvelous melody. The river becomes great and wide, a triumphant meandering force that eventually reaches the gates of Prague before vanishing in the distance.

IN AUGUST 2008, I STARTED TO RECEIVE CELL PHONE CALLS FROM PEOPLE I did not know, wanting to discuss my brother Barack. I ignored them.

Then, just a month after Xue Hua and I married, the *Times of London* published an attack on me, identifying me by my full name and claiming

I ran an illegal business in Shenzhen that sent cheap products to America. It attacked me as a shady capitalist, a destroyer of American jobs.

American politics is vicious and the last thing I wanted was to be involved in it. For one, I valued my privacy and my simple life in Shenzhen. But there was also another reason I did not want to be involved. There were mistakes I had made in my life that I was still coming to terms with. I believed that under close scrutiny from the press these would be exposed and I would shame my brother and my family. I was so proud of what Barack was achieving, and yet I always felt I was the bad apple that would spoil everything. The shame ran very deep, intensified by years of trying to forget the ghosts of my past.

After the *Times of London* article, I was hounded by forty-plus phone calls a day from reporters. With the help of a good friend, my wife and I left Shenzhen for two weeks, hoping things would calm down eventually.

One night, as my wife and I were hiding out in a hotel room in Hainan, a seaside province famous for its beaches and tropical climate, I knew what I had to do. High above the ocean, the moon slashed across the slate-black sky like a bright white hook. Below, the beach was a long, thin strip of silver. A lone gull circled high above, occasionally cutting across the moonlight. It was a beautiful night, but I was feeling almost suicidal.

"Will he understand?" I said to my wife.

She nodded her head. "He is your brother. He must."

"I'll shame him and all the people around him."

She did not say anything. With a heavy heart, I sat down in front of my computer to e-mail him.

"I must tell him. I can only be honest. What else is there?"

Subject: Confession
Barack:
> *In my early-twenties before I came to China I made two major errors in my life that may affect you negatively. I have to tell you because I just cannot bear to hurt you, my family and the country more by keeping these long-harbored secrets.*
>
> *1) In 1991 I cheated in a Stanford doctoral exam and was suspended. Although I later received a Master's I decided not to return to Stanford.*

2) When I came to China I couldn't get a job (had lost my American job during 9/11), and incurred debt by trying to save my house (which I lost). Since then I have never made enough money to even begin paying off the debt. My plan is to make enough one day to pay them off (right now I make about $700 a month despite erroneous newspaper reports that I am rich). I could have moved back to the US and searched for a higher-paying job but I stayed because I loved the people, the country, my wife and the orphanage children. Ecce homo.

McCain's war room probably has this information and is waiting for the right time to spring it on you. Since the LT article Xue Hua, our friends and I have been besieged by reporters. I have had to leave Shenzhen with her and today they published my photograph on the Internet. I dread returning to Shenzhen next week. I do not know what I should do.

I have learnt from my mistakes but have often blundered into them. Since I have lived in Shenzhen my focus has been on charity and teaching the kids piano, learning Chinese and calligraphy and finding my better half. I came to China to start a new life and have been happy here until now.

It would be devastating to me if we never meet again, Barack, but regardless I am so very sorry I disappointed you and my country.

Let me know if you would like me to work with you on an advance response to counter the inevitable Republican attacks.
Love always,
Mark

There. I had said it, spilt the beans as it were. I waited for his reply, but I didn't know if he cared. I couldn't believe that he didn't. He would have known, as only a brother must, how hard it had been for me to share this with him. Normally he took days to reply as he was so busy. This time he answered me almost instantly.

Mark
Do not worry—your life is your own and will not affect my election. Just remember that you have no obligation to talk to reporters,

and in fact should avoid talking to them if they approach you. In time,
the interest will wear off.
Sorry that this is having an impact on you.
All the best,
Barack

He had urged me not to worry and to go on with my life. During this most despondent of times it was family—including Barack—that continued to console me, and for that I will always be grateful. I cried on my wife's shoulder that night but found the strength to go on.

During the US presidential campaign my Chinese friends were alternately amazed and skeptical, but mostly the latter. However, I best remember the words of a close friend, David, the man who had helped me bring those first gifts to the orphanage and to set up a business. When the press discovered I was living in Shenzhen and gave me no peace, it was David who drove my wife and me away for a week's peace in Hainan. By that time it seemed obvious to me that Barack would win the election. More and more people were coming to believe the once impossible would occur.

During the trip, David and I discussed starting World Nexus again. I had always thought that he was essential to the success of the company and, if the two of us became partners again, we could build it up.

"Can you get your friends to invest?" I asked him.

David looked at me, his expression inscrutable. I knew he was thinking of how he could turn this worldwide attention into something tangible.

"I talked to my friends," David said. "They still don't think a black man can win. They say McCain has a fifty-fifty chance."

If there was anyone I had felt would recognize my brother's true potential, it was David. But even he seemed to be hedging his bets. He would not express his doubts to me directly but shared them anyway through his friends' opinion. I was surprised. I had forgotten that, in China, business is business, and businessmen are the most conservative thinkers of all.

"Of course he will win," I protested. I wasn't thinking about the business. I felt I had to defend my brother, and I really believed he would do better than McCain.

"Maybe, but it is hard to get money from my friends, you know." And David's voice trailed away. I knew then that even my best Chinese friends could not believe a black man could win the presidency.

Many Chinese did not know of my family connection, and I preferred it that way. Some of them did not see me as black and were unguarded in their comments before me, saying things like "You're not black, your skin is too light!" A number of Chinese acquaintances said many whites wouldn't vote for him in the general election.

With the election, something remarkable happened. From Montana to Texas, Florida to Illinois, Massachusetts to California, Americans of every background joined together in a common cause. With a surge of hope, through the ballot box, we clawed back our country.

Against all odds, my brother was elected president of the United States. A new America was indeed emerging.

That day, November 4, 2008, my wife and I celebrated the final election results in our modest Shenzhen apartment with a bottle of champagne. We had subscribed to CNN just for that evening, and were looking at the huge crowd in Chicago's Grant Park. Tears were running down our cheeks as we saw those other wet, happy, and ecstatic faces from far across the Pacific.

As I saw my brother emerge onto the podium, I texted a message to my friends in Shenzhen.

新美国来了
The New America Has Arrived.

To me it was a private message, but my life had changed. Little did I know that my text would be quoted on TV stations across China and Hong Kong and even in the United States.

Many of my Chinese friends were elated. It was as though the doubts they had privately nursed about America had vanished, or at least been ameliorated. On the buses local Chinese looked with astonishment at the

TV monitors, flabbergasted by the sight of a dark-skinned US president. A friend of mine who was in Beijing on election night told me he saw a middle-aged Chinese woman standing in front of a TV outside a little shop, tears running down her cheeks.

How surprising it must have been for many Chinese. I remember a time a few years back when I was on a late-night Shenzhen bus, returning after a day trip to Hong Kong. The conductress, seeing my travel bags and a little surprised that I spoke Mandarin, had struck up conversation with me.

"Where are you from?" she asked.

"America."

"You're American?" Her ruddy young face looked at me doubtfully.

"Yes, I'm American." I smiled.

"But all Americans have blue eyes and yellow hair. You do not look like an American," she protested, fingering an edge of her blue jacket in embarrassment. I just smiled, understanding a little of the astonishment she felt.

I certainly did not have blue eyes or blond hair. And now someone who looked just like me would shortly occupy the most powerful office in the world.

<hr />

Soon afterward I too realized a long-held dream. It was mid-January 2009, little more than three months after Barack's election, and just a few days before his inauguration ceremony, that an event I had long prepared for came to pass.

Before the tumult of American politics interrupted my life, my dream had long been to introduce music to orphans through a program of musical events, and above all through classes that could be taught in orphanages across China. I had never forgotten this dream.

One day back in 2003, four people met in a room above a piano shop in Shenzhen. I sat in front of a small wooden table, drumming my fingers on top of it. To my left was David, clutching his portfolio. To my right, my friend Alicia was sitting nervously, and across from me was the owner of the piano shop, Mr. Ye. We were discussing how to set up a concert to raise money for the orphans. Mr. Ye had always made his shop available for me to practice piano and I knew he was eager to help.

"We can make this happen!" David said. "We can get sponsors from the business community to help us," he continued, clutching his portfolio even tighter and gesticulating energetically.

Alicia, naturally more circumspect, listened carefully. She had just graduated from college, was young but wise, and I valued her opinion. After all, it was she who had first introduced me to the orphans and guided me through the necessary government paperwork before I could work with them.

"I will help too," Mr. Ye said, dabbing his brow with a handkerchief and more often than not taking off his spectacles to wipe them clean. "I can arrange the concert hall and get a good piano."

"Everyone should donate money or resources. No one should have to pay anything. It's for the kids," I said. It seemed we were all on the same page.

Only Alicia didn't say much.

After the meeting, she counseled caution, saying "It might be difficult. China has so many rules and regulations about foreigners."

I didn't listen. I stayed positive. It was that hope thing. I felt that with the help of my friends, their energy and knowledge of Shenzhen, anything was possible. David and I explained our proposal to the orphanage director. Afterward, David was upbeat.

"Very, very good news," he said. "The director said that they would take care of all the paperwork. That is a big thing. Dealing with the government paperwork is a big thing."

I noticed that in China whenever government was involved with anything, people tended to be very wary. The bureaucracy there is highly convoluted, and many Chinese dislike and distrust it, preferring not to divulge their personal and business information if they can avoid it.

I put together a detailed plan but realized we were missing something—foreigners.

"Sure, I know what you want," a friend said when I asked her to join. "I'm good at these dog and pony shows. The Chinese love to see the *Lao Wai** make fools of ourselves. Count me in!"

---

* Foreigners.

An American working at the Guangzhou consulate offered to play guitar. Three women friends offered to sing. Some Chinese friends also offered to play violin. My program still felt lacking because I just did not have many friends in China yet.

Then one day I got off the bus at Windows of the World and saw a beautiful Russian woman reading a book. I walked over and explained what we were trying to do. I knew that the theme park employed a number of foreign dancers, many from Eastern Europe. She was absolutely gorgeous, and I didn't know if she would think I was a crank and brush me off. However, the fact that she was reading a book gave me courage.

"Are you a dancer here?" I asked.

Without skipping a beat, she answered, "Yes, I dance at the evening show."

"Could you perform at a charity show we're putting together in Shenzhen to support orphans?"

"Of *course*. If it is for a good cause."

We were ready to go. I waited for further news from Alicia and David. And then nothing.

I knew one needs patience in China so I wasn't alarmed. I thought perhaps they were just busy.

Then weeks passed by, and there was still no news about the concert. Now I was worried. Finally, David called me.

"I talked again to the director. He asks me if we can postpone it until next year."

"What? We are all ready!" I was burning to go.

"I know," David said. "But, you see, it's the way things are here. He is giving me excuses. I don't think he really wants to do it. Maybe it is too much paperwork for him and this is really an excuse not to proceed."

I was devastated. So much for ordinary people getting together and making things happen. I had yet to learn that Chinese government workers have a built-in reluctance to innovating and taking risks. There's a rampant fear of failure that comes from a culture where achievement is rarely rewarded but failed experiments severely punished.

But six years later things had changed. I had built credibility with the orphanage. With the election campaign, and eventual election, of my brother, I had increased visibility. I felt no compunction about using this visibility to help people who needed it. I decided to set up a charity concert with some of my Chinese friends, but it fell through. In desperation, I called Harley Seyedin, the president of the American Chamber of Commerce of South China.

"We can do it. I have a great team here. Just tell me when," Harley said over the phone from Guangzhou.

"In a month."

"Let me talk about it with my team and I will get back to you." A few days later he texted me.

"We can do it. Just say the word."

"Let's go," I replied.

This time the stars aligned in our favor. On January 16, the night before I flew to the presidential inauguration, I gave a piano concert to raise money for, and build awareness of, orphans in China. Harley, who shared in the jubilation at my brother's victory, together with his team, pulled out all the stops to help my dream become a reality. Through Chen Kai Zhi, former mayor of Guangzhou and head of the China Poverty Alleviation Fund, we obtained the necessary government approvals and support.

I performed three piano pieces at the event: a nocturne by Chopin, a famous Chinese folk tune, and a jazz piece by Fats Waller. I remember walking through a blinding series of camera flashes before the relief of finally sitting down in front of the piano. The sound of the clicking cameras was deafening, like thousands of crickets magnified in stereo. Flashbulbs blinded me and forced me to close my eyes again. From the crowd, questions were shouted out at me.

"Mark, how old are you?"

"Do you talk with your brother?"

"Are you going to the inauguration?"

I ignored them and started to play the beautiful Hunan tune "Liu Yang River." At once I was in my own private world, a place of pure sound and meditation, peace and inner strength. In the 1950s, this lovely melody was set to words praising Chairman Mao. I had been worried conservatives in the United States would consider me a traitor for playing it. I had even e-mailed my concern to my contact at the White House Press office, but he had calmed my fears.

"Hmmm, if it's obvious enough for the reporters to notice it might be an issue," he said, "but sounds like you are mixing it up enough that they would really have to do their homework to notice."

"Liu Yang River" is a piece much loved by the Chinese people. Toward the end of the piece that night, during its rousing climax, I heard Chen Kai Zhi, behind me on the podium, singing loud enough for everyone to hear him.

When I finished, somewhere behind the whirring cameras and reporters' cries came the sounds of clapping hands and the babble of conversation. I prefaced each piece with a few words of introduction.

My next piece, "Viper's Drag," by the great black stride pianist Fats Waller, was a work that Judith Stillman, a well-known American pianist, had taught me when I was an undergraduate at Brown University. The title literally refers to a drag of marijuana. My wife and I had debated explaining this to the audience. In the end we decided to do so, but I paraphrased the reference to marijuana as simply "having a good time."

The final piece, the one closest to my heart, was the Chopin Nocturne Op. 9 No. 1, his first published nocturne. I learned this marvelous romantic work in high school just when I was starting to perform publicly. I still remembered the first time I had played it in the school auditorium and Father Cormac had told everyone to be quiet and listen. It has been one of my favorite performance pieces ever since.

After I stood to take a bow, there was applause from the concertgoers and even some of the photographers. A lanky reporter with piercing eyes stood up and repeated his question:

"Mark, how old are you?"

I ignored him. It was Bill Foreman, bureau chief of Associated Press in China. Ironically, he would scoop my first interview almost a year later. But this time, I was taking no questions, particularly about my personal life.

The concert was a great success. We raised almost forty thousand dollars in cash and gifts for orphans in Shenzhen and survivors of the Sichuan earthquake eight months earlier. Most important, thanks to the media coverage, millions around the world were more aware of their plight than before. With this success behind me, I could then focus on the coming week in Washington, DC, where Barack Obama would be sworn in as president of the United States. I, too, would be there to share in his happiness.

I frequently speak out against domestic violence. Here I am at a Speak Out Against Abuse initiative of a Shenzhen NGO I helped promote. I want the world to realize that even the American president's family had specific, extreme experiences with domestic violence. Just as I would speak out, so could others. c. 2012

David Sui and me in Hainan during the 2008 campaign. Contrary to news reports, I have not and never had any relationship with his barbecue food chain.

In 2010 I gave a benefit piano concert in Guangzhou's Xinghai Concert Hall, organized by the American Chamber of Commerce in South China. Chamber President Harley Seyedin (right) is pictured here with his brilliant son, nine-year-old co-presenter Dylan Sterling. Philip Chan, the other co-presenter, stands on the left. Dr. Xia, the children's hospital director, is in the middle of the photo. The local audience and sponsors raised enough money to fund more than one hundred heart operations for poor children in need of immediate lifesaving procedures.

CHAPTER TWENTY-ONE

White House Family Reunion

MUSICAL EVOCATION

Adagio for Strings: Samuel Barber
The string quartet is the most personal of musical ensembles, and the orchestra the most public. Copland's "Fanfare for the Common Man" and Dvořák's "New World Symphony" are more popular as representations of American music, but Barber's work symbolizes the essence of America through its magical reworking of a simple melody, in a smaller and more intimate setting. America, at its core, like this famous melody, is about reinventing itself, creating hope where once there was none.

IT WAS THE MIDDLE OF THE AFTERNOON IN SHENZHEN. A BREEZE FROM the South China Sea rustled the white cotton blinds of my apartment and sucked them partially out the open window; they fluttered like the wings of angels over Mei Lin Road. I knew it would rain shortly.

I was holding a bunch of photos taken during the inauguration, cheap Kodaks mailed to me in China by my relatives.

There was gold everywhere. It weaved in and out of objects, a sinuous gleaming presence like a beautiful snake. The color yellow was once the Chinese emperor's sole prerogative, and unauthorized use, in feudal times, punishable by death. In the photos it shone from the exotic hijab of my eldest brother Malik Obama's wife, on Kezia's scarf, in the luminous background, and the gilded interiors of the Mayflower Hotel. Revisiting this scene felt bittersweet. Those joyful times seemed far away now. We all looked so happy, so exhilarated.

In one photo of just the two us, Bobby, who now calls himself Malik, loomed over me, his face so black I couldn't see his features properly. His arm pointed to the left, as though commanding someone. His eyeglasses and round shining cheeks seemed to give him two pairs of eyes. For a moment, I remembered the taunts of my schoolmates: *Four eyes! Four eyes!*

I was pictured standing gingerly next to him, as though afraid he would fall and crush me. We were both holding an inscribed gold plate I had brought for him from China.

During inauguration week, the Kenyan Obamas had gathered each day on the second floor of the famous Mayflower Hotel in Washington, DC. Realizing several of his kin were too poor to make the trip, Barack had paid out of his own pocket for their accommodation and plane fares. Outside the hotel, Washington was in a frenzy over the inauguration. Inside the hotel it was quieter, but just as joyful.

Another photo showed me with Kezia, her son Bernard, Malik's wife, his two children, my brother Joseph, and others. We all looked elated but with a sort of shell shock in our eyes, too, as though we could not believe what had happened. Kezia's eyes, in particular, seemed bemused and a little afraid, as though she saw in this spectacle a grand but evanescent dream. Malik's son, dressed in a red cardigan, his hands in his pockets, had a sweet, glorious smile, shy and unperturbed. He seemed lost in a secret world overflowing with lilacs and daisies, marshmallow trees and rivers of chocolate.

Notable were the people missing from the shots, such as Granny Sarah, who does not get along with Malik and stayed in another part of the hotel. Aunt Zeituni was then battling immigration officials in Boston, and afterward she walked around the hotel lobby with her lawyer, slightly stunned and ignored by several family members. Throughout the inauguration, Auma and her daughter Akinyi would keep away from Malik and his group, remaining with Granny Sarah. "Those people in Kisumu, they always have these power struggles," my mother would say to me. "I just keep away from them. I don't need all that useless *maneno!*"

In one photo my arm is around Kezia while Joseph hugs Bernard. My younger brother and I were blissfully naive about the internal power struggles of extended families, let alone the grand politics of Washington.

For a brief, glorious moment in our lives, all of us had come . . . from Kenya, Britain, China . . . to the capital of the United States, to dream of a united world.

———

January 17, 2009

On the plane from Shenzhen to Washington, DC, I idled away the time by observing the passengers next to me, mostly Chinese families and some business people. I looked out the window. Hong Kong and its various islands, called the New Territories, were already far behind.

The inauguration would mark the end of my own journey across three cultures. Little did I know that this plane trip was, in fact, only another stage of the odyssey, and that my meeting with the Obama family members would mark the beginning of a new chapter in my life, one that would lead to redemption and heartbreak, joy and catharsis.

I was to be in Washington for approximately a week. There were concerts, ceremonies, and other events to attend, and lots of catching up to do with the extended family.

"Okoth, Umerudi." Granny Sarah's familiar voice greeted me in Swahili. *Okoth, you have returned.*

The matriarch of the Obama family, Granny had cared for my father, Barack Obama Sr., after his own mother left him and rejoined her own family. The last time I had seen Granny I was about five years old, visiting Kogelo. Then, under the mango tree, next to the chickens and children playing, her grizzled face had looked to me like the bark of a mahogany tree, another harsh detail in an alien landscape.

In her Mayflower Hotel room in Washington, DC, she was sitting on a small stool, chatting with the family members clustered around her. Light from the window behind her cast a shadow over her face, but her smile shone out across the dark hotel room. She said a few words in Luo, which I did not understand. I sat down on the edge of the bed facing her.

"Granny, how are you?" I said in Swahili. I did not know Luo, and even if I had, I would not have known what else to say. It had been so long.

She smiled again and said a few words to a young woman next to her, who translated.

"She has waited a long time for you to come back. She is sorry for what happened."

As my gaze turned from the translator back to Granny's smiling face, I thought I had heard wrong: *She is sorry for what happened. What made her say that?* I thought. She could have talked of my life in China, or of the weather outside. She could have asked me about my mother, or even chatted about recent extraordinary events. She could have mentioned how her back hurt in the cold January weather, or how she missed her *nyoyo* (corn and beans) or herbal medicine. Yet, instead, her first words were about those days long, long ago, full of dark memories that marked the thorny, trampled road of our Obama family. I realized all at once that my own unhappiness had not existed in a vacuum. Something inside me cracked then. I knew that Granny still loved me, and she was welcoming me back.

"Bring me your wife. I want to meet her," she added.

Brushing back tears, I grasped her hand in both of mine. Her teeth were very white in her ebony face, which seemed smooth-skinned and gleaming, no longer the harsh, scored surface of a child's bad dream. At that moment she was my light in the darkness, welcoming me, forgiving me for my long absence. I promised her I would take Xue Hua to visit her in Africa.

I heard Malik's loud bellows of laughter before I met him again. Walking up the steps to the second floor of the hotel, I recognized him at once, looming above a group of other Kenyans, all talking excitedly. His deep voice resonated in the air and across the years.

"Bobby, how are you doing, bro?"

He looked at me, eyes wide in disbelief. "Okoth, it's you. How are you doing, brother?"

We gave each other a long hug. It felt natural, as though we were seeing each other after a short time apart. I was surrounded by other Obama family members, including aunts and uncles, nephews and nieces that I barely remembered. The family had practically taken over the entire mezzanine. Bags and cell phones were scattered across the furniture, and Luo, Swahili, and English peppered the air. I looked again at my eldest brother.

"It's good to see you, Bobby. It's been a long time."

He shook his head. "It's Malik now. Ma-LIK."

Dressed in a Muslim *kofia* [hat] and long white robe, he lowered his large frame heavily on to a sofa and stared at the blank screen of the TV.

"I think of him every day," he added in a quieter voice. "I see David and it breaks my heart." He did not look at me. He might have been crying; it was hard to tell.

I met his mother, Kezia, who had come with her younger son Bernard from the UK. She peered at me closely, as though looking for the vestiges of a boy whose face was only a dim memory.

"Okoth, Okoth, it's you! Come here." She tried to get up but fell back in her chair, clearly unable to stand easily. I bent down and she gave me a hug. I also greeted Bernard, and I learned Kezia's other son, Abo, was not yet in the United States. I would bump into him later during the week. He needed money so I gave him a little. I learned later that he had had a rough week, detained in the UK by the police.

My sister Auma had her own demons to deal with. I was one of them. She was like Patience, the character in *Dreams of Red Mansions* who serves the matriarch of the royal family. Upset after receiving a slight, she refuses to talk to Bao Yu, the young boy, and walks away instead. When I had visited Granny at the Mayflower, Auma was there but my sister had refused to look at me directly. We had hugged, but it felt like I was touching a model in a window.

"Granny and Auma want nothing to do with Malik, and Malik wants to control everything. They don't talk to each other," someone later explained. Why this meant Auma could not welcome me remained unclear.

Behind the smiles and bright eyes of other family members, I sensed a history of aggrieved feelings, small and petty jealousies, and subtle and not-so-subtle power plays. While I wanted to join their circle, I hoped I would not be drawn into these dark conflicts.

I walked out on to the streets of Washington, DC. Throughout the city, there was a special feeling in the air. Washington—and America—seemed free for the first time in a long while. It was as though something had driven away the fear and suspicion that had settled over the country since 9/11. A new beginning had dawned with this new president.

"Do you feel ostracized because of your race?" Barack had asked me long, long ago when we first met in Kenya.

"No, I just ignore those things," I said. "I have a thick skin. I forge ahead and ignore them."

He had looked at me slowly, as if he didn't believe what I was saying, but made no comment.

"What about in America? Do they accept you?" I asked him in return. He hadn't answered. Barack kept many secrets, but I felt then as if I had touched a nerve.

My brother understood race relations far better than I did. For so many years I had, like my mother, willfully blinded myself to any problems arising from differences in skin color.

Yet over the course of many years, I had discovered for myself the way that race affects so much of who we are, what we do, and how we progress in life. Like Barack, I had refused to be pigeonholed. Unlike me, he had been welcomed everywhere he went. He was what I had never been: popular.

At one time, I had resented him for this.

That day I was attending his day of glory and transfiguration as a member of his extended family, one that he himself had described as a "mini–United Nations." My mother was white, my father black. I was married to a Chinese woman. One of my brothers (through my stepfather) was married to a Mexican American. I had Christian and Muslim brothers, a sister who had married a white Briton, a half-Indonesian sister. My maternal grandmother had emigrated from Lithuania. Indonesia, Kenya, China, England, the USA, Mexico, Lithuania. Jewish, Christian, Muslim, Agnostic. We were a truly global family, and this global family was now represented in the White House. To me this signified the greatness of America, the defeat of racism, and the emergence of a truly global multiculturalism.

I stayed at my friend Paul's house just outside of DC. Around nine o'clock on the morning of the swearing-in ceremony, Paul drove me to the metro station closest to his house. I estimated it would take about an hour to get to the National Cathedral for the morning prayer, after which Barack would be sworn in around noon. When we discovered the roads were closed, we wasted precious time backtracking to another station. Waving a quick good-bye to Paul, I dashed down the steps to the crowded platform. A few minutes later a train arrived. It was heaving with passengers, so crowded that the doors would not close.

"Get out and take the next one!" someone yelled. I was roughly pushed out when I tried to squeeze in. The train moved only a few feet and then stopped.

A voice came on the speaker: The train into Washington is delayed.

Before the announcement was finished, I had already run up the station steps and made a beeline for the waiting taxicabs. I opened the door of the first one.

"I need to get into Washington!"

The driver, a man with a mop of thick hair and a Rude Dog T-shirt was listening to earphones and filling out his newspaper crossword. He looked up at me and shook his head.

"DC?" His accent was faintly Middle Eastern. "No. All the roads are blocked."

"Can't you try? I must get there!" I pleaded. He shook his head again. "No. No way to get in."

An icy shiver ran down my body. I looked at my mobile phone. It was already closing on ten o'clock. I was in danger of missing the inauguration.

"Please, you must try to get me there. I have invitations!" He shook his head and turned back to his crossword. I dashed to the next cab in line. A portly man with a salt-and-pepper mustache looked at me with some puzzlement.

"Washington, DC. Very hard get there." His accent was Greek or Middle Eastern.

"Please, please, you must help. I'll pay whatever you want," I said. He stared into my face. I must have looked desperate because his head shake turned into a slight nod.

"I take you to Virginia. Maybe metro not crowded there."

I jumped in the back and we were off to try another station. This one was even more crowded. It was almost impossible to move on the platform, let alone get into the train, whose doors were opening and closing as if broken.

"The metro is blocked down the line," someone explained to me.

I jumped back into the cab. The driver looked at me pityingly. "You really need to go to DC, I can tell!"

"Yes!"

"Let me call and see what is going on." He talked to someone on his cell phone.

"It is not good," he said. "The police have closed every road into downtown."

"I have invitations," I said, waving my brown folder of tickets. "They will let me through. I know I can get through."

He scratched his head for a moment, then thrust his chin up and looked at me fiercely from behind his thick glasses.

"Okay, we go!"

The roads were devoid of traffic. Every few hundred feet, police cars with flashing strobes sat on the buffer lanes. Were it not for these, I would have felt we were the last people on earth. We drove for about fifteen minutes and came to a freeway on-ramp filled with several patrol cars. We were flagged down and a beefy officer peered through the window.

"I'm sorry, gents, you have to turn back. The road is blocked from here on in."

"Officer," I said in my most charming voice, "I have an invitation to the inauguration and other events. We must be there on time." I desperately did not want to say I was the president's brother.

"I'm sorry, sir," he said, politely but firmly, "no one can get through."

I handed him the invitations and said with as much emphasis as I could politely use: "Officer, please call the White House. You can check with them. The president is my brother."

For a moment no one said anything. The officer looked at me as though he hadn't heard me right. I didn't say anything. He took my envelope of documents and started to open it, while other officers grouped around the cab looked on in silence. Then, without looking inside, he handed the envelope back to me.

"Are you really the president's brother?"

"Yes, officer," I said meekly. "I came all the way from China to see this."

I handed him the brown envelope again. He waved it aside and laughed.

"Go on. I don't need to see them. You look like him!"

He talked with another policeman. A sergeant walked up to me. "We'll radio on down for them to let you through," he said.

Some of the officers then saluted.

At that moment I felt an immense rush of pride. It was as though some of Barack's glory had rubbed off on me, and I, too, had an honored role to play on this momentous day.

The taxi driver was quiet as we continued down the deserted roads. If he was surprised he did not show it.

"You know, I have a PhD back in Syria," he said abruptly. I nodded, wondering where this was going. "I came to America with my family, and I am driving a taxi. I have a PhD."

"Congratulations!" I did not know what else to say.

"My children are now studying in America, and they are Americans, like me. I am proud to be American, and when I have time I can teach people as well. Today is a good day. One day I will get a better job, but today anything is possible in America."

We started chatting, about his daughter who was studying for a doctorate, his determination to build a home and a future for his immigrant family. At about eleven o'clock we entered downtown Washington, DC. Near the cathedral we were stopped by a soldier standing next to an army tank on the road. Again I explained the situation. He didn't bother to check any credentials but took a long look at me and waved me on.

"Okay," he said. "No problem. Please go ahead."

Then, just before we drove off, he bent down to me. With his face close to mine, and in a low voice, he said, "If you get a chance to talk to him, can you please tell him that Don't Ask, Don't Tell doesn't work. Everyone in the army hates it."

I nodded. "I understand."

The cathedral was before me. As I scrambled out of the car, the driver gave me his card. I grabbed his hand.

"Thank you so much. I will never forget this." He nodded.

"E-mail me. Thank you, sir. Thank you."

Everyone in America knew this was a day for the history books; indeed, it was a day on which the whole world watched and marveled. People on five continents had waited breathlessly for the outcome of the campaign. A few days after 9/11, the French prime minister, Jacques Chirac, had said "We are all Americans" in a gesture of solidarity. Now, with this election, billions of people around the world could feel and share in America's battered but enduring spirit of optimism.

The election had dealt a stinging retort to the spirit of racism that had tainted so much of American history. It had upended conventional wisdom and shattered decades of ossified thinking. Every American minority had had to deal with the burdens of race, and for those who were unschooled in the rituals and etiquette of racial relations, like myself, it had been painful. Inspired to seek change, millions voted for the first time in their lives in a testament to my country's ability to reach that "more perfect union" spoken of by the founding fathers in the American Constitution, and during the campaign by Barack himself.

I once had told a good friend, "America has a marvelous, and perhaps unique, ability to pull itself out of problems by remaking itself anew."

Now I attended a prayer session to celebrate that process and stood on the platform before my brother's podium. On that chilly January day at the Lincoln Memorial, with an icy wind biting into my jacket, someone remarked to me:

"Look behind you. Isn't that something?"

I turned my head around to face the Washington Monument. A vast rectangular pool stretched hundreds of feet across the park toward the lofty white obelisk. What looked at first to be a flat brown pancakelike substance surrounded the still, icy water. My eyes were misty from the cold and my whole body was shivering. Focusing my gaze, I realized the "pancake" was people, countless people filling the park, so numerous they were like cascading levels of ever-lighter colors, eventually vanishing into the horizon.

When my brother was finally sworn in, on the steps of the Capitol, I was filled with a sense of wonder and gratitude, humility and pride. I felt happy and honored to be there, but my real goal was to see my brother again.

The day after the inauguration, I met him at the White House. That morning Reggie Love had called me to say, "Come over about four. The president will give you a tour and take time for some photos afterward."

Joseph, Dora, and I were thrilled. I so wanted to see and congratulate Barack. In particular I wanted some private time with him, even if just for a few minutes. I wanted to tell him how much I supported him and how I would never use our family connection in a dishonorable way, as some in the press and others had started to say. But it was not to be.

At the White House, as we waited in the West Wing, the door opened and Bernard, Malik, and Kezia walked in, followed by Bernard and Malik's children.

"You guys thought you could see him without me? Sorry to disappoint you!" Malik said triumphantly to Dora. He seemed a little upset, though, eyes wide behind his glasses.

This was another point of friction that tended to appear at the oddest times in our dysfunctional family. I sighed but resigned myself to a family event. I realized that, from now on, as long as Barack would be president, he would hardly ever have time to be alone with just one or two individuals. For the remainder of his term of office, perhaps even after that, there would always be an aide or adviser around him, and his every action and comment would be explicitly or secretly monitored. Furthermore, family members, including myself, would become almost possessive about access to him. It was like we were jealous wives in a harem, all angling for time with the emperor. It would take time for each of us, including me, to moderate our behavior and rid ourselves of this empty jealousy and possessiveness.

Our small group waited in a room in the West Wing. The White House struck me as much less colorful, smaller, and much more staid than in photos I'd seen: almost like a museum. I didn't care. I would be seeing my brother again and it was a wonderful feeling. It was as though he was sweeping away all the hurt, shame, and regrets of my life. I had only to think that my brother was with me both in spirit and in this great house, helping to change the world.

It was as though the words of the ancient Chinese saying were carrying across the Pacific and the fifty states to this day and time.

爱屋及乌
Love for a person extends even to the crows on his roof.

I had been the crow; perhaps I could fly away and become a swan. As I looked around at the members of my family gathered in the White House, I was suddenly swept up by a feeling of such ebullience I believed anything might be possible.

Suddenly the door opened and Barack walked in. He wore a dark-gray suit with dark shoes and moved with that familiar, comfortable ease, sliding over the ground with a light swagger that reminds many of our father. Dora, Joe, and I were in the corner to the left of the door. Malik and the others were directly in front. Perhaps because Malik was the tallest in the room, Barack moved toward them and at first didn't see the rest of us. Then he looked around, saw me, and came up. We hugged. I looked carefully at his expression. It was abstracted, as though he was thinking of something else.

"How are you! Good to see you!" His baritone was strong and distinct, full of authority.

"Good to see you too, Barack. We are so proud of you, bro!"

I introduced Joe and Dora. She was beaming. I had never seen her so happy. My Mexican-American sister-in-law loves Barack. Dora would always tell everyone how, when they last met in Austin, Barack had remembered her upcoming wedding and even asked her how the preparations were going.

We all gave him our gifts.

"This is a photo of my wife, Xue Hua." I handed him the framed photo I had brought from China.

"Yes, I remember her. Please give her my regards."

"She really wanted to come and meet you, but the media glare was just too intense. We hope we can meet when you are in China."

"I understand. I'm sorry she could not come."

"This is for you and Michelle."

I handed him two porcelain Mandarin ducks, which symbolize eternal love, a hand-stitched silkscreen portrait, and some herbal teas.

"When you are in China, can you visit our house for dinner?" Only later did I realize how absurd that statement must have appeared. He didn't laugh, however, but said: "I don't think that will be possible, Mark. They won't let me."

This was the confirmation of the fact that even the most powerful man in the world had limits set on him. There were places even he couldn't go. But it hadn't yet sunk in with me that my brother was no longer an ordinary man. I so wanted him to visit Shenzhen.

Before I could continue, Reggie Love chipped in: "Mr. President, we only have about thirty minutes. Maybe we should start the tour."

"Right. Everybody, let me show you around this place."

And with that my brother led the way. We passed through a room decorated in red furniture and fabric.

"I'm getting my bearings so Worthington can correct me, okay?" He turned to Worthington White, the White House usher. A pudgy, smiling man standing next to us gently nodded.

"This is the Red Room," Barack said, and then at a loss for words, added, "I think it is because everything in it is red." I thought he was joking and waited for him to say more. He didn't.

The Red Room is one of four official White House reception rooms. The richly carved and beautiful furniture was created by the French-born cabinetmaker Charles-Honoré Lannuier. It reflects Napoleonic motifs of sphinxes, dolphins, lion's heads, and other characteristic designs. The draperies are made of gold satin with red silk valances and handmade gold-and-red fringe.

We went into another room, which was all decorated in green. Thomas Jefferson used to cover the floor with a green canvas for protection, hence the name.

"This is the Green Room. I wish I could tell you more about it," Barack bashfully added, "but I really am still learning."

As we walked into the room, a young Secret Service Officer looked up at him. "Where are you from?" he asked her.

"Arkansas, Mr. President."

"I like Arkansas. Many good people there."

She beamed at him, her eyes shining. It was as though Barack had touched a personal chord with her, even though he wasn't obliged to. It was this sense of connection and empathy that had been important in helping my brother attain the love of the American people and, by extension, the presidency.

In the State Room there was a portrait of Lincoln, sitting cross-legged, chin in hand, staring thoughtfully into the near distance. We stood looking at it for a few seconds. I asked who the painter was. No one knew. Worthington stepped out and rushed back a few seconds later, his face flushed, as though he had just come back from a jog.

"William Cogswell!" he said triumphantly.

In one room there were scores of paintings of Barack and Michelle. There were so many, several had been placed on the floor. We gingerly tiptoed around them.

"These are paintings people have given us. I don't know what to do with them," Barack said.

Although none of the paintings seemed to be of great artistic merit, each reflected the dreams, hopes, and aspirations of someone in America who had passionately supported him.

"Look after Kezia. These steps are a bit steep," Barack said quietly.

Even on this momentous day, he was thinking of his father's ailing first wife. With help from some of us, Kezia moved slowly up the steps to the second floor of the White House. By now Barack looked preternaturally serious, as though the weight of the world was on his shoulders. Other than when some photos were taken, he wouldn't smile once throughout the tour. Unlike our earlier meeting in Austin, a few months before he was elected, this time he seemed to be distant, almost in another world. That he nevertheless found time to welcome family to his new home on the day after the inauguration was a sign of the largeness of his spirit.

When we walked into the Oval Office, Barack cautioned everyone: "My lawyers have asked me to tell you that any photos you take in this room cannot be posted on the Internet." We all nodded.

Malik didn't say much. He just chewed an apple he'd picked up from the desk and with his other hand clutched a card that Barack had signed for the townspeople back in Kogelo. He seemed totally underwhelmed. Though the room was smaller than I'd expected, the desk, however, was imposing. And the chair! What could one say about that chair? High back, leather upholstered, simple and utterly magnificent. Almost as though there was an invisible force about it. Everyone in the room would sit on the sofa, try out the fruit, touch the plants, but not one person, even the kids, would go near that chair.

At that point I made a big mistake. I pronounced my brother's name with the accent on the first syllable: *Ba*rack.

He immediately said, "You should pronounce it Ba*rack*."

I apologized but he wasn't having any of it. He went on: "After two years you should know by now!"

I was stunned into silence. I had used the pronunciation of our father's name, BARack, as seemed natural to me. I realized later that even when we had met in the past, I had probably mispronounced his name. Why hadn't he ever corrected me before? Perhaps he did not want me to be publicly embarrassed. Perhaps he hadn't thought it important at the time. Now we were among family, and family members tend to be direct among themselves. "Sorry, Barack," I said to him a while later, when we were alone. Astonished, he looked at me.

"Sorry for what?"

"For getting your name wrong!"

He softened his tone, took me aside, and said, "Don't worry, Mark. Because of security issues I cannot have dinner with you in Shenzhen, but I will definitely meet your wife."

I felt much better then. I wanted him to like and accept me. It was taking me a while to realize that this would take time and much patience.

"You are brothers," Xue Hua told me, "you cannot change that. He cares for you but he is also like you. He is hard and tough."

I remembered how I, too, had been hard with my mother those years ago at Brown, that day when we were crossing the street and I had cruelly lashed out because I was ashamed of her. It was that hardness in me that sometimes attacked the softness in people around me. Barack had a little of this, too, but he was also, I honestly believed, a much more decent person than I was. How could I expect to turn up after so many years and at once start a relationship with him, and others in my family, as though nothing had happened in the interim?

"Life flies by faster than the blink of an eyelid," said the Bahai prophet Bahá'u'lláh. I had dreamed that, in the blink of an eye, I could repair relations with my siblings, and by doing so come to terms with myself. The process would take a little longer than that, but attending my brother's inauguration was a significant first step.

"My brother has given me confidence to start this journey," I told Xue Hua. "I am proud of him."

What Barack had brought to my life—the sudden global exposure, the pride in my family, the awareness that I could amplify the impact I had on helping those who needed help—was without price. There was no room in my heart for the bitterness of envy, or the swift and passing pleasure of retribution. A new life had opened up before me. My brother and I would no doubt continue to have a bumpy relationship, but what was that next to my newfound confidence in stepping out into the world? I now had the courage to be open about my past, and to cast aside the burdens of regret and failed promises.

Yes, my brother, you opened my heart to the world again. And for that I thank you.

———

As I flew back to Shenzhen, I thought not only of the extraordinary week that had just passed but also of the concert that had preceded it.

Would the money make a real difference? Would it truly improve the children's lives? Was music even the right path to take with them? I did not want all my efforts to be just a passing impression in a child's mind.

"Music helps to build confidence. Your students were very shy before. Now they have much more confidence," the teachers and staff at the orphanage had told me many times.

After passing through the proper channels, the money was finally released to three Shenzhen orphanages: in the Bao'an, Meilin, and Long-gang areas.

Yet I still did not see any tangible results. No new music program. No instruments. It seemed nothing much had changed. In time things fell back to the old rhythm, although I visited now about twice a month, rather than every week, as I was a little busier outside the orphanage.

Fallon was one of my newer students. She had been brought to the orphanage from another institution. She was about eleven years old, cut her hair short, and was tiny for her age. The expression on her face constantly veered between astonished and sulky, as though she had been wronged. However, every so often, when she was playing with other children or was seized by a fresh idea, her black eyes would light up and she would flash me a dazzling smile. I knew next to nothing about her background, but I guessed that she had been shunted from institution to institution and had little chance of being adopted at her relatively late age.

"She is smart but doesn't practice," Teacher Li complained. "She sometimes does not want to learn."

"Why?" I asked.

She shrugged. "Maybe she is not that interested in piano."

But I knew Fallon was drawn to music and vowed to be patient with her. A few weeks later, Teacher Li sent me a short message telling me that Fallon had run away from the orphanage and been gone for several hours. She suggested I not teach her that week.

I worried that my teaching had upset her in some way. Later, Teacher Li explained:

"She has been having trouble with the other children. She left the orphanage in the morning and the teachers went frantic trying to find her. Then, eleven hours later, the police found her almost outside of Shenzhen."

Perhaps Fallon had a loved one she was looking for, or perhaps there was something she was running from. I did not know. The workings of the orphanage, and of wider Chinese society, were still nebulous and mysterious to me.

I feared Fallon would stop learning piano. When I came in the next week, though, she was sitting glumly, looking at her music book. The lesson proceeded as usual, as though nothing out of the ordinary had happened.

A few weeks later I arrived at the orphanage and couldn't find her. Since it was later in the afternoon, I thought perhaps she was at dinner. After waiting several minutes I asked one of my students, an older boy, where she was.

"She is in the clinic downstairs," he said.

"What? Why?" I asked, shocked.

"I don't know."

I headed down to the clinic. At the end of a long corridor, past empty rooms filled with medical equipment, I found Fallon. She lay on a white bed; a long tube snaked from her arm to a drip bottle above her head. Her neck was terribly inflamed, swollen up to almost twice the normal size and painfully red. She looked at me and covered her eyes with her free hand, as though ashamed. She wouldn't talk to me.

"My God, what happened to her?" I asked one of the staff.

"She was in a fight with other children," I was told. They would not tell me more. Or perhaps they did, but I didn't understand.

I entreated the people in the clinic to take care of her. Before I left I walked over to her bedside.

"Fallon, don't worry, you'll leave here soon."

She just looked at me, her hand still over her eyes. Her swollen neck seemed to pulse in and out.

"You are doing great at piano. I am really proud of you. But," I added, "I want you to remember something."

She removed her hand and stared at me. She looked lost. Her eyes shifted restlessly about the room, as though she had run out of places to look.

"Respect other people. If you respect them, they will respect you."

The following week, when Fallon came into the room, she sat down demurely at the piano and wordlessly started to play. As usual, while her face remained stony, her hands darted nimbly over the keyboard. I thought I would try to pry a few words from her. I knew that she and some other children had recently traveled to Guilin, a province not far from Guangdong.

"I heard you went to Guilin? Did you like it?"

"Yes." The word came out as slow as treacle.

"What did you like about it?"

I waited while she looked expressionlessly at the keyboard. Then, just as I was about to change the topic, she lifted her chin.

"I could use the telephone."

"What?" Surely she had made telephone calls before, I thought.

"I liked making telephone calls," she repeated, and then she added something I didn't understand.

"She says she liked calling people in the other hotel rooms," another girl explained.

Fallon started talking in a rapid staccato, so fast I couldn't make heads or tails of her words. She said more to me in that minute than she had in almost a year. She had left the monosyllables behind, it seemed. But that wasn't all. She called in a young girl I had never seen before.

"She wants to play piano," Fallon said firmly, her chin lifted high.

Just as abruptly, she lowered her head and again lapsed into silence. I took my cue and taught the girl a few elementary exercises. I was surprised to discover she had already learned some simple pieces.

"You've played before. How did you know how to? Who taught you?"

"Fallon helped me play piano."

A strange, happy feeling washed over me. It was as though I had started something in these children that was bigger than me, something that would continue of its own volition and momentum. This girl who had run away two months ago and been in hospital was now expressing herself and helping another child.

It was hot inside the room, and I was sweating. I dabbed my forehead with some tissue. Just then one of the girls placed a cup of water on the piano.

I looked at the cup, and in a flash I remembered the first time I was there. I remembered the cup of water they had given me.

I could theorize without end why I was so happy to learn of what Fallon had done, but nothing seemed to answer the question. Years back, I had sought a fifth force, akin to gravity. Yet even physics could not explain the why, just the how. Charity, like love, was such a force, springing forth without reason, like a leaf reaches for the sun, or the sound of the wind through the leaves lulls one into a gentle sleep, or a cup of water brings forth memories.

The desire to help others can lie dormant within us, and then, without apparent reason, it burgeons like a flower. This happiness could also wash away the hurt and guilt of decades. My students' actions were now independent of me. The great river of life was continuing, from me, through me, and yet without me, and this gave me peace. They had taught me, and healed me.

Yet I was still waiting for the orphanage to do something with the money we had raised. I wondered when the director would get teachers and instruments for the children, as he had promised.

One day, as I walked in to give my regular piano lessons, Fallon rushed up to me, nervous and agitated, fluttering her hands like she was waving away flies.

She wore a pink cardigan that seemed to overwhelm her slight frame. The anxious expression on her face was particularly intense.

"Come down. You must come down!" she blurted out, as though petrified I would not hear.

I followed her down from the fourth floor. Almost forty people had gathered in the main reception room. Mr. Tang, the director, came up to me, a huge smile plastered over his face.

"Mr. Mark, come and see what we have done." Without waiting for a reply, he grabbed my hand and led me toward the podium.

The reception room normally looked empty and cavernous, filled with a conference table and some skimpy chairs and decorated with the occasional red banner draped over the proscenium. That day it looked gloriously different.

A small crowd of children and teachers had gathered. A boy was playing the piano. Laid out in neat rows were brand-new musical instruments such as violins and drums, even Chinese flutes and zithers. I recognized another boy, Zhen Qing, energetically playing the drums. Whenever I talked to him in the past, he had squinted as though he could not see me clearly before grabbing my hand, opening his eyes wide, and plaintively saying: "Teacher Mark, I want to play piano."

The few times I had coached him, I had never really felt his heart was in piano playing. But now it seemed as though he had found his instrument. He was a blur of motion, hair whipping from side to side, arms akimbo, and a huge smile stretching from ear to ear.

On one side of the room a group of what looked like punk rockers lounged on some seats. Mr. Tang led me over to them.

"These are our volunteers. They want to teach the children music and dancing."

Four men stood and I shook their hands while two women sitting beside them looked on and giggled.

"Help the kids. Please do what you can," I said. They nodded. A huge crash on the drums startled us. Zhen Qing had launched into an amazingly fast and precise rhythm, egged on by the small group of adoring kids next to him.

"I never even knew he could play," one of the teachers shouted above the din.

Music takes many forms and each child can find his or her own preference—so long as the opportunity to explore is made available at the right time.

Teacher Li, the organizer of the newly formed troupe, was ecstatic as he told me, "Teacher Mark, we will set up many classes for new students who want to learn music. Flute . . . recorder . . . we have many instruments that they can use. And now we can afford to find a piano teacher."

A few days later there was a concert at which I was honored by the orphanage. It was wonderful. City leaders came to express their support, and I learned that I had been appointed honorary director of a troupe of about eighty child musicians across the city.

One of my students then performed a Chopin nocturne. He was dressed in a tux. A little over the top, I thought, but he looked happy enough. Later he complained about his own performance, like a proper musician.

"Terrible! Terrible . . . The piano keys were sticking. I couldn't play and had to stop."

"Always check your instrument before you play," I advised him. "You must take control. Try not to let others choose your instrument for you. But you did well so don't worry too much."

He nodded and looked a little relieved. He then smiled and talked about other things, like how he was going to start a restaurant business and how difficult it was to do the volunteer piano teaching he undertook every Sunday. As I listened to him I realized that my time in China had not been wasted, that it had been a joyous thing to get to know this boy and his peers.

Although I had seen them only for brief periods every week, I felt I had played my part as they had grown. I remembered when Zhen Qing was half this size, his mouth gaping when he was curious. I remembered how another child, now a strapping teenager, once rushed up to me in the courtyard, grabbed my hand, and pointed to the object I wore on a chain around my neck.

"What is that?"

"It's a lion's tooth."

"I want it!"

"Well, I cannot give it to you, but you can hold it, okay?"

I handed it to him. He grasped the gold-mounted tooth and reluctantly handed it back to me.

"Is it really a lion's tooth?" he asked.

"Yes," I said, and he scampered off grinning.

Now he was much taller, up on the stage, eyes alight with inspiration and happiness. I'd heard he was due to go to university.

All these faces . . . how some have changed, how fast time has gone by, I thought. Seven years in the blink of an eye.

A few days later at our next lesson, I asked little Fallon why she wanted to play piano. She said, after much coaxing from me and Mr. Li, "Because I like music."

So simple and to the point. This was the outcome I had wanted all along.

Performing at the Mayflower Hotel. During Inauguration Week I
found some time to play on the wonderful piano at this historical
hotel where several family members were staying. c. 2009

At the White House I gave
Barack a framed photo of
Simeon and Ruth.

Barack and me at the White
House, sharing a light moment.
c. 2009

Inauguration 2009. Barack gave a tour of the White House, including the Oval Office. Here we both admire a painting of Abraham Lincoln. (PHOTO: DORA ZEPEDA NDESANDJO)

To Ruth – Wishing you all the best!

Barack gave us a tour of the White House in 2009. When my stepfather, Simeon Ndesandjo, passed away in 2011, I asked Barack to sign the attached photo for my mother as she was extremely depressed and needed a lift. He promptly did so.

CODA

Kenyan Spring

Musical Evocation

Okok Okok: Luo Song

*Okok okok miya kodi marachar, Okok okok miya kodi marachar, Mondi
wawil kodi gi maga, Adhigo ka wendo mabor*

*(Bird, Bird. Give me your white nails. Bird, bird. Give me your white nails.
Let me exchange mine for yours,
fly far, far away)*

*In January 2011 I flew to Nairobi, and visited my hometown, Alego-Kogelo,
for three days. My last visit there had been in 1972. In a few intense days, I
helped make up for more than three decades of absence. While I was there, I
learned this Luo tune, which is sung by children as they herd cattle around the
shores of Lake Victoria. The words cross cultures, to speak of a universal sense of
identity, self-discovery, and redemption.*

"If my hands were black, they wouldn't stop!"

My mother's hand fluttered from the car window like a white flag. The
small minibus, or *matatu*, whizzing toward us slowed down immediately.

In January 2011 I went back to Kenya for a short visit. I was determined to catch up on my many years of absence and reconnect again with

my relatives in Alego. I also wanted to understand more about my early life in Nairobi.

"What is with this identity thing of yours?" Mum asked me.

"I want to understand where the different aspects of me came from. It's like a mosaic. I'm unique, but each part of me came from somewhere ... someone. The process of finding out helps me learn more about myself, what I can do and where my life should lead."

So one Saturday morning, at my request, my mother drove Xue Hua and me to the house I'd lived in as a young child. It was a tortuous route. She steered her car deftly through the traffic, using the less-traveled, ignominiously named rat routes to avoid bottlenecks. She zoomed past the Technical Centre where I sat for my SATs twenty years before, then charged straight along Ngong Road into Adams Arcade, a busy commercial strip of shops including a supermarket and gas station. Our noses were assailed by the pungent smoke from burning garbage and charcoal fires. Occasionally a *matatu* whizzed directly toward our car, and each time she would flutter her fleshy white flag of a hand and it would slow down in response.

"Woodley used to be a nicer neighborhood," she proudly exclaimed amidst the din of blaring horns and screeching tires. "I still remember where to go though!" She drove fast for a woman in her seventies.

At the Adams Arcade roundabout, we took a sharp right into a warren of roads that used to be surrounded by green fields. All that was visible now were tarpaulin-draped squatters' camps and shops made from leaning corrugated-iron sheets. Further into the warren I saw the area's neat thick hedges and remembered foraging in there for tasty yellow tomatoes.

Then we rounded a corner and I recognized our hedge. A closed, looming black gate hid the house, but it was there—like a ghost. The house where I had lived for years with my mother, David, and Barack Obama Sr. had been waiting for me all this time.

It was now occupied by a frowning Kikuyu woman who opened the door to us reluctantly.

"Three people have come here already. Auma Obama and a woman ... Sally someone," she said, frowning at us. Her house was now linked to the American president. It was clear she resented our intrusion, but she chatted with my mother as I inspected the outside of the house.

A massive iron gate was itself dwarfed by the long-established hedge, like a green belt wrapped tightly around the house. The iron grilles behind the windows had not changed, despite a recent coat of paint. Their hollowed eyes peered back at me. *Like a prison,* I thought. I looked furtively to the side of the house. The two women were still chatting. I walked up to the front door and jiggled the handle. Locked. I found it strange; for so many years I wanted to be on the outside and could not be. Now I wanted to enter but could not.

My prison had shrunk. Or perhaps it was only that I was no longer seven years old. The spot behind the house where Rita, Bobby, and I dipped for apples at birthday parties was now partly a maize *shamba** and partly a makeshift garage of propped-up wooden poles and sheets of iron.

Next to the kitchen door, a young girl, perhaps six or seven years old, stood forlornly looking at us.

"*Jambo.*" I smiled at her, saying hello. She did not answer. "*Habari gani?* (How are you?)"

She continued to stare at me.

Slightly perturbed, I looked away. In the center of the garden, once just a grassy space, a large tree loomed.

"In China it is called a *rong yang shu,*" Xue Hua later told me. "It signifies wealth and good fortune."

There was a time I knew its Swahili name too.

My mother and the lady were still chatting, and Xue Hua was taking photos around the garden.

"Ogola still lives here," the woman said suddenly, "just a few houses away."

Mum started, eyes wide. "Gladys? My old friend Gladys Ogola! I must go and see her!"

"Wait, before you go, give this lady a little *uchumi.*" The householder rubbed her fingers together and held out her hands. "I have to buy some milk this morning."

Her forced smile was half ingratiating, half pleading. "Some *uchumi,* for the milk," she repeated.

---

* Garden.

My mother gave her two hundred shillings, and we left feeling a little saddened, as though this last act had turned us into mere tourists. With a clang of the black metal gate, the scene of my most intense childhood memories disappeared from view.

———

Gladys Ogola indeed still lived across the street. She was stunned to see us, after thirty years, particularly Mum. The old woman sat across from us on her sofa, like a mirage.

As we sat in the living room, chatting, the women's talk turned to the newspaper coverage of Barack's presidency.

"I was so surprised and sad that they never talked about you or your children," Gladys said. She turned to me then. "I remember how your father used to stand outside your fence every night, yelling and shouting. Your mother came running to our house for help when he beat her. My Boaz would try to talk to your father and calm him down. And you were such a bright, naughty boy, so handsome, always so curious about everything."

Then, her eyes moist, she looked at my mother, who, just as emotional, smiled back gently and nodded her head.

"Kezia was talking in the newspapers so much but she never mentioned you. It made me feel sad," she said.

I asked her why.

"You know in Luo culture, when a child takes on the name of another man, it means he has separated himself from his origins?"

I nodded and looked up to see, just above her left shoulder, a placard on the wall:

The family that prays together, stays together.

A postcard with President Obama's face on it was placed among a bouquet of flowers on the mantelpiece. Photos surrounded the flowers. It looked like an altar to Barack. Grace's husband had been a Harvard classmate and close friend of my father's. Books were everywhere in this small house.

"But my brother David loved the Obamas," I answered, "and often hung out with Rita and Bobby. Yet he still used the Ndesandjo name. Did they reject him?"

"Your brother was a sweet boy, always happy and pleasant," Gladys said. "They would have liked him and been with him, but deep inside they would have felt he was not one of them, because, like I said, in Kenya taking another man's name means rejecting the original family. By doing it you have separated yourself from them."

"You see, I thought it was natural to take Simeon Ndesandjo's name when I married him," Mum said ruefully. "I did not think of the implications for the boys." Then she added, "And of course I wanted to shut Obama out of my own life forever."

I saw my mother, her face flushed and eyes bright.

Gladys nodded, as though she understood. *You have separated yourself from them.* Her words tumbled around in my mind.

I did not want to be separated from them. I made my choice perhaps twenty years too late, but it was my choice regardless. In the end I had taken back the name Obama, without reservation, without permission, and without regret.

My return to Kenya would have many such stories, cutting across family and tribes, acceptance and rejection.

———

Back at Simeon's home we had two domestics, Rose and Gracie. They were Luhya, but Rose had a Luo grandfather and gave me a few lessons in the dialect before I left for Kogelo. The Luhya is Kenya's third-largest tribe, behind the Kikuyu and the Luo.

"Gracie, do you know any Luo?" I asked her as she stood by quietly.

"No, I am Luhya." She smiled a little uncomfortably.

Rosie interrupted. "We are the same tribe, but different clans."

"Really?" I asked.

"Yes, George, the *shamba* boy, is also Luhya, but we have different clans."

"How many clans are there?"

"I do not know. Many. I think eighteen. I read it in a book."

So many clans, I thought, *and always the tribal differences.*

"Next week you will go up-country. *Utasafari mashambani.* And you will be visiting your own clan," Rosie added.

I nodded. A part of me wanted to have "my own clan," as Rosie said, but another part of me resisted being placed within this endless spectrum of cultural and racial boundaries. *Where do the categories stop?* I wondered.

I met a local politician over lunch. "How do you navigate the tribal complexities of Kenya as you do your work day-to-day?" I asked him. He was widely respected in Kenya as being generally above the fray of tribal politics and nepotism.

"I make sure I have all sorts of people working in my office," he said. "I am Kisii. My secretary is Luo. My department managers are Luo and Kikuyu. My security detail is Kipsigis. I know when something will work because they tell me. Officials who hire only from their own tribe end up closing themselves off from the world."

"That's the way it should be," his wife said. "You Americans are always thinking of laws. A product that sells for one thousand dollars in Kenya goes for four thousand in Europe and America because of litigation and insurance."

I agreed with her, but I particularly noticed she referred to me as one of "you Americans." I am an American, but I was born in Kenya and lived here for eighteen years, my father was a Luo, my stepfather also a Kenyan.

Later, at a bank, an old man stared solemnly at me. I did not know him but as I discussed some matters with the teller, he stared persistently at me. Finally, in exasperation, I said, "Hello." I looked at him, eyeball to eyeball, daring him to say what was on his mind.

"Don't worry. It's okay about that thing in your ear," he said finally, referring to my gold earring, "More people wear them these days."

It seemed I would always be a shape-shifter. I was a human chameleon, appearing in different colors and hues, sometimes blending in, other times sharply standing out, learning how things worked yet always on the outside, engaged in a never-ending odyssey.

"I obtained a full scholarship to Harvard, but I had no plane ticket."

Hilary Ngweno, a leading Kenya intellectual, sat awkwardly in the big sofa in my parents' home, careful not to put pressure on his bad back, as he recounted the early days of the airlift that brought many of my father's friends and associates to America. Hilary had helped me edit *Nairobi to Shenzhen*, and my parents had known him a long time. He remembered Barack Obama Sr. well.

"It was two years before your father left," he said, carefully sipping his tea. His whiskery beard was whiter than I remembered, but the almost beatific smile was still the same: quizzical, unassuming, eternally optimistic.

"I knocked on the door of an important government official. He had lots of connections and a big house. I thought he would help me get a plane ticket. The first question he asked was, 'What tribe are you?' When he learned I was Luhya, he said, 'You should ask the Luhya for help.' Every tribe had its own leaders, but I was seventeen. I did not know these things then."

Hilary had a smile on his mouth, but his eyes were a little sad. He bent forward slightly, a little tense in his comfortable seat.

"So I asked my father what I should do. He took me to a community gathering of Luhyas here, where many other students were also looking for money. Then each student was asked to speak. There was only one condition. Everyone had to speak in Luhya. I did not know Luhya. I had lived in Nairobi all my life. My father was a train driver, and our house was ten foot by ten foot. How could I spend the day inside? I had always been outside playing, talking to my friends in Kiswahili. We hardly ever spoke the tribal languages. This was Nairobi. My father and I left the gathering empty-handed. I still had to get a plane ticket. I used to go to the US Information Service Library to read, and one day while I was there, I met Gloria Hagberg. She encouraged me. Helped me write letters. 'It will be slow but we will get it done,' she said."

He put down the cup and paused. I noticed how carefully he moved his hands. They were long and bony, always working, like those of a craftsman or a pianist. My ears pricked up at the mention of Gloria Hagberg, my father's mentor and a good friend of Simeon and Ruth's. Gloria was now in her nineties, well-respected, and living quietly in the capital.

"One day a visiting American helped me write a letter to the Society of Pullman Engineers, which was founded by William Randolph Hearst, to ask for help. I had no time to waste. It was only months before school started. Eventually I got not one, but two tickets to America. I could go! Before I left I got a phone call from the counselor I had first sought help from. 'I hear you have an extra ticket to America. You know, there are some students here who still need tickets. Can you help one of them?'"

Hilary leaned forward sharply, as though ready to attack the biscuits on the table, but only took a sip of water. He resumed his story.

"There was a student I knew who had been accepted to Caltech. He happened to be Luhya. Now, I didn't care if he was Luhya or not, but he was going to Caltech and was a friend so I gave him the ticket."

Kenya and America. My two countries had come to each other's aid.

Just as important, I was realizing, decades later, the extent and magnitude of racism and tribalism throughout Kenyan society, affecting even my darker Kenyan brothers. Hilary's story exemplified the challenges and triumphs of tribalism in modern Kenya, itself a form of ostracism just as hurtful as the rejection of mixed-race children or segregation in the States.

After Hilary left I looked at my mother. "Can Kenya ever get past tribalism? Look at Hilary. A brilliant guy, and even he couldn't escape."

I expressed doubt about Kenya ever healing these tribal fractures.

"We're getting better, little by little," my mother said. "Kenya has already improved a lot. Some people come here for only two weeks and they think they know everything about the place."

"You're talking about me, aren't you?" I said, hurt.

"No, just some people . . ."

She had denied it but I knew she had been referring to me. I had become a stranger in my own land. How little it took. Now it seemed I could pass obliviously through the eye of Kenya's needle, without seeing the complexity of her fabric and colors. In fact, the Kenya I'd known from childhood had not changed; my eyes had.

I was looking forward more and more to seeing Granny Sarah. It was as though she stood at the eye of this swirling storm of personalities, landscapes, history, and tradition.

When Ida Odinga, wife of the Luo Prime Minister of Kenya, Raila Odinga, heard I was in Kenya, she invited me to her office for a brief visit.

Her assistant welcomed us. Double doors opened to reveal a room containing a huge desk at which the prime minister's wife was seated before a Sony notebook computer. She stood and came around to shake our hands. She was shorter than me but grasped my hand like a wrestler, not letting go, and eyeballed me for a full thirty seconds. Just as I was about to lose my balance, she let go. I introduced my brother Joseph, and we sat down to chat for a bit.

A big-boned, tall, and gregarious woman, she talked easily about her family, her work helping disadvantaged young women, and her beloved garden in Karen, exuding a sense of comfort and ease. When I mentioned my grandmother had a similar name and had emigrated to America, Mrs. Odinga told me she was named after Ida Betty, the American feminist and civil rights supporter. "You can call me Ida," she said and laughed.

"The Chinese are the new kids on the block," she said diplomatically when the issue of Chinese business in Nairobi came up.

"Your wife is Chinese. You like Chinese women, I think." She laughed offhandedly. "I would like to meet her one day."

We chatted about family, and about the social projects we were involved in.

"The women of Kenya need help," she told us. "We organized a project where we handed out thousands of water-purification kits. Clean water is one of our biggest problems."

"Maybe we can do something to help women and children here in the future," I said. She nodded, but I knew she was still sizing me up.

Then, abruptly, she mentioned having lived in Woodley herself once.

"Yes, I used to live there. We knew your father, and I remember seeing the two of you when you were young. You and your brother. What was his name?"

"David . . . David Opiyo."

"Yes, and my husband was a good friend of your father's. He particularly admired Obama because he was so . . . articulate."

Facing this clever, commanding woman, I had a brainstorm.

"Ida, I will be visiting my granny Sarah in Kogelo next week. Is there something meaningful in Luo that I can say to her? I want to tell her I have come home, finally."

"I have just the thing." Ida Odinga stood and headed briskly to her desk. She wrote down some words on a memo pad, tore off the sheet, and handed it to me.

"It means, 'Granny, I have come home.'"

I looked at the words. Although they were written in Luo, I knew they were just right. I repeated them sound for sound. She nodded approvingly, coming as close to me as when she had shaken my hand.

"You must pause after the first word. That way she knows you are talking to her," Ida told me. "Then you say the rest."

I folded the paper and put it in my pocket. As we were about to leave, she invited us for tea at her home. A few days later, we were at her expansive Karen estate, sipping tea and nibbling biscuits.

During a pause in the conversation, I mentioned a phrase I had recently spotted in a Luo language book: *Okok Okok Miya Koki Marachar.*

Ida sat up excitedly. "Bird! Bird! Make my nails white before you fly away!"

She waved her hands in the air, mimicking a bird, while her assistant explained that white nails were considered a sign of beauty.

I remembered how I hated the white spots on my nails when I was growing up. The nails of the white people I knew had always seemed perfectly pink by comparison. Only black people have this problem. I thought there was something wrong with my diet.

Ida's Karen estate was a beautiful place, so peaceful and serene. Yet I recalled how the country had exploded into tribal warfare during the last elections in 2007. Not too far from here, hundreds had died, thousands had been hurt, and hundreds of thousands displaced. Any notion that we were peacefully living together, black and white, brown and yellow, Kikuyu and Luo, Kamba and Kipsigis, was blown apart in those weeks after Christmas. I looked around her beautiful garden. The jacarandas bloomed and the cypress spread its boughs high above us, yet Kenya's heart had bled into the earth beneath. I asked Ida if there was hope for the country, considering the ethnic violence of 2007.

Like my mother, Ida Odinga was hopeful.

"We will get over it," she said. "We can do it. I first really began to be aware of these things in 2003. I was perhaps naive, maybe shielded, for a long time. I had a Kikuyu student who was always getting in trouble with the authorities at Nairobi University. I would protect and defend her. Then these riots started and she was agitating with the others. I talked with her one day and said: 'Why are you causing trouble like this? I have taught you and been your friend for so many years. Why are you against the Luo?' She said, 'Oh, it's not you. It's all these other people.'"

She suddenly stopped talking and became pensive, leaning with her chin resting in her hand as though she had run out of words. Ida's grandchild, who has a Luhya father and a Luo mother, shouted happily from a distance as she played with Xue Hua. My wife seemed to have fallen in love with the beautiful, precocious four-year-old.

"I must tell you, Mark, although he had many problems later, because of drink and all that, I remember your father as a great man. He was very impressive. When he talked everyone listened. My husband respected him very much. Please send my regards to your mother and your father."

Later that day, referring to the 2007 election riots, my mother commented that Ida likely helped reconcile her husband with the then-president Kibaki, thereby halting the violence.

However, my mind was on other things. I remembered Ida's advice about what to say to Granny Sarah, and I casually looked at my nails. No white spots. Not anymore.

———

I was looking forward to flying to Kogelo. In the meantime, I was finding out more about my father.

Ogosa Obama, one of my relatives, was a short, thickset man in his sixties, with the energy of someone much younger. We were sitting in a small cafe at Sarit Centre, a large shopping mall in downtown Westlands, a wealthy part of Nairobi. There was sadness in his red-rimmed eyes, as though he had fought with his own nature throughout much of his life, and may have doubted himself too frequently.

"Do you remember the time I came to visit my father?" I said. Ogosa lived with Barack Obama Sr. for years after the divorce.

"Yes, of course," he said, sipping his tea.

"I gave up … and turned back when I reached the door of the apartment."

"It was evening," he said slowly. "I saw David come in and he said, 'Mark is outside. He won't come in.' I saw you beside the building, walking away very fast. I think you were wearing some nice clothes. You even had a tie."

I nodded my head. How could I forget the day I lacked the courage to visit my own father? I tried to explain: "David had asked me if I wanted to come, but I stopped at the fence. I was afraid. I could not enter. It felt as though I was going back to a time I had erased from my mind."

Ogosa nodded in understanding.

"When I told your father you were not coming, he said, 'Don't worry. He will come home one day. He is my son.'"

I had never heard of my father saying anything about me. If he talked about his children, according to what I had long known, it would have been about Barack in America, never about Okoth.

My father's words were like rays from a long-dead nova, arriving eons after the explosion. They warmed me, touching me in a way I had never expected. I realized, in that moment, that I cared what my father—the man I had hated for so long—thought of me, as his son. He could have cursed me, he could have kissed me, but any acknowledgment would have touched me deeply

Characteristically, he had showed neither regret nor remorse.

He will come home one day. He is my son.

"Your father," Ogosa continued, "would be very proud to know that you are returning to Kogelo, and that you will bring your wife."

Would I want him to be proud of me? Would I care? I had never loved Barack Obama Sr., but I was learning to respect him more. I was his son, and he was my father. Our relationship was a matter of fate, not choice. I could see in my father's history an image of my own failures and fears, thoughts and dreams—themselves often consequences of my father's choices. It was as though we were separated by a cracked mirror, and love, or at the very least, acceptance, was the glue that would reconstitute it.

"He wanted to return to Kendu Bay, where his mother is buried. He said he would build there and perhaps remain."

"Did he say he wanted to be buried there?"

"That I do not know. There are some things he would not tell me."

———

Some say the real Obama homestead is in Kendu Bay, but I have no experience of that place. Alego-Kogelo, faintly remembered, was my ancestral home, the place I had visited often as a child, and Granny Sarah was at its core.

On the plane ride there my heart was beating rapidly. The Luo words and phrases I had learned rolled through my mind.

Amosi . . . Wabironenore . . . Nyasaye omedi ngima.

The flight was short, lasting about thirty minutes. When Xue Hua and I stepped off the double-propeller plane, the faint blush lighting up the horizon beyond the acacia trees was long gone. The blazing noonday heat of western Nyanza Province surrounded us like a furnace. For some reason, I thought of my mother stepping off a plane in Africa in 1964, her white face and hands smooth and unlined, and being immediately seduced by her surroundings.

As with Ruth before me, there was no one at the airport to greet Xue Hua and me. As if from nowhere, a woman in a bright yellow jacket came up to us, smiling broadly.

"I have seen you before," she said. "You are Obama's brother. Welcome home."

"Excuse me," I said. "Who are you?"

"My name is Bright," she said. "I am a supervisor here at the airport. I know Mama Sarah and your family!"

I thought of the supervisor Mary Radier, a Luo woman, who had befriended my mother when she arrived in Kenya. How similar some things were here, even forty years later.

Others stepped out of the shadows and into the bright sunlight to welcome us. A man in airport yellow came up to us, a toothy smile on his swarthy face.

"Do you remember me?" he said happily. "I am Abong'o. I knew you when you were very young!"

We hugged instinctively.

"I often drive Granny's guests to see her. Your father's sister was my mother," he said. Abong'o was one of many cousins I would meet that day. All of them would welcome us home.

The owner of the "canteen," a small cluster of plastic chairs set under the mango trees, introduced himself next.

"I knew your father. I had to go abroad to study, and he helped me get authorization for a passport. He was a very friendly man . . ."

This was the warmth of Africa, the reaction of family. We chatted while we waited for my uncle Said Obama, who arrived shortly afterward.

Saying farewell to the small crowd, we sped off toward the lake, leaving behind the sun-spangled tin roofs of the airport. We checked into a local Kisumu hotel and drove off to see Granny Sarah.

Okok. Okok.

The white-crested egrets that live beside Lake Victoria called out again and again, as though repeating my Luo name, Okoth. Said Obama confirmed Ida's explanation of the song.

Said Obama is the youngest son of Barack Obama Sr.'s father, Hussein Onyango. He is tall, his face somewhat aquiline. His eyes are remarkable, always wide and inquiring, as if surprised, even a little taken aback, by life's unpredictable turns.

"These birds always used to be around the cattle," he said. "They would wait for them to stir up the insects in the grass, and then eat them." Our car rattled over frequent potholes. Overhead, the equatorial sun shone without remorse as we left the buildings and paved roads of Kisumu for Kogelo.

Kogelo lies in a once-forgotten part of Siaya District, off the rain-ravaged Bondo Road, about thirty kilometers from Kisumu. Kogelo is a place where the candelabrum and mango trees hover over the scrub, and the huge boulders of Maseno seem about to topple over but never do. Every so often the wind, like the breath of a genie, blows a swirl of yellow dust.

"Your father walked eighteen kilometers each day to school," Said remarked from the front seat. "He would get up at four or earlier to go to the *shamba*, milk the cattle and the goats. At around six-thirty he would walk to school, then return in the evening. He would do various chores, including tending to the cattle. Then from about seven to nine he would do his homework."

Today he was my teacher. I listened carefully to him. Who else would tell me these things? Most of my relatives knew nothing of me. Even if they did, the ones who really knew, like Granny Sarah, could not speak English.

"I believe that a hard life is what makes us appreciate the small things," he said, and lapsed into silence.

We stopped at the high school my father had attended, where school had already started in Siaya District. Except for the schools and government offices, Kisumu and Alego were sleepy places, like dusky holograms stuck in slow motion. There were few people on the streets, and half the businesses had their doors shut.

"In January everyone has spent money on school fees, and there is none left for buying things and eating out," the driver, a friend of Said's, explained.

We met the assistant headmaster inside the school. He was a young man, in his late-thirties perhaps, who sat with an air of authority behind a creaking wooden desk.

He told us we'd be welcome to see my father's records and photos if we returned the next day. But Auma Obama, who had control over Barack Sr.'s records, called the headmaster and told him I was not welcome there.

But I did not need to see photographs or other records. I just wanted to experience the surroundings. After the meeting we walked around the campus. Maseno's magnificent trees loomed over the corrugated-iron roofs of the low-level mud-and-brick school buildings. Students in green cardigans and dark slacks walked about urgently to myriad appointments.

At moments throughout the day, I thought of Barack Obama Sr.'s other surviving children: Barack Jr., Auma, George, and Malik. All of them had struggled to make sense of a life filled with a dizzying range of choices, complicated by nature and nurture. My brother Barack now occupied a rarefied sphere, ever-more remote from our lives. I had never met George, but I knew he, too, had been struggling with the sudden and shallow glare of the world's attention.

When Said told me Auma was in town, I decided to text her, because she may not have known I was coming. She sent an angry reply, accusing me of opportunism regarding our father and adding that she had nothing more to say to me. She still had not forgiven me for publishing *Nairobi to Shenzhen*, in which I had used fiction to come clean about the domestic abuse my father had inflicted on us. I still remembered that night many years ago when Auma had unlocked the main door of the house, and my furious father rushed in and held a knife to my mother's throat. I wondered if she regretted this, and perhaps felt that I was striking back.

I realized with some sadness that Auma formed absolute judgments, without nuance, perhaps because for so long she was forced, by circumstance and misfortune, to choose between black or white, without the option of gray. I held no malice toward my sister. Her only fault, if it can be called one, was having loved our father absolutely.

I looked at the motto above the gate of his school: Perseverance Shall Win Through. The school badge was a red cross, an open book, and a tree.

The school was located exactly on the equator. A small roundabout, planted with flowers and with the word Equator painted on a border of white bricks, seemed like a symbolic link between the worlds of America and Kenya, which my father inhabited and struggled with for much of his life.

"He had one foot in the west and one in Kenya, and it was not easy for him," a family friend had told me. "When he came back it must have been a huge change. And things were not easy for white women married to blacks then. Even after independence, there were rules and regulations, zoning laws that made it illegal for people to live in some places. If a black and a white wanted to live somewhere, they had to get special approval."

I remembered what my mother had told me when we'd visited our first home, the house in Rosslyn where I was born. "It was very lonely. There was a white couple next door but they wanted nothing to do with a white woman married to a black man. I didn't care," she added ruefully. "I used to ignore those things."

Perseverance. We all need perseverance. She lived seven years with Barack Obama Sr. She did not quit.

Back in the car Said told me, "Sometimes Granny would take your father by bicycle to school. Bicycles were a luxury then, and we were lucky to have one for a while. My mother had a hard life. She would grow beans, *sukuma*, and carry ninety-kilogram bags on her back to the market fifteen kilometers away, to sell them. She would come back to attend to the homestead and look after my father, your grandfather, who was working for the British or out of the country. Then she would take your father to school. She did this every day for many years."

"What about my grandfather?" I said, thinking of the stern man who had driven away my grandmother.

"Later he was very old and not easy to look after."

After driving through a dusty, hilly area of scrub vegetation and ever-thicker copses of trees, we entered a flat area of gated homesteads with small *shambas* of crops and brick-built houses. Women carrying pails on their heads looked at us curiously as we drove by. Some schoolchildren seemed to start with surprise on seeing my relatively pale face.

"That is where Malik lives." Said pointed out one of the houses to me. The blue-roofed building stood in a large meadow surrounded by a tall iron fence. If time permitted perhaps my brother and I would meet again.

Granny's homestead lay ahead. A police officer opened the gate for us and we drove up to the small brick house set before a huge mango tree. We walked straight into a modest living room. After a few minutes Granny entered. On seeing me she rushed over.

"Okoth, *umerudi* [you are here]!" she roared in her deep, strong voice.

Without waiting for an answer, she hugged me, grasped my hand, and pulled me down on the couch. Xue Hua sat beside me, Said across from us, translating.

We held each other's hand throughout the visit.

"My knee is acting up," Granny said. At first she had not looked straight at me, as though a direct gaze was too powerful a thing, and only the touch of hands, the feeling of skin against skin, could be borne. When our eyes finally met, I said what I had come to say, words that completed a dialogue between me and Kogelo that had existed off and on for almost forty years.

"*Adwogo Dala*," I said. I have returned home.

The Luo phrase I had memorized, that Ida Odinga had written down for me, flowed effortlessly from my tongue. I had practiced the words so many times. Like a Buddhist mantra, they had resounded in my mind for days.

She smiled and we hugged silently. I kissed her on both cheeks. She gave me a robust peck on mine, almost like a bashful lover.

"*Mae Jaoda,*" I said, introducing Xue Hua. *This is my wife.*

Xue Hua also hugged my granny. For she was indeed my granny. I did not need the permission of others, like headmasters, record-keepers, and bitter family members, to call her this. With her support I had returned, just as I had taken back the name that was my birthright.

"I asked you to come and bring your wife, and you have done the right thing today," Granny Sarah told me.

A young woman entered the room and took my hand. One by one, others came in. We greeted each other in Luo. There was a powerful energy in the room. It was as though Granny's enthusiasm and honesty filled everyone around her. Every so often, particularly when I laughed, she would laugh too. It was a deep throaty sound. Her teeth gleamed, her whole body shook, and her wrinkled face was wreathed with joy.

"Why did you leave me so long, Okoth?" she said. She looked at me sidelong when she spoke, as though still not fully trusting what her eyes told her.

"There was much I wanted to forget about this place because of the pain I had gone through," I tried to explain, "Because of what my mother had seen and felt. I wanted nothing to do with my father or here."

"But how could you just turn your back?" she persisted. "I loved you so much, and you loved me. I remember you used to play with the chickens and dogs all the time, and with me. Then, all of a sudden you never came back."

"I'm sorry for the pain I caused you, Dani."

I had prepared this phrase in Luo beforehand. Part of me had always recognized the pain she must have felt when her youngest grandson had stayed away for more than forty years, the absence marked by the white birds that annually cross Lake Victoria in long, white ribbons, threading their way to far-off lands.

Xue Hua also said a few words in Luo, which everyone in the room appreciated. Later they gave her a Luo name, *Achieng*, which means "born during the daylight."

"You were on the wrong path," my grandmother told me. "And in that you did wrong, but let bygones be bygones. We are now starting again."

"Why didn't anyone let me know my father had died?" I asked her. She and Said discussed this spiritedly. Xue Hua and I listened without comprehending the fast flow of Luo.

"I think your mother knew," Said translated for me.

Somewhat carelessly, I told Granny I did not remember my mother telling me.

"If your mother did not tell you, then she was wrong," she said.

"I do not know what happened. I think maybe this is something she may have told you but you did not remember," my uncle said slowly.

I nodded. Finally it made sense.

<hr />

Guests arrived, and Granny left us to greet them. Meanwhile Said took me to see me my father's grave. With a shock, I saw that it was within feet of the house. I had expected we would need to drive elsewhere. I had also not been sure I wanted to see it. Next to visiting Granny, everything else, even my father's resting place, had seemed peripheral.

I stood before his headstone.

BARACK HUSSEIN OBAMA
BORN 1936–1982
IBED GI KWE

The Luo words for *Rest in Peace.*

I removed my sunglasses. I do not know if it was the blazing heat that affected me, or something within, but tears trickled down my face. I stood for several minutes before the white-and-yellow-tiled grave that seemed to look back at me, neither accusing nor absolving.

A few feet behind was the larger gravestone of my grandfather:

Jaduong
Hussein Obama Onyango
1870–1975

Jaduong means "the old man."

Later we rejoined Granny, talking to a group of men and women, all seated in a circle under the shade of the mango tree. I introduced my wife and myself in Luo to the village chief, family friends, and relatives, including brothers of my father, and men who claimed to know me but whom I did not recognize. My mind was still reeling from the shock of seeing my father's grave.

"Granny, what do you remember of my mother?" I asked her eventually.

"I remember her. She was with us for only a short time, but I think she was a good woman. But we did not know her very well."

"Some people told me that because I had used another man's name, the Obama family had cut me off and that's one reason we stayed apart so many years."

The chief vehemently shook his head. "That is not our custom."

"Perhaps some clans have their own traditions, but we do not do that. But let us hear Granny," Said replied.

"Your brother David was among us, and played and talked with us. He was one of us, no matter what his name." Granny looked at me as she said this, and everyone nodded in agreement. "You are of this land."

You are of this land.

"Granny," I said, "I believe that too. I have come home. *Adwogo Dala.* My name is Mark Okoth Obama Ndes . . ."

Before I could finish, she interrupted me. "Okoth Obama, in this place!" she said and laughed.

It was late afternoon when I let go of Granny's hand and bid her farewell. My eyes were wet. I still felt incomplete. As I was sitting in the car, she heaved herself up with difficulty on her walking stick and came over. She was still beaming. I stepped out of the car again and hugged her for a long time, this woman I truly loved.

"*Oriti Dani.*" Good-bye, Granny.

"Don't forget to come back home," she answered, pressing me close. Her tear-filled eyes were inches from my face, sharp and clear.

"*Wabironenore. Nyasaye omedi ngima,*" I said. I will be back. God bless you.

⎯ ⎯

As we drove off, I considered stopping to say hello to Malik but decided not to do so. It would be too casual, too rushed, the moments spent together too superficial after the joy of my reunion with Granny Sarah. I remembered Auma's words, uttered during the campaign: There is a time for everything.

I remembered the cafeteria owner at the airport, who had told me how Barack Obama Sr. had helped him. On my trip I would hear many other stories of my father's warm and gracious side, the good part of him I never knew.

"How could he have been this way outside the family and so bad to us?" I asked my uncle.

"We were far away so we could not see. But we knew of the good things too," he said.

Said recounted many tales of my father while he was growing up. One stuck with me in particular.

"We had once gone drinking in the evening, and were driving back to Alego when we saw a neighbor on the street." Said talked slowly, plainly moved by the memory. "She waved us down and told us her nephew had just died. We helped us bring the body back to his hometown, far, far away. We barely had enough petrol and thought we would not make it. In those days no one else would help her. She was poor and alone."

As I left Kogelo, I was not bitter. I did not hate my father. There was not even any sadness. It was as though I had left that part of my life behind, and a new chapter had begun. It was not the good stories about my father that now gave me succor and wiped away the hurt. Nor was it just this place. It was mostly the people, and the sense that I was back where I had come from.

My story is one of fathers and sons, of forces that impel boys—like birds with white feathers—to fly away and leave their homes, returning like prodigals years, or even decades, later. It is a story of Kogelo, my home, and of China, and of America. It is a story of regaining a piece of my life, part of a larger puzzle in which there still remain many gaps and jagged edges. But one piece at least is finally in the right place.

Adwogo Dala. Ibed Gi Kwe.

A few days later, on the red-eye back to Shenzhen, I looked down over the airliner's humming Rolls-Royce engines. The city's lights sparkled across the peninsula like a vast jeweled belt, and a familiar feeling of elation washed over me at the sight of them. *This place has been my home for more than ten years,* I thought. I would be returning to my lessons at the Welfare Center, continue my calligraphy, practice piano, and tend to my business, with my wife beside me and the backing of my family around the globe.

The city's shared minibuses are gone now, but taxis swarm for fares around the exits of the new subway lines. Swaying on the balls of their feet, old men and women still walk their grandchildren past the mahjong players in the streets. The electronics market at Hua Cheng Bei is still an open, yawning mouth, crowded with DVD hawkers and agile, chain-smoking young men. At the bustling Luo Hu entry point, doe-eyed, raven-haired girls still arrive lugging huge plastic bags of possessions from their villages in the provinces. Multitudes from all over China and abroad are drawn to Shenzhen—just as I was—winding their way through grassy fields or along tracks of smoke and steel, in search of fame, or money, or love.

In my personal odyssey I have found every sort of love: selfish and magnanimous, lustful and chaste, innocent and opportunistic, returned and unrequited, all-consuming and petty, divine and lusty, serious and humorous—love that reaches across race and religion and extends back as far as time itself.

A children's refuge has become a place where I can sink back into anonymity or face the glare of the spotlights, equally without fear. In the streets outside, the magnificent mangroves of Jing Tian Road claw their way into the concrete below, their gentle boughs shading slow-walking families from the spring rain. Like drops of water on a leaf, or pearls on a vast jade plate, my life retains its familiar outlines while ready at any moment to slide into the unknown. But always it reflects light from three great sources, three cultures, the three places I call home.

At the 2009 inauguration I met Granny Sarah. The last time had been around 1970. It was freezing on the steps of the Capitol, but we were together again as a family.

In 2011 I reunited with Sarah Ogwel (Granny Sarah) in Kogelo. Sarah was Obama Sr.'s stepmother. Now in her nineties, she delights in tending to her *shamba* (farm) and looks after orphan children living close by. Granny and her son Said were among the first Obamas to welcome me back after my long absence. Here, Xue Hua initiates a family hug.

In 2011 I stood before my father's grave in Kogelo, on Granny Sarah's home-stead. Close by was the grave of my grandfather, Onyango Hussein Obama, whom I consider the Obama family's first Global Citizen.

Said Obama helped bring me back to Kogelo in 2011.

APPENDIX I

Obama Family Genealogy: 1700s–Present

This chart is based on research by Obama family members, focusing on my father's side of the family. As such, it is a generally accurate description of the Obama genealogy.

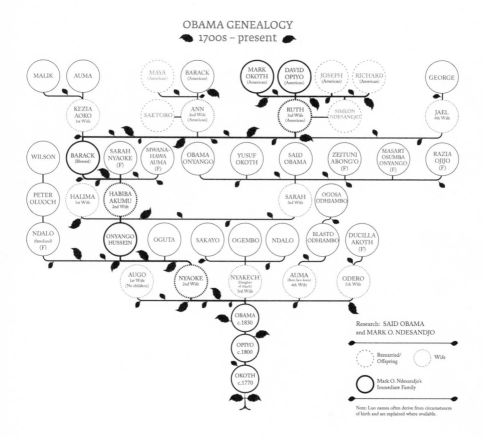

OBAMA GENEALOGY
1700s – present

APPENDIX II

On *Dreams from My Father* by Barack Obama— Setting the Record Straight

The following notes are based on my recollections and descriptions as well as those of certain Obama family members. They are not intended to represent the views of the family as a whole, or to disparage the opinions of others, but are a re-evaluation of common ideas and assumptions. (Source text: Barack Obama, *Dreams from My Father*, Canongate 2008.)

As the author and Barack Obama biographer David Maraniss pointed out to me in early 2010, although my brother's book has a number of historical inaccuracies, it can nevertheless be seen as an accurate psychological portrayal of Barack Obama's life. Here I have detailed some points in it that need to be finally corrected, as they have led to years of rumors and false assumptions about intrafamily relationships, which, in some cases, have hurt people.

> *[Auma Obama says to Barack]: "I was scared of him. You know, he was already away when I was born. In Hawaii with your mum, and then at Harvard. When he came back to Kenya, our oldest brother, Bobby, and I were small children. We had lived with our mum in the country, in Alego, up until then. I was too young to remember much about him coming. I was four, but Bobby was six, so maybe he can tell you more about what happened. I just remember that he came back with an American woman named Ruth, and that he took us from our mother to go live with them in Nairobi. I remember that this woman, Ruth, was the first white person I'd ever been near, and that suddenly she was supposed to be my new mother."*
>
> *"Why didn't you stay with your own mother?"*

*Auma shook her head. "I don't know exactly. In Kenya, men get to keep children in a divorce—if they want them, that is. I asked my mum about this, but it's difficult for her to talk about. She only says that the Old Man's new wife refused to live with another wife, and that she—my mum—thought us children would be better off living with the Old Man because he was rich." (*Dreams from My Father, *p. 213)*

Two corrections here. First of all, Auma was sent to board at Mary Hill Girls' School near Thika by her father at age five. It is quite possible that at that young age, the shock of this sudden change in her family situation caused Auma to resent Ruth Ndesandjo, even though, according to my mother, "It was entirely Obama's choice/decision," and, Auma implies, done with Kezia's agreement. In any case, at that age Auma was not living with my mother as she implies here.

Second, Kezia and Barack Obama Sr. were never divorced. According to Luo tradition:

*Prior to the Mission influences, it made little difference to a man if his wife went away with someone else, because he knew that she must some day come back to him because her father would not dare to accept second bride wealth animals, and all the children born out of the illegal association would be his children by the right he established by bride wealth payment. The essential feature which distinguishes "divorce" and "separation" is the return of the bride wealth. (*Luo Customary Laws and Marriage Law Customs, *Gordon Wilson, p. 134)*

According to relatives, the dowry was not returned, so it was a separation, not a divorce.

[Auma Obama says to Barack]: "And he had an American wife, which was still rare—although later, when he was still married to Ruth, he would go out sometimes with my real mum. As if he had to show people, you see. That he could also have this beautiful African woman whenever he chose.

Our four other brothers were born at this time. Mark and David, they were Ruth's children, born in our big house in Westlands. Abo and Bernard, they were my mum's children and lived with her and her family up country. Bobby and I didn't know Abo and Bernard then. They never came to the house to see us, and when the Old Man visited them, he would always go alone, without telling Ruth." (Dreams, p. 213)

We were born in Woodley, not Westlands. Relatives note that Abo and Bernard were Kezia's children with another man, and not Barack Obama Sr.'s. According to Luo tradition, because they were separated but not divorced, Abo and Bernard would be regarded as Barack Obama Sr.'s children.* Others dispute that Obama visited Kezia while married to Ruth. Auma suggested otherwise, implying without any evidence that I am aware of that Barack Sr. fathered children while still married to Ruth Ndesandjo. I feel that this is a disservice to all of us.

[Auma Obama says to Barack]: "I told you that Ruth's divorce from the Old Man was very bitter. After they separated, she married a Tanzanian and had Mark and David take his name. She sent them to an international school, and they were raised like foreigners. She told them that they should have nothing to do with our side of the family." (Dreams, p. 339)

Simeon Ndesandjo was a Kenyan, not a Tanzanian. I also am not sure what "international school" means here. We went to Kenyan schools, including St. Mary's, which has been a Kenyan school since 1939. My mother never discouraged me from contacting the Obamas. It was my decision not to do so. On the contrary, it was my mother who encouraged me to keep the name Okoth that my father gave me, although I did not want to do so. It was also she who encouraged me to come out of my room and meet Barack Jr. when he visited.

------

* (See Wilson, op. cit; also *A Study of the Economic and Social Life of the Luo of Kenya*, John W. Ndisi, 1973.)

But only a few days later, Auma and I came home to find a car wait-
ing for us outside the apartment. The driver, a brown-skinned man
with a prominent Adam's apple, handed Auma a note.
  `"What is it?" I asked*
  "It's an invitation from Ruth," she said. "Mark's back from America
*for the summer. She wants to have us over for lunch." (*Dreams, *p. 340)*

My mother did not send a car to pick up Auma and Barack. I have
never known her to do anything like this. I also do not recall us having a
driver. My mother also had no way of knowing or even wanting to know
where Auma lived. Furthermore, according to my mother, we did not have
lunch together that first meeting. Barack's arrival at our house was a total
surprise to my parents and me. We never expected guests that afternoon,
and to see Barack Obama Sr.'s other son from America was surprising
and unsettling! Perhaps Barack was using poetic license, or his memory
was unclear. It is also possible that the author wanted to emphasize that
we were wealthy and stretched the truth a little.

We came to one of the more modest houses on the block and parked
along the curve of a looping driveway. A white woman with a long
jaw and graying hair came out of the house to meet us. Behind her
was a black man of my height and complexion with a bushy Afro and
*horn-rimmed glasses. (*Dreams, *p. 341)*

As I recount on page 145 of this book, we did not come out of the
house to meet him. They walked in. While I was reading in my room my
mother announced we had guests and I walked from there directly to
the living room. Again, it was a complete surprise to see my American
brother, Barack.

"Yes, yes," the man said, standing up. "Come on, Joey . . . it was nice
to meet you both."
  The boy stood fast, staring up at Auma and me with a bright,
curious smile until his father finally picked him up and carried him
out the door. "Well, here we are," Ruth said, leading us to the couch and

pouring lemonade. "I must say it was quite a surprise to find out you were here, Barry. I told Mark that we just had to see how this other son of Obama's turned out. Your name is Obama, isn't it? But your mother remarried. I wonder why she had you keep your name?"

My mother denies ever saying this.

I smiled as if I hadn't understood the question, "So, Mark," I said, turning to my brother, "I hear you're at Berkeley."

"Stanford," he corrected. His voice was deep, his accent perfectly American. "I'm in my last year of the physics program there." (Dreams, p. 341)

I did not say this. In fact, I was about to start my studies at Stanford and was certainly not in my last year there. Perhaps Barack was referring to Brown University, where I graduated that year with a BSc. in Physics. On a more positive note, his reference to me as his brother, and not half-brother or some other unfamiliar term, was nice of him. It is possible that Barack confused what I told him here with what we discussed at a later meeting in San Francisco, just after I had left Stanford.

That's how the next hour passed, with Ruth alternating between stories of my father's failure and stories of Mark's accomplishments. Any questions were directed exclusively to me, leaving Auma to fiddle silently with Ruth's lasagna. I wanted to leave as soon as the meal was over, but Ruth suggested that Mark show us the family album while she bought out the dessert. (Dreams, p. 341)

According to my mother, and from what I recall, she said very little at this meeting and it lasted much less than an hour. "I was shocked and did not know what to say," she later told me. "Seeing Barack there from America made me completely shut down. I basically sat down on the couch and said very little."

As explained above, we did not have lunch together, although we did look through the family album.

"Don't be so modest, dear," Ruth said. "The things Mark studies are so complicated only a handful of people really understand it all." She patted Mark on the hand, then turned to me. "And Barry, I understand you'll be going to Harvard. Just like Obama. You must have gotten some of his brains. Hopefully not the rest of him, though. You know Obama was quite crazy, don't you? The drinking made it worse. Did you ever meet him? Obama, I mean?"

"Only once. When I was ten."

"Well, you were lucky then. It probably explains why you're doing so well." (Dreams, *p. 342)*

My mother denies ever making these comments.

[Auma Obama says to Barack]: "Soon after Barack [Sr.] came, a white woman arrived in Kisumu looking for him. At first we thought this must be your mother, Ann. Barack had to explain that this was a different woman, Ruth. He said that he had met her at Harvard and that she had followed him to Kenya without his knowledge. Your grandfather didn't believe this story and thought that again Barack had disobeyed him. But I wasn't so sure, for, in fact, Barack did seem reluctant to marry Ruth at first. I'm not sure what finally swayed him. Maybe he felt Ruth would be better suited to his new life. Or maybe he heard gossip that Kezia had enjoyed herself too much during his absence, even though I told him that this gossip was not true." (Dreams, *p. 423)*

My mother arrived in Nairobi, not Kisumu, to meet him. Also, my father invited her to come to Kenya before he left Boston, and she agreed to do so.

[Auma Obama says to Barack]: "Or maybe he just cared for Ruth more than he liked to admit. Whatever the reason, I know that once Barack agreed to marry Ruth, she could not accept the idea of his having Kezia as a second wife. That is how the children went to live with their father and his new wife in Nairobi. When Barack brought

Auma and Bobby back to visit, Ruth would refuse to accompany him and would not let Barack bring David or Mark. Onyango did not discuss this directly with Barack. But he would say to his friends, in such a way that Barack could hear him, "My son is a big man, but when he comes home his mother must cook for him instead of his wife." (Dreams, *p. 423)*

David and I visited Alego off and on until the divorce. I also remember my mother accompanying us there. According to my mother and other relatives, Kezia wanted nothing to do with her children by Barack Obama Sr. and, because Barack Sr. had asked her to look after them when they were dating in Boston and no one else would, Ruth looked after them. According to my mother: "BO Sr. never mentioned Kezia to me in the sense of her living with us—it never entered my mind, or his, I believe." It was Kezia who felt the children would be better off living with the Old Man because he was rich, in Auma's words.

On another note: Obama's relatives sometimes lived with us. For example, Aunt Zeituni, the relative charged with illegal immigration into the United States, claims she looked after me while I was growing up. In fact, she lived with us only about one year. It was a sign of Ruth Ndesandjo's kindness and tolerance that she agreed to these arrangements.

In a recent e-mail to me, Ruth wrote: "I know I was not aware of the many complexities that you have unearthed of that situation—my innocence at that time protected me—also, I have not really cared that I was portrayed unfavorably in BO's book—he didn't know the true situation either."

The following week, I called Mark and he suggested that we go out to lunch . . . He was more relaxed than he had been during our first meeting, making a few self-deprecatory jokes, offering his observations about California and academic infighting. (Dreams, p. 343)

In the early nineties, at his request, I met Barack for a few hours in San Francisco, when I was working at AT&T and shortly after I had left Stanford. At that meeting I might have commented about California and academic infighting at Stanford. It is possible that Barack met me to research his book, and he may have mixed up some of the things I said then with his recollections from our first meeting. He met so many people in Kenya that he may have honestly not remembered some of the specifics of our references to Stanford. Nevertheless, a lot in these pages simply did not happen.

Other Notes:
- "Nidesand" is a misspelling of Ndesandjo and was first mentioned in an AP report. My mother's maiden name is Baker.
- After our 2009 Beijing meeting, President Obama said he had first met me "two years ago." We first met in 1988 during his trip to Kenya.
- Joseph Ndesandjo has no blood relationship to President Obama, but he and I share the same mother.
- In our family we do not refer to each other as half-this or half-that.

ACKNOWLEDGMENTS

This book is the culmination of ten-plus years of blessings, failed starts, and unexpected events. The list of people who helped me write this book is endless, but it is a pleasure for me to thank the following groups and individuals who made it possible.

Friends and associates who helped me research and understand historical terrain include Eric and his wife for welcoming me to Israel, Peter Munves for loving music, Konstantin Tsakonas for being a magnanimous and kindred spirit, Reggie Love for his unflagging support, Paul Liu and his family for welcoming me during the first inauguration, Natsuhiko for remaining friends across oceans, Alicia and Rebecca for their warm welcome those first few weeks in China, Cheng Wei and her family, and Mr. Wu Chengwei for making that first visit to the Welfare Center possible. Jaleh Ehsani for helping me know myself, Jacob Barua for following his dreams too, Jeff Koinange and his family, Debbie Malik and her family for supporting my mother many years, Aidan Williams for helping me through endless edits and proofs of the book. Honorable Bob Goldberg and Sally Goldberg for making that Beijing visit possible, Honorable Brian Goldbeck and Nara, Sally and Jaz and their family, Itzhak Perlman and Rohan Dasilva for sharing music with children, Director Wu of the Shenzhen Foreign Affairs Department and his staff, Mrs. Liu yan and her family, Honorable Consul Jennifer Galt and her family, Honorable Ida Odinga for her Luo lessons, Hilary Ngweno for his insights into 1960s Kenya, and Gloria and Paula Hagberg and their family for their helpful comments on my grandfather and my father's early years. I also want to thank my friends at Brown, Stanford, and Emory who patiently supported me and the priests, teachers, and staff at St. Mary's School in Nairobi. Thanks to the friends and colleagues at Nortel, AT&T, and Lucent, including Rob and Ruth, two special evangelists.

I want to also thank many in the Chinese community and others like myself who made China home. These include my students at the Welfare

Center, Shenzhen Welfare Center Director Li, Director Tang, Director Zhang, and their amazing teachers and staff, Mrs. Li Ting who helped set up the Music Troupe and Mr. Wu who first assisted me teaching piano at the Welfare Center, Director Tao and Mr. Mo for their insights into China's welfare system. Chairman Huang and his family, Mr. Zhou and Joe Lu for their tremendous insights, David Buxbaum, and Mr Peng for their invaluable help and insights, Alice Chiu and her family, the American Chamber of Commerce of South China and its extraordinary leader Harley Seyedin, Hui and Sterling Seyedin, Dr. Luke Liu for his photos of my calligraphy, Mr. Li Zhong for his calligraphy teaching, Mr. Qin for his insights into writing Chinese and classical poetry, Jeff and his support team of student volunteers, Mr. Yi Songguo for his domestic violence awareness leadership, Rex Liu, Steven Song, Chairman Li, and the Hua Yi Company, Mr. Harry Zhong, and Ballen Ma. Last but not least are the Chinese people who welcomed me from the beginning and helped me understand their deep and great culture.

The book would not have been possible without the enthusiastic and active support of my agent, Marleen Seegers, who believed in the book from the first, as well as the professional and dedicated team at Lyons Press, including my editor, Jon Sternfeld, who has been incredibly supportive and reassuring under real-time pressure in the process of producing this book.

Last but not least, I would also like to thank my family, who helped me understand more of our history, or inspired and supported me, including Ruth, Simeon, Chloe and her family, Joseph, Dora, Richard, Barack and Michelle Obama and their family, Said Obama, Ogosa Obama, Granny Sara, Malik Obama, and Zeituni Obama.

—M.O.O.N.